ISLAM AND POWER

ISLAM AND POWER

EDITED BY ALEXANDER S. CUDSI
and ALI E. HILLAL DESSOUKI

THE JOHNS HOPKINS UNIVERSITY PRESS
BALTIMORE AND LONDON

First published in the United States of America, 1981, by
The Johns Hopkins University Press, Baltimore, Maryland 21218

First published in Great Britain, 1981, by
Croom Helm Ltd, 2–10 St John's Road, London SW11

Library of Congress Cataloging in Publication Data

Main entry under title:
Islam and power.
Includes index.
Contents: Introduction / A.S. Cudsi and Ali E. Hillal Dessouki — Activism and quietism in Islam / Michael Cook — A Moslem theory of history and its relevance to Islamic reform movements / Thomas Naff — [etc.]
1. Islam and politics — Addresses, essays, lectures. 2. Islam — History — Addresses, essays, lectures. I. Cudsi, A.S. (Alex S.) II. Dessouki, Ali E. Hillal.

BP173.7.184 1981 291'.1977 81-47608
ISBN 0–8018–2697–7 AACR2

Printed in Great Britain

CONTENTS

FOREWORD

The Hellenic Mediterranean Centre for Arabic and Islamic Studies was founded in December 1976 as a postgraduate and research institution — the first of its kind in Greece. In addition to teaching Arabic and Turkish, the Centre trains Greek postgraduates in the history, economics, politics and international relations of the Arab and Islamic countries.

In addition to its teaching and research activities, the Centre holds occasional conferences, seminars and international symposia. In the last two years, this aspect of the Centre's work has focused on various aspects of Islam. The present volume is an outcome of the seminars and conferences held on this topic.

Special thanks are due to Professor I. Georgakis, Greek Ambassador at Large. The foundation of the Centre is a result of his efforts over the years to introduce in to Greece the study of the world of Islam and the modern Arab world. As chairman of the Centre's Governing Council, he continues to offer his active service, support and encouragement to the Centre.

The Centre is also grateful to our colleagues from the Middle East, Europe, the United Kingdom and the United States of America. Their participation and support have contributed greatly to the early work of the Centre.

PJV

INTRODUCTION

The 1970s witnessed a mushrooming of Islamic movements and ideas which was described variously as Islamic revival, Islamic resurgence and Islam on the march. Whether as part of the majority or minority, whether under capitalist or socialist regimes, Muslims have been moved by this reawakening.[1]

The massive demonstrations which led to the victory of the 'Islamic Revolution' in Iran have now brought into sharp relief Western interest in Islamic resurgence, especially with the increasing importance of oil-producing Arab countries to Western economies. The probable political repercussions to a number of neighbouring Muslim countries of the Islamic revolution in Iran have raised serious strategic questions. At the same time, Soviet military intervention in Afghanistan and the rise of an Islamic resistance movement, whose members are known as *al-mujahidin*, have presented Western analysts and policy makers with a golden opportunity to incite Muslim anti-Soviet feelings.

But what really are the causes and nature of this Islamic resurgence? Is it a purely religious revival? Or is it a social and political movement that must be understood in the context of the Muslims' conditions and milieu? Or is it a combination of both? What are the social classes to whom Islamic groups appeal most? Will it really lead to the establishment of an Islamic socio-political order or will it end up as an instrument of struggle between Muslim ruling elites and their opposition?[2] And finally what are the foreign policy implications of these developments? Do they necessarily lead to a more militant and hostile attitude towards the West?

It is beyond the scope of this introduction to attempt an answer to all of these questions. A number of them are treated by the various contributors in this book. An important point, however, is the role of Islam as an instrument in the political struggle between ruling elites and opposition groups. Islam has been used by various rulers to acquire and sustain legitimacy, or to mobilise masses, in support of particular policy options. In such situations, rulers usually effect an alliance with the religious establishment. But Islam has also emerged (as in the case of Iran, Tunisia and Egypt) as an expression of political opposition and social discontent. It is this framework of the use of Islam as a political instrument that we should like to deal with in more detail.

Islamic Resurgence

Islamic resurgence must have bewildered a number of theorists of modernisation who view this process from what one might call a 'displacement-transformation' perspective.[3] This group of theorists perceives the process of modernisation in post-colonial countries as one of fundamental change from a traditional socio-political order, including of course religion and religious values, to a modern one. This view is shared by liberal, marxist and revolutionary writers alike. Liberal authors used the images of the passing of traditional society (Daniel Lerner),[4] the shattering of the glass (Manfred Halpern)[5] and social mobilisation (Karl W. Deutsch).[6] Some revolutionary Arab thinkers such as Hisham Sharabi and Jalal Sadiq al-Azm took a critical view of religion and its role in society. Notwithstanding ideological differences, both groups depart from a dichotomous vision of social reality.[7]

The thrust of this view is that the modernisation process generates new integrative symbols and structures which replace the old ones, leading to a new basis of community, identity and legitimacy. For the revolutionaries in the group, the modern and progressive structures and values can only replace the traditional conservative ones through a revolution. For both liberals and revolutionaries religion and religious values are destined to lose their overt social role. This view, however, fails to explain the persistence, let alone the resurgence, of religious movement.

A second perspective which has a particular appeal to sociologists and anthropologists is the concept of 'dual or hybrid society'. It refers to the persistence of traditional loyalties, social structures and norms in the midst of social change. It underlines the ability of traditional orientations and structures to survive through adaptation, to acquire new roles and, in many cases, to make use of modern technological devices to reinforce tradition (witness, for example, Saudi Arabia). The eventual result is a society in which two social structures and value-systems co-exist. The complex network of interactions, in conflict and co-operation, is bound to arise and the 'balance of power' between the two changes from one time to another, depending on the situation, without either one being able to score complete victory. This contradiction is inherent in the situation with which most post-colonial countries have to grapple. Hence, according to this view, Islamic resurgence reflects the particular conditions of the Muslim world, or more precisely a number of Muslim countries, and their respective 'balance of forces'.

A third and final point of view which is held by the adherents of Islamic groups is the 'Westernisation-authenticity' perspective. This departs from the belief in the centrality of Islam and Islamic traditions in the history and life of their societies. According to this perspective, the introduction of modern 'Western' structures, codes of law and ideas were in fact part and parcel of the colonisation process. It follows that many aspects of what was considered to be modernisation are now perceived as a colonial legacy, a symbol of dependency and a function of Western domination that must be eliminated. A return to Islam, therefore, is a return to authenticity (*aṣāla*), an assertion of national pride and independence of thought.

Islamic Resurgence: Four Propositions

Islam has always been an important element in the public life of most Muslims, perhaps with the exception of Muslims under communist rule. It remains a major component of mass culture, and a bond for social solidarity.

Our argument is that Muslim reawakening does not simply reflect the reaffirmation of Muslims in their faith, but rather expresses deep-seated social concerns that are reflected in a situation of a 'society-in-crisis'. The features of this crisis are well known: rapid urbanisation and an economic crisis that involves fundamental social change, affecting the lower middle class in particular; the disillusionment with Western ideologies and political systems; and the problem of legitimacy surrounding the existence of a corrupt or ineffective leadership.

To understand more fully how these problems are evaluated from a Muslim perspective, we need to present a brief outline of Islamic thought and its system of ideas. Muslims distinguish between two types of society: the natural and the true. For them, the natural society is one that is ruled by custom, evolved by men for their own purposes and in ignorance of God's commandments (*jahiliyya*). In such a society, social solidarity is based on natural relationships (*'asabiyya*), and political power is institutionalised in natural monarchy (*mulk*), which is created by human process, controlled by human sentiments or purely human calculations of means and ends, and directed towards worldly goals.

Such a society, however, cannot be free from divisions and strife. In order to be so, Muslims believe, it must be permeated by a stable ethic that can only be provided by the revelation of the true religion. It is precisely for this purpose that God has revealed Islam to mankind, and it is primarily through the application of its comprehensive system of morality (the *shari'a*) that the true society could be established and maintained. Common obedience to the *shari'a*, as well as the mutual acceptance of the reciprocal rights and duties laid down in it, provide the moral relationships on which a stable social integration can be founded. In this context, political action must have as its objective the execution of God's will, and consequently political power is essentially a delegation by God (*wilaya*), controlled by His will and directed to the happiness of Muslims in this world as well as in the next.[8]

It is precisely this organic relationship between the realms of religion and politics that characterises the Muslim *umma*. In contrast to Christianity, Islam is not a private affair, the domain of which is the conscience of the individual. Rather, it is both a religion and a social order (*din wa dawla*), which pervades all aspects of human conduct. It is, in short, the essential attribute of the Muslims' true society.

Inherent in this view, there is an equally important concept of history. For Muslims, history is a process by which the natural society is replaced by the true Muslim society. It is a struggle that had been going on throughout history and had culminated in the establishment of the first Muslim community under the Prophet Muhammad. With this fulfilment, history had no more lessons to teach. If there was change, it could only be for the worse, and the worse could only be cured, not by creating something new, but by renewing what had once existed. In this sense, the struggle has extended into Muslim history whenever the ordering of Muslim society diverted from the true model. This need for a renovator (*mujaddid*) has become the launching pad for revivalist movements.

This is what is happening with the present resurgence of Islamic orthodoxy. Judging from similar movements in previous centuries, some observers have viewed the present trends in terms of a fundamentalist reaction to modernisation or a reassertion of medieval thought and practices. While such aspects are undoubtedly present, the new revivalism is not essentially a rejection of 'Westernising' influences. Rather, it is basically the product of new thought-forces that have been generated *within* Islam itself as a result of, and in response to, profound changes in the twentieth century.

'Western' ideas have indeed had some impact, sometimes positively and at other times negatively. One such influence is the Western concept of political obligation. In traditional Muslim thought, while political power was an essential function of the Prophet and his legitimate successors, true sovereignty in the *umma* rested only with God as the source of all authority. Muslim rulers, like all other Muslims, were equally called upon to submit to God's will, and accordingly the *shari'a* was established as the supreme authority in Muslim society. In this view of things, the ruler of the *umma* was thus responsible to God and his own conscience alone for the way in which he ruled. By implication then, the first duty of the community towards the ruler was one of obedience. But this obedience was neither passive nor without conditions. The duty of obedience held so long as the ruler ordered nothing which was contrary to the supreme law in the land, the *shari'a*. In later periods, and as a result of political changes in the Islamic world, this concept of political obligation had undergone an important modification. Obedience ceased to be conditional and became instead an absolute duty. It was henceforth argued that even an unjust ruler was better than none at all.

During the twentieth century, this concept of obedience has undergone further change. Under conditions of alien rule and nationalist mass movements obedience could no longer be considered an absolute duty. The concept of conditional obligation re-emerged, finding expression in experiments with liberal constitutional, democratic socialist, and nationalist one-party systems. That these experiments failed was not due to any incompatibility of this concept with Islamic thought. Rather, it was due primarily to the fact that the *secular* principle on which these systems proposed to re-order society was alien to, if not in conflict with, Islam as *din wa dawla*. Despite such failures, however, the belief in the principle of conditional obligation persisted and is now finding expression in a call for the revival of Islamic *political* orthodoxy.

Another Western influence that has contributed to Islamic revivalism has been in the impact of the polemic between secularism and Islamic fundamentalism. In earlier Muslim society, it was mainly through the influence of Sufi orders that tendencies to worldliness (and hence deviation from the true model) among urban classes were counteracted. By discrediting the aberrations and superstitions of popular Islam, secular education has had the effect of profoundly weakening the Sufi role in this delicate balance within Muslim society. At the same time, the arguments presented by Muslim apologists in favour of the social virtues of the Islamic system, and against the social evils prevalent in Western societies, have had the additional effect of neutralising secularist tendencies and strengthening instead orthodox fundamentalism. All of this was happening at a time when the central theme of 'development', associated with nation-building in the twentieth century, was increasingly impressing the Muslim world with the necessity and goodness of social progress. But progress in the Muslim perspective must have as its aim the restoration of the true community, and thus nation-building has come to acquire an Islamic framework.

In connection with development, there is another idea that has contributed to Islamic revivalism. The old Islamic view of knowledge was not a search for the unknown, but a mechanical process of amassing the known, which was conceived as 'given' and eternal. As a consequence, nothing in Muslim tradition could be discarded as antiquated, superseded or disproved.[9] At the same time, Muslims recognise that the solutions to present-day social problems are very complex affairs involving new legislation, which in turn raises very fundamental issues as to who is to legislate and by virtue of what authority. The entire philosophy of Muslim law becomes involved in this, raising furthermore problems of the political constitution of the state, of representation and the nature of political authority. A new framework of knowledge is thus required, one that must include modern ideas that are acceptable to Islam. This would involve the selection of some concepts and the rejection of others, as well as the modification of those which are accepted in the light of the teachings of Islam. This discrimination between what can and cannot be absorbed into Islam is not alien to Muslim tradition; it was effectively carried out by *ahl al-sunna wa'l jama'a* under the authority of the early caliphs. To be able to do likewise in the twentieth century presupposes the restoration of a duly recognised Islamic authority. It is the search for this much-needed institution that has inspired much of the present Islamic revivalism.

The 1980s are likely to witness a proliferation of Islamic revivalist groups in a number of Muslim countries. The mosque is indeed coming back as a centre for political agitation and mobilisation. Whatever paths these Islamic groups might take, their programmes and fortunes will undoubtedly contribute further to the endeavours of political Islam to accommodate itself to the process of modernisation. There is probably no reason to be pessimistic about the outcome. Eventually, the Muslim peoples will find their own appropriate solutions. 'These solutions might not necessarily coincide with anticipated Western solutions, but they will at least be based on Muslim experience and needs.'[10]

Alexander S. Cudsi
Ali E. Hillal Dessouki

Notes

1. Manifestations of Islamic resurgence in Israel, Turkey and the Soviet Union have also been reported. For Israel see the *Washington Post* 30 January, 1980; for Turkey the *Los Angeles Times* of 6 July, 1980 and for the Soviet Union see Alexandre Bennigsen, 'Soviet Muslims and the World of Islam', *Problems of Communism*, vol. XXIX, no. 2 (March–April 1980), pp. 38-51. See also Bennigsen's contribution to this volume.

2. There is a growing literature on the subject, see for instance G.H. Jansen, *Militant Islam* (New York, Harper and Row, 1980), Special issue of *Current History* on the World of Islam, vol. 78, no. 456 (April 1980); Raphael Israeli, 'The New Wave of Islam', *International Journal*, vol. 34, no. 3 (Summer 1979), pp. 369-90; Susan E. Marshall, 'Islamic Revival in the Maghreb: The Utility of Tradition for Modernizing Elites', *Studies in Comparative International Development*, vol. XIV, no. 2 (Summer 1979), pp. 95-108 and Ralph Brainbanti, 'The Recovery of Islamic Identity in Global Perspective', in Bruce Lawrence (ed.), *The Rose and the Rock: Mystical and Rational Elements in the Intellectual History of South Asian Islam* (Durham, Carolina Academic Press, 1979), pp. 159-98.

3. The conceptualisation of the first two perspectives is found in Michael C. Hudson, *Arab Politics: The Search for Legitimacy* (New Haven, Yale University Press, 1979) pp. 7-11.

4. *The Passing of Traditional Society: Modernizing the Middle East* (Glencoe, The Free Press, 1958).

5. *The Politics of Social Change in the Middle East and North Africa* (Princeton University Press, 1963) pp. 25-30.

6. 'Social Mobilization and Political Development', *American Political Science Review*, vol. LV, no. 3 (September 1961), pp. 493-514.

7. For their views see Ali E.H. Dessouki, 'Arab Intellectuals and al Nakba', *Middle Eastern Studies*, vol. 9, no. 2 (May 1973), pp. 187-95 and also by the same author 'The Views of Salama Musa on Religion and Secularization', *Islam and Modern Age*, vol. IV, no. 3 (August 1973), pp. 23-34.

8. Albert Hourani, *Arabic Thought in the Liberal Age, 1798–1939* (Oxford University Press, London 1970), pp. 6-7.

9. H.A.R. Gibb, *Modern Trends in Islam* (Octagon Books, New York 1975), p. 64ff.

10. Ibid, p. 105.

PART ONE:

ASPECTS OF THE ISLAMIC TRADITION REGARDING POWER

1 ACTIVISM AND QUIETISM IN ISLAM: THE CASE OF THE EARLY MURJI'A

Michael Cook

This chapter is concerned with establishing the political character of early Murji'ism; I shall argue, against the prevailing view, that it was activist. By way of essential background, I shall begin by sketching the little we know about early Murji'ism in general. At the end, I shall place my findings in the context of the wider question of activism and quietism in Islam. The research on which I am drawing here is presented in detail in a forthcoming monograph on the sources for the study of the Murji'ite and Qadarite controversies in early Islam.[1] The source-critical character of my research will be obvious even in the summary treatment given here: there will be more discussion of sources than of politics. Sources are less interesting than politics; but this presentation may at least help to bring home how thin are the threads from which our modern interpretations hang.

Early Murji'ism

The classical doctrine of Murji'ism is that faith consists in belief to the exclusion of works. There are well-behaved believers and badly-behaved ones, but all are believers. This doctrine is discussed at enormous length in the second- and third-century sources, and no Islamicist can avoid having heard of it. Occasionally, however, our sources speak of the 'early Murji'a' (*al-murji'a al-ūlā*) or 'early Murji'ism' (*al-irjā' al-awwal*). They do this with reference to a doctrine that might be categorised as historical rather than theological: that one must suspend judgement on the rights and wrongs of the first civil war. It is this doctrine that will concern us in this paper. Whether it really was historically anterior to the 'classical' doctrine is a good question, but one that we can at this point leave aside.

The content of this 'early Murji'ism' is best attested by two early epistles. The first is the *Kitāb al-irjā'*, an open letter ascribed to Ḥasan, a son of Muḥammad b. al-Ḥanafiyya; a Medinese 'Alid, he flourished (and perhaps died) in the days of the Caliph ʻAbd al-Malik. His epistle contains a brief and somewhat obscure Murji'ite *prise de position*. It has been edited, with an extended discussion, by Professor Josef van Ess, who argues for its authenticity.[2] The second relevant epistle is an Ibāḍī text ascribed to one Sālim b. Dhakwān, to which attention has been drawn in other connections by Dr A.K. Ennami. It contains a sustained anti-Murji'ite polemic which I am publishing in the monograph referred to above. This epistle, if authentic, dates to the early 70s — comparable to van Ess's dating of the *Kitāb al-irjā'* to *c.* 75. Whether these epistles are in fact authentic is a question which I discuss at length in my monograph; the important point for the present argument is that they stand or fall together.

The Murji'ite doctrine attacked by Sālim is remarkably close, in diction and content, to that propounded by Ḥasan, and contributes significantly to the restoration and understanding of the text of the *Kitāb al-irjā'*. The core of the doctrine consists in a simple epistemology: one must suspend judgement on events unless either (a) one has witnessed them oneself, or (b) there is unanimous testimony regarding them. (The origin of this epistemology is incidentally a question of some interest: either it is home-made common sense, or else it derives from a survival of the Sceptical-Empiricist tradition into late antiquity.) The crucial application of this epistemological razor is to the events of the first civil war: since we were not there, and hear only conflicting testimony, we cannot judge who was right and who was wrong. Since the first civil war is a favourite ground of sectarian self-definition in early Islam, it does not take much empathy to see this Murji'ite doctrine as anti-sectarian in purpose.

Into what historical context should we place this doctrine? Who invented it, when, and where? It is at this point that our sources begin to confuse us. It is easiest to begin with the question who first propounded Murji'ism, since this is a question which our sources explicitly set out to answer. More specifically, they provide three competing answers:

(1) The most widespread answer is the above-mentioned Ḥasan, to whom the *Kitāb al-irjā'* is ascribed. This is a commonplace of the biographical literature of the third century onwards; it has been taken up by several modern scholars, notably van Ess, who (without discussing the alternative answers) considers it correct.

(2) A second answer is ascribed to Awzaʿī (d. 157) and transmitted by Abū Dāwūd al-Sijistānī (d. 275). The first to propound Murji'ism is here said to be one Qays b. Abī Muslim al-Māṣir, a Kūfan who fought at the battle of Jamājim in 82. This answer has received brief discussion from Helga Brentjes and W. Madelung.

(3) A third answer, which dominates the early Ḥanbalite material, names Dharr b. ʿAbdallāh, a slightly better-known Kūfan who likewise fought at Jamājim. This answer, though associated with much interesting material, has not to my knowledge been discussed by modern scholars.

We have, then, three different candidates for the role of the originator of Murji'ism.

The question of when Murji'ism was invented is not one to which our sources often address themselves. We can say that in general they invite us to think in terms of the 70s or 80s of the first century. If we seek more precise indications, we again find contradiction. The fullest tradition on Ḥasan's originating role is closely associated with our placing his (rather slippery) death-date before Jamājim. So *irjā'* began *before* 82. Yet the only explicit chronological statement in our sources is a tradition assuring us that *irjā'* was only invented after the defeat of Ibn al-Ashʿath, i.e. *after* 82. We need not pursue this further.

The question where *irjā'* was invented is answered implicitly by our sources when they identify the putative originator. Ḥasan is Medinese; whereas Qays and Dharr are Kūfans. It is in this form that the issue requires that we ourselves take a stand. In favour of Ḥasan, and hence of the Ḥijāz, is the popularity of his candidature with the later sources, supported by his authorship of the *Kitāb al-irjā'*. But the endorsement of the later sources should not weigh with us unduly; and the epistle is an argument of substance only if we accept the ascription to Ḥasan which is given by the *isnād*. This *isnād* is in fact suspect, for a reason I shall touch on. Here it suffices to note that our materials on Ḥasan as a Murji'ite are almost entirely of Kūfan provenance — notably the text of the epistle. No independent confirmation is to be had from the traditions of the Ḥijāz itself, where indeed the Murji'ite record is virtually a blank. A Kūfan origin for *irjā'*, by contrast, fits well with the overwhelmingly Kūfan character of the movement as we know it from our sources.

My own preference, then, is for a Kūfan origin for *irjā'*; and I would go on to explain the alleged role of Ḥasan as a projection on the part of the Kūfan Murji'ites. If we remember that the primary antagonists of the Kūfan Murji'ites were the Kūfan Shī'ites, then such an invocation of a minor Ḥijāzī 'Alid in the role of founding father seems an apt polemical move. But if one believes in the historicity of Ḥasan's role, one can perfectly well reverse the interpretation: the materials on the role of Dharr, though Ḥanbalite in provenance, have *isnād*s of a marked Kūfan Shī'ite colouring, and could be seen as a secondary Shī'ite fabrication. In what follows I shall keep both a Medinese and a Kūfan origin in view as alternative hypotheses.

Early Murji'ite Politics

The political reputation of the Murji'ites in the bulk of the secondary literature is unenviable: at best they are quietists, at worst compliant supporters of the existing regime. This reputation rests primarily on evidence relating to the second century, and in particular to early Ḥanafism. How far it is fair to the Ḥanafites need not concern us here. The issue I want to discuss is whether it can justifiably be projected back to include the 'early Murji'ism' we have been discussing.

There is one text, unambiguous as it stands, which would indicate that it can. In the *Kitāb al-irjā'*, Ḥasan in one passage denounces extreme Shī'ites for slandering the Umayyads and God: *wa-a'lanū 'l-firya 'alā banī umayya wa-'alā 'llāh*. Van Ess has also interpreted in a philo-Umayyad or quietist sense other passages of Ḥasan's epistle and other aspects of his heritage (his hostility to the Qadariyya, his appearance in the *isnād* of a well-known tradition against *mut'a*, his — unfortunately rather garbled — report of disagreement about the division of booty after the death of the Prophet). I do not want to discuss these in detail here; the point I want to insist on is that none of these provides independent evidence of philo-Umayyad or quietist attitudes on Ḥasan's part. In other words, the evidence of the reference to the *banī umayya* in the epistle, while unambiguous, is also isolated.

What of the evidence *against* the thesis that early Murji'ism was philo-Umayyad or quietist? First, there is the striking fact that, as Madelung pointed out, the Murji'ites appear at the battle of

Jamājim on the *rebel* side. This includes both Qays and Dharr, the Kūfan candidates for the role of first Murji'ite. It requires an awkward *ad hoc* hypothesis to reconcile this with the philo-Umayyadism of Ḥasan's epistle. We must suppose, with Madelung, that the Murji'ites in joining the rebellion were betraying their own principles; or, with van Ess, that they liked and adopted Ḥasan's doctrine regarding the first civil war, but had no use for his contemporary politics.

Secondly, there is the clear testimony of the Ibāḍī epistle referred to above. From Sālim we learn that the Murji'ites dissociated from Mu'āwiya. (He mentions this in order to point out that in calling on the younger generation to join them in this position, they are violating their own epistemology: the younger generation have no direct knowledge of Mu'āwiya.) We learn further that there was a difference of opinion among the Murji'ites regarding the status of the rulers of the day: some considered them sinful believers (*mu'minūn ḍullāl*) affiliation to whom was forbidden; others considered them as plain infidels. Sālim makes apt polemical use of this disagreement to set one group off against the other. He makes no reference to Murji'ites taking a more favourable view of the regime — a significant silence, since any such views would have been grist to his polemical mill. Again, it would require an awkward *ad hoc* hypothesis to fit Ḥasan's concern to vindicate the Umayyads into such a picture.

What then are we to make of the favourable reference to the Umayyads in the *Kitāb al-irjā'*? Two possible lines of interpretation suggest themselves. The first arises from considerations regarding *isnād*s. As I have said, almost all the material bearing on Ḥasan as a Murji'ite is of Kūfan provenance (what little is not Kūfan seems to be Baṣran). But within this, two classes of material can be distinguished. First, we have what we may label 'pure Kūfan' material, where the *isnād*s show Kūfan transmitters already in the first half of the second century. Some part is played in the transmission by Kūfan Shī'ites (an example is a tradition expressing Ḥasan's disapproval of the Qadarites). But the most interesting items come from Kūfan Murji'ites — precisely the sort of people in whose hands we would *expect* to find the heritage of the real or alleged Ḥijāzī founder.

Secondly, alongside this 'pure Kūfan' material we have what we may call the 'adopted Kūfan' material. The traditions in this group are transmitted by Kūfans of the later second century (I have my reasons for including here the great traditionist Sufyān b. 'Uyayna who, though of Kūfan origin, was domiciled in Mecca). But the authorities from whom these Kūfans transmit are Ḥijāzīs of the dim and distant past: the Meccan 'Amr b. Dīnār (d. 126), and his perhaps slightly younger contemporaries, the Meccan 'Abd al-Wāḥid b. Ayman and the Medinese 'Uthmān b. Ibrāhīm al-Ḥāṭibī. This 'adopted Kūfan' material has two interesting features. First, the *isnāds* are very suspicious; for example, 'Abd al-Wāḥid b. Ayman, an early Meccan, is quoted only by Kūfans who die in or after the 190s. Secondly, this material contains all references to the *Kitāb al-irjā'*, including the text itself, with the single exception of a hostile tradition which has the author, Ḥasan, repent of having written it. One of these references, moreover, contains the explicit categorisation of his doctrine as *al-irjā' al-awwal* — a commendable attitude to the first civil war, it is implied, as opposed to a nasty heresy about faith.

The hypothesis I would venture in the light of these considerations is roughly like this. At some time in the second half of the second century, when hard-core Murji'ism of the classical sort went into decline in Kūfa, an attempt was made to rehabilitate what could be rehabilitated of the Murji'ite heritage; this salvaged component either was, or was presented in the guise of, the original Murji'ism of the Ḥijāzī founder, whose role was accordingly played up. It is thanks to this attempt that we have the text of the *Kitāb al-irjā'*. But we cannot accordingly rely on having the text in its original form; and one aspect of the price it may have paid for being preserved at all may have been a measure of political editing. We could construe the tradition that Ḥasan died before Jamājim as a further attempt to dissociate him from Murji'ite activism. In this context it would be of great interest to know who it was who wanted Ḥasan to have repented of having written the *Kitāb al-irjā'*. Unfortunately, the *isnād* is too chequered to allow us to answer this question: it is hard to say whether the tradition is Kūfan or Baṣran, and if Kūfan, whether Murji'ite or Shī'ite.

All this, however, is rather in the nature of using a sledgehammer to crack a nut. A more straightforward interpretation of the *banī umayya* of the *Kitāb al-irjā'* is textual corruption. The epistle as we have it is manifestly corrupt in several passages, which can rarely be restored with assurance. Our passage could be such a one. The simplest conjecture is that at some stage in the transmission of the text the phrase *nabiyyi 'llāh* was misread *banī umayya*.

Whether one takes the early Murji'a to be activists or quietists, one is left with something to explain away. My contention is that the activist assumption leaves us with less to explain away than the quietist.

Activism and Quietism in Early Islam

Islam, as everyone knows, is a political religion. *Umma* and imamate are at once political and religious conceptions with an ongoing significance in Islamic society — a situation to which no real equivalent can be found in Christianity. If there exist in this way intrinsically Muslim political values, then *prima facie* the political duty of a Muslim may be expected to lie in doing something about them. To that extent activism is given in Islam; here, in contrast to Christianity, it is the quietists who have to work to provide themselves with excuses. Consider, for example, the contrast between two major Shī'ite sects, the Zaydīs and the Imāmīs. The political thought of the Zaydīs, a sect of persistent activists, is straightforward and unstrained. That of the Imāmīs, by contrast, is marked by an extraordinary elaboration of the notions of *taqiyya* and *ghayba*, each a testimony to the amount the Imāmīs had to repress in becoming a quietist sect.

This activist heritage reflects the fundamental importance of tribal society in the history of Islam. It was tribesmen who conquered what was to become the Muslim world. They have also done much to keep the activist tradition alive down the centuries; witness the tribal environments of the Omani, Yemeni and Moroccan imamates, or the careers of Ibn Tūmart and the Sudanese mahdi. Unlike any other major religion, Islam is a highly successful ideology of tribal mobilisation; witness the profusion of Muḥammad's lesser imitators.

But the politics of the Muslim world at large could hardly sustain this spirited character. In the settled lands of the Muslim Caliphate, two processes operated to transform the social basis of politics. One was the gradual demobilisation of the tribal armies of conquest as new and quite different political and military elites were created. The other was the onset of large-scale conversion among the subject populations, from the point at which there could no longer be any pretence that to adopt Islam was to join the privileged ranks of the conquerors. The result of these two processes was the emergence of the Muslim masses — large numbers of Muslims who lived their lives with no part in the exercise of political power and no realistic expectation of achieving it.

Under such conditions it is not surprising that it should increasingly be pointed out that, if politics is none of your business, you had best keep out of it. When there is *fitna*, lock the door and sit quietly at home. At some time in the second century, a mass of injunctions of this type comes into circulation among the traditionists; in the early third century it sets the tone of the apolitical politics of the Ḥanbalite movement in its confrontation with 'Abbāsid heresy.

The case of the early Murji'a fits well into this general perspective. The milieu is Kūfa, a major settlement of the tribal conquerors in Iraq. Iraq was the greatest province of the empire; but the outcome of the first civil war, confirmed by the second, had condemned it to be no more than a province. Increasingly, the real military role in Iraq was taken over by the more professional Syrians. Having failed against the Syrians, the Kūfans did no better in their assignments against the Khārijite rebel Shabīb and the pagan Zunbīl of Sīstān. The Kūfans were becoming rather useless. The process issued in, and was accelerated by, the revolt of Ibn al-Ash'ath and the disaster at Jamājim. Thereafter, real power was not to be found in Kūfa — only the memory and the fantasy of it. On the Shī'ite side, Kūfan sentiments varied through sulkiness, half-hearted activism, to gnostic extravaganzas; it was perhaps here that Imāmism evolved into the quietist persuasion that was to exist for so long in symbiosis with the 'Abbāsid state. The conversion factor may have operated in the same direction. By the second civil war a whole army could be created out of converts — but it was an army armed only with sticks. In the subsequent period such men could well have been among the first to cast down their arms and take up civilian roles. The converts undoubtedly provided some extravagant gnostics; they may also have provided a milieu for the development of quietism.

Against this background, both an initial Murji'ite activism and a subsequent evolution towards quietism make good historical sense.

Notes

1. *Early Muslim Dogma: A Source-critical Study* (Cambridge: Cambridge University Press, 1981).

2. A convenient English summary of his views may be found in his paper 'The beginnings of Islamic theology' in J.E. Murdoch and E.D. Sylla (eds.), *The Cultural Context of Medieval Learning* (Dordrecht and Boston, 1975), pp. 93-7.

2 TOWARDS A MUSLIM THEORY OF HISTORY

Thomas Naff

Every Muslim society is under a moral obligation to know and understand its past, above all that unique past created by the Prophet Muḥammad and the first Islamic community (*umma*). From the days of the Prophet, the preservation and transmission of the past, in a variety of forms, has been of utmost concern to Muslims, especially to their religious authorities. This interest is understandable since for Muslims salvation depends fundamentally on knowledge of their religious history. In Islam, salvation demands correct Muslim behaviour (*'ibada*), which requires understanding God's rules of religion and law, which comes only through accurate knowledge of the words, actions and customs of Muḥammad, his companions and his early successors; that is, knowledge of the *hadith* and *sunna*. Thus, historical memory (or historicism) and salvation are cognate in Islamic belief.

This interlocking relationship is a basic theoretical construction in Islam. It is integral to the theocratically conceived political and social organisation of Muslim societies, since it is upon the base of this special kind of historical knowledge that the structures of Islamic theology and law are built. As bodies of knowledge, Islamic history, religion and law not only derive from, and were formed by the same primary sources — the Qur'ān, *hadith* and the *sunna* — but they share a common object, which is to make possible the attainment of salvation through the fulfilment of God's will, towards which end history stands in the service of religion and law. By this Islamic formulation, history and religion are inextricably bound and cannot stand independent of one another, with the result that the Muslim concept of historical knowledge is shaped by theology. The logical corollary is also true.

This organic linkage leads to a basic hypothesis for an Islamic theory of history: if history and religion are cognate and the function of history is to serve religion and law, then it follows that within Muslim thought, history is a moral science whose purpose is to give an ethical meaning to life that will lead man to God.

In the Islamic universe, the governing principle of all thought is that God, not man, is the source and object of history. Islamic history is formed by God's revelation to the Prophet Muḥammad of the perfect existence. By living in obedience to God's will, Muḥammad and the first Islamic community created for eternity the perfect social model. After the death of the Prophet and the end of revelation, complete knowledge of that perfect experience degenerated with time and human misunderstanding. Thus, the process of history for the Muslim could only become a constant striving to regenerate and immortalise that ideal moment. This endeavour was a command imposed by God.

In response to so compelling a need as comprehending God's will, there evolved the doctrine of *ijma'*, that is, the consensus of the *'ulamā* — technically, 'the unanimous doctrine and opinion of the recognised religious authorities at any given time' — or, in the absence of recognised religious authorities, something resembling generally accepted opinion by leading ecclesiastics and ruling powers. By providing an effective means for true and accurate interpretation of the Qur'ān, *ijma'* became the foremost instrument of classical Muslim legal theory and practice. This complex doctrine was construed differently by the various schools of law, but in the matter of divine guidance for the *umma*, it was a self-fulfilling proposition. *Ijma'* allowed the Muslim community to receive divine guidance through the special ability of its religious authorities to interpret God's word. They determined by consensus what was spiritually or legally correct for the community, and, reflexively, it was generally agreed that what the *umma* as a whole accepted and acted on represented a valid consensus of what God intended. Nevertheless, in a system of belief where history proceeds from a divinely-ordained immutable perfection of existence, with perfect rules for living in an imperfect human society, serious difficulties arise.

Remedial theories such as consensus mitigate but do not solve the problem. Without the guidance of a true prophet, it is impossible to know God and understand His will perfectly. Since God gave man free will as well as obligations, this Muslim concept of history, even with its established prescripts, symbols and principles, is not a closed, static or predetermined system. In a condition where divine revelation ceased and where the only resource left to man was his own fallible intellect, God's work could be given limitless interpretation and the striving for perfection could take any form or direction. The Muslim community was rescued from spiritual chaos by the leadership of religious authorities, the *'ulamā*, who preserved the word of God and the tradition of the Prophet, elucidating them for the true believers. That divisive centrifugal forces operated on the early generations of Muslims is seen in the major controversies that divided the community after Muḥammad's death, such as the disputes over the recension of the Qur'ān, the nature of the *khilafa* (leadership of the community) which produced a heterodox Islam as a separate branch from orthodoxy, and in the more than 100 schools of religious law (*sharī'a*) that burgeoned. In time, guidance was also offered by Muslim saints, sufis, zealots and mystic sects that claimed esoteric knowledge of God's word.

Still, without a living prophet, a definitive understanding of God's will is beyond the capacity of ordinary human intellect. Lacking such a precise knowledge, man is incapable of comprehending and controlling perfectly his actual social world, that is, his immediate history. So, in each generation, man gives moral relevance to his immediate history by directing his actions toward recreating a God-given ideal state which he can only imperfectly grasp, and which he perceives through the prism of the realities and needs of his own time. In both *sunni* and *shī'i* belief, man is in permanent need of guidance, but for the *shī's*, divine guidance is given only through the sin-cleansed *imām* (spiritual leader of the faithful), making the existence of the *imām* a 'metaphysical necessity'.

However, unlike the fixed sanctified past, the historical process as an immediate reality is forever evolving, a shapeless unchannelled flow of experience. For every society, history is made 'real' by time, perspective, selectivity and the imposition of meaning through the medium of a religion, ideology or theory. The range of historical meanings a society can give to its actions is limitless, in constant process of creation. For Muslims, actual reality must somehow be made to harmonise with the divine ideal, or at the very least, must symbolically project an Islamic vision which imitates the ideal. But there will always be discordance between the historical ideal, defined and maintained by religious authorities, and immediate historical reality. While there is universal acceptance in Islam that Muḥammad, with God's inspiration, created a perfect society — that is the fixed part of the historical ideal — notions of the exact nature of that state change constantly in accordance with the empirical, experiential, ideological and ecological exigencies of contemporary living societies. Although Muḥammad's society is a permanent historical reality for the faithful, its religious representation will always be unstable because religious expression is ideological and ideology is, over time, in constant flux, changing to fit the 'historical moment of its use'.

Yet every society exhibits a compelling need to define itself by imposing a stable meaning on the history of its own time. The effort may or may not take the form of an independent intellectual pursuit, which produces historical literature or a conscious historicism as conceived in modern intellectual or scholarly terms. In Islam, this is a religious struggle which is manifested in faith and in the symbols and metaphors of an idealised past. The process involves a combination of religious and historical experience: the ritual reenactment of certain spiritual exertions deemed essential to recreating the prescribed past; selecting and redefining various aspects of social history which determine social conduct in the present; the reworking of religious symbols or the creation of new notions for the attainment of present goals or satisfaction of present needs; all in the cause of understanding and controlling immediate history.

The process reshapes and gives each current social order its own particularity which, being religiously defined, is thus ideologically justified. By applying religious conventions in specific ways, and through careful control of ideology, Muslim rulers and ecclesiastics together could claim to be preserving and maintaining the traditions of an ideal past. Nevertheless, despite a universal and constantly renewed avowal by Muslim societies that God's will is the cause of all that happens in the world, the very nature of historical evolution precludes the possibility that a living social structure can ever be in complete congruity with its conceptualised model. If one accepts that all social structures are the product of historically determined social relations which form the substance — the empirical reality — from which existing societies fashion their institutions, then this incongruity is logically preordained. For every Muslim community there were and are certain realities that overwhelm any other possibility: the unique historical experience of different Islamic societies; the tendency of Muslim societies to mould Islam to the contours of their immediate historical experiences thereby giving Islam as many meanings as there are local historical settings; the deep-rooted instinct of all peoples to select from among the general concepts of religion those precepts which most conform to daily experiences; the demands of survival whether from ecological or human causes; and even the obligatory change-producing struggle to understand and accommodate one's actions to God's will.

It is the tension generated by the incongruity between the received God-perfect immutable past and the ever-changing commonsensical reality of the present that gives history in Islam its moral purpose and imposes on Muslim communities the obligation of spiritual struggle. This fundamentally religious rationale of history has formulated the Muslim attitude toward change in the social order. In Islam, the only legitimate change is change which results in the moral betterment of the Muslim community. The validity and quality of any structural variation of Muslim life is measured by its conformity to God's law and by the degree to which it is believed to direct the community back to that perfect model of existence created by the Prophet. It follows that, as a concept, history cannot be for Muslims a natural organic or rational scientific progression, either by evolution or revolution, towards a yet to be realised ideal sprung from human vision. Ibn Hanbal argued that believers must simply take some things on faith. This would appear to be one of those propositions in Islamic thought covered by that dictum. For the faithful Muslim, the ideal (Muḥammad's original community) has already happened, it has been revealed, it is real, it is continually reaffirmed by symbol, metaphor and ideology, and it is of an infinitely higher order than any man-made realm since it comes from God.

Therefore, Islam, being the creation of God, cannot be reformed and needs no reform — reform in the sense of improving or altering its basic truth. Within a strictly Muslim interpretation, the concept of reform entails a process of purifying Islam of those excrescences of human misunderstanding which have been attached through the centuries, restoring Islam to the pristine state in which Muḥammad left it. This mentality explains the basic religious nature of reform — and revolution — in Islamic history, strikingly so in Ottoman times.

Such an attitude also reveals why Islamic reform is always governed by and drawn inexorably to the past: to the Muslim mind, nothing in the present or future could possibly ever be as good as that exquisite society erected by Muḥammad and transfixed forever by his death. The object of true Islamic reform cannot be to create a new society; rather, it must have as its ultimate end the re-establishment of the Prophet's ideal community. Of course, a mortal society of believers, however pious, is incapable of literally recreating what was in the last analysis a creation of God. But by the process of fulfilling its obligations to God, rendering service to God (*'ibada*), and understanding and controlling its moral history, the Muslim polity could hope to rediscover and realise, at least by imitation, Muḥammad's divinely-inspired vision of the perfect society. Only by such a process, grounded in faith, could Muslims change their immediate condition and attain an improved moral state. Change for any other cause would be to no purpose and even contravene God's will. al-Ghazali (d. 1111), a towering figure in Islamic theology and philosophy, argued that in Muslim society, reformers had to be religious authorities or religiously inspired because the *ulamā* possessed the deepest insights into God's purpose and only they could give the truest meaning to God's word as set forth in the Qur'ān. The reflexive religious response of Muslim societies to deep crises meant that Islam in its various parts and settings has always been subject to a kind of ongoing reformation, which is why it never underwent an experience precisely like that of the historical Reformation of Christianity in the sixteenth century. Unlike Christianity, Islam has never possessed the structural elements for a great institutional and doctrinal Reformation. There were no synods or church councils in Islam to decree who was a Muslim or to legitimise doctrine and ritual. In Islam, doctrine is interpretable but untouchable.

If there is a single paradigm common to the history of all Islamic nations it is this: the belief that Islam is a way of life inherently superior to all others; that power and prosperity are conferred on those Muslim communities that conform to the true path leading to Muḥammad's ideal existence and thus to salvation; that straying from the path to pursue false notions and mundane ambitions results in degeneration; that regeneration requires a spiritual purification which is attained by cleaning the community of its corruptions, by the fulfilment of its obligations to God, and by living in accordance with God's word, all of which will result in the restoration (or imitation) of an idealised past existence (identified and expounded by the *'ulamā*).

There is within this paradigm internal evidence of a false assumption. Because of the historically consistent, all-pervasive religious ambiance of the social and political modes of Muslim societies, it has been contended that there is no duality of religion and state in Islam. This is not historically correct. The conflict between immediate historical reality and the religious ideal of a fixed past, the ever-widening gap between *shari'a* (the theoretical bond of all Muslim societies) and secular law, and functioning of the paradigm itself, all of which have been a part of the Muslim polity from its beginnings, are testimony that the ideal of an integrated Islam encompassing all facets of life never became a reality. From the outset, after the death of the Prophet, whatever hope had existed for an ideal unity of religion and state was shattered by the long controversy over the *khilafa* begun during the early formative years of the Islamic nation. The classical concept of an *umma* with an ideal *khalifa* was unrealisable because it presupposed a caliph who is both spiritual and worldly ruler over a universal Muslim *umma*, a condition never achieved. However, in this connection, it should be recalled that the ultimate duty for the *umma* and for the individual Muslim is the act itself of striving for this ideal — to 'strive in God's path' — for the perfection that was made historically real by the Prophet. Nor was the notion of a politically and religiously monolithic Islam immune from the divisive effects of the continuous struggle between temporal and religious authorities for the primary and higher loyalties of the Muslim citizenry, a contention also dating from an early Islamic era.

Despite the persistence down to modern times of the ideal of a temporally and spiritually integrated Islamic community, the *umma* has in fact historically been treated as a segregated polity by various Muslim dynasties. Under the Ottoman *millet* system in which the non-Muslim subject population was constituted into religiously defined political and administrative entities, the Muslim subject became a *de facto* Islamic *millet*, especially from the seventeenth century onwards, by virtue of the government's policies of taxation, land tenure, administration and other regulations. With the growth of the nation-state, the concept of *umma* underwent changes of emphasis, with greater stress placed on its being a religious community as opposed to a political or national body; but the ideal, though often faint and distant in most of the modern Islamic world, has never faded entirely from existence.

However, although Islam did not really function as a wholly unified religious, social and political system, historically religion has emerged consistently as the primordial structural element in Islamic public life. Because in Islam religion is both theoretically and, in many respects, actually the determinant of social and political conduct, religion has been constantly a central public and international issue. This is not a latter-day phenomenon, stimulated by the impact of Western influences or by European insistence on the right to protect Christian communities in the Ottoman Empire, although these factors did reinforce the public and international character of religion. Religious laws and sensibilities were always integral to the conduct of Islam's international relations and domestic affairs. Even though, in the modern age, religion has receded to the background in the exercise of foreign and domestic policy among most Muslim nations, it remains an element of reckoning, a touchstone, and is always capable of a rapid, often revolutionary, revival.

The Islamic concepts of history and reform are rooted in the same theoretical soil and nurtured by the same theoretical principles. Since the impelling event of Islamic history is the advent of Muḥammad, and since the primary moral purpose of every Muslim country is to attain salvation in the next world by emulating in this one Muḥammad's first community, and since that obligation can be fulfilled only by striving 'in God's path' to recreate that perfection of existence fixed in the past by the Prophet's death, then the study of history is also a moral imperative for it is an integral part of the struggle to revive a particular God-willed past. It was through history, not necessarily always as a recognised independent intellectual endeavour but often subsumed as a branch of theology or law or philosophy, or in the form of biography, geography, annals, genealogy or as *hadith* — but none the less history — that the tradition of the Prophet and the cultural heritage of Islam was preserved.

Muslim historical literature has on the whole consistently reflected the influence of the Islamic concept of history, even in its modern 'scientific' scholarly modes. Those modern and contemporary Muslim historians who have not altogether abandoned Islam frequently exhibit a traditional, morally didactic purpose in their writing, even when espousing a particular secular ideology. The practice of employing a religious argument to promote and justify a secular idea has a particularly long and rich tradition in Islamic history.

Early and classical Muslim historiography focused on Muḥammad and the meaning of his message, his life and times, and his death. In Muslim and non-Muslim historiography, Muḥammad is a real historical figure who is connected to pre-Islamic times by his association with the established chain of prophecy in Judaism and Christianity, and with all ages after him by the universality of his message and the obligations God placed on his community. Since God obliged the *umma* to know and understand the Islamic past, the study of history in its various forms is, hypothetically, also a requirement for the attainment of the Prophet's perfection. Hypothetically so, because there appears to be no hard incontrovertible historical evidence that the formal study of history *qua* historiography, is a doctrinal or legal obligation, nor, on the evidence, does it appear that the obligation was one normally or consciously urged by the *'ulamā*.

The paradox here is more apparent than real. Several obvious factors demonstrate that the duty to study history is implicit in God's command to know the past, and that Muslim communities have always perceived that this received first principle contained its own corollary. Among the deduced evidence to this effect is the traditional importance given to history in the education of Muslims, but the most conclusive proof lies in the sheer quantity of historical writing in all epochs of the Islamic past and in the moral ambience of that historiography. Despite certain Aristotelian and Byzantine influences, Muslim historiography, down to recent times, is consistently religious in its stated purpose and presentation. It is permeated by references to God, the Prophet, the Qur'ān, the *hadith*, the *sharī'a* and salvation. Major and minor historians alike, whatever their genre, down to the nineteenth century, rarely failed to advise their readers (or hearers) of the moral purpose of their labours and to reiterate that object throughout the text — history is useful 'to prepare man better for the life after death and for his religion'; the purpose of history is *hisba*, 'to create a desire for good actions'; a good historian must be a good Muslim because then he will be 'reliable in religious matters and (therefore) trustworthy'. The same mentality pervades the great epics of Muslim literature.

The moral object of Muslim historiography is reinforced by Muḥammad's own sturdy interest in and ideological use of history to authenticate his prophecy and to strengthen his leadership, as well as by the fact that for the Muslim historian, the primary source document of Islamic history is the Qur'ān. These elements have been influential in the development of Muslim historiography. One aspect was a tendency among classical Muslim historians to attempt universal histories in parallel to Muḥammad's universal message, works which on examination turn out to be general histories of their own times and places, that is to say, of their own Islamic realms.

This focus is not a reflection of disinterest or ignorance of other cultures. Muslim geographers, travellers and chroniclers contributed significantly to knowledge of world history. It is, rather, a matter of stress determined by the pervasive moral mission of scholarship and by the concomitant view that other cultures simply did not compare in importance to that of Islam. The proper, the essential focus of study had to be the Islamic *umma* and its salvation. Everything beyond was potentially corrupting. But because Muḥammad is linked to a pre-history of his era through the Bible and the earlier prophets, this past and its related places could be woven into the tapestry of Muslim history as a kind of border to the central design.

This theoretical construct of Islamic history as a moral science in no way denies or contradicts the other documented realities of Muslim historical literature. The writing of history as a separately identifiable humanistic and social science did not emerge in Islamic scholarship until around the tenth century. Muslim historians, like their non-Muslim counterparts, in general concerned themselves with the deeds of their contemporaries and with other worldly affairs, often in the role of official court historians recording and magnifying the accomplishments of their patrons. The best of the great histories and chronicles stand forth all the more in relief against the bulk of ordinary historiography, because they were transcendent in quality and scope.

Even so, normative historical writing was consonant not only with the tradition of oral history, often as epic narrative or epic poetry, rooted in pre-Islamic Middle Eastern tribal societies, but as well with the tradition of recording the particular reigns and actions of Muḥammad's companions and early successors. The historical record of their lives and times were essential for the creation and authenticity and transmission of *hadith*, for establishiong geneologies and for providing precedents for legitimising legal theory and practice.

Consequently, with rare exceptions, Muslim historians focused almost exclusively on the Islamic past until the sixteenth century when the demands of state compelled the Ottoman authorities to acquire more knowledge of their European adversaries. It is important too, for understanding the nature of Islamic historiography, to know that Muslim historians in pre-modern times did not devote themselves solely to the writing of history. They were also theologians, philosophers, jusrists, statesmen, bureaucrats and teachers. (At-Tabari and Ibn Khaldun are outstanding examples of great historians who combined in themselves several of these professions.) These other backgrounds and experiences give a particular coloration (and, often, special insights) to their histories.

But whatever the approach, there was within the profession (if it can be loosely designated as such) a generally demonstrated concern with the authenticity of sources — which included a wide variety of documents, primarily but not exclusively Muslim and Arabic — accuracy of detail and fact, and a care for truth as it was perceived by each practitioner, despite much fabrication of *hadith* and polemical writing. In these matters the moral purpose of history exercised an influence, for if the study of history was to serve its function, the tradition of the Prophet and the events of the first and subsequent early Islamic states had to be recorded accurately.

In sum then, as history, in its conceptual role, was to provide ethical guidance to the *umma* for its moral betterment, and as the *umma* could be reformed only for moral improvement, then in the Islamic scheme, at least theoretically, history is both an integral part of and a directing force in the process of change itself. This logic also encompasses Muslim historiography which, true to its theoretical base, was morally didactic.

Reference Abbreviations

'Anthropology of Islam' — Abdul Hamid el-Zein, 'Beyond Ideology and Theology: The Search for the Anthropology of Islam', *Annual Review of Anthropology*, no. 6 (1977), pp. 227-54

Bayan — al-Jahiz, 'Amr b. Bakr, *al-Bayan wa-t-Tabyan*, (ed.) Hasan al-Sandubi, 4th edn (Cairo, 1956), 3 vols

Bidayah — Ibn Kathir, Isma'il b. 'Umar, *al-Bidayah wa-n-Nithayah fi-t Ta'rikh* (Cairo, 1932-9), 14 vols

Dakhirah — al-Ghumri, Sa'ad ad-Din al-'Uthmani ash-Shafi'i, *Dikhirat al-I'lan bi Ta'rikh Umara' al-Misr fi-l-Islam* in Rosenthal, *Historiography*, p. 546, Arabic text (see GAL, II, p. 297, S II, p. 408)

Historiography — Rosenthal, Franz, *A History of Muslim Historiography*, 2nd revised edn (Leiden, 1968)

Ihya' — al-Ghazali, Abu Ahmad, *Ihya' 'Ulum ad-Din* (Cairo, 1939), 4 vols.; also, the most recent edition (Cairo, 1967-8), 5 vols

I'lan — as-Sakhawi, Shams ad-Din Abu al-Khayr Muhammad b. 'Abd ar-Rahman b. Muhammad b. Abi Bakr b. 'Uthman as-Sakhawi ash-Shafi'i, *al-I'lan bi-t-Tawbikh li Man Dhamma Ahl at-Tawrikh* in Rosenthal, *Historiography*, pp. 263-499 and Arabic text, pp. 584-610

Kamil — Ibn al-Athir, Ali b. Muhammad 'Izz ad-Din, *al-Kamil fi-t-Ta'rikh* (Beirut, 1965-7), 13 vols

Khitat — al-Maqrizi, Ahmad b. Ali Taqi ad-Din, *Kitab al-Muwa 'idh wa-l I'tibar fi Dhikr al-Khitat wa-l A'thar*, 2 vols. (Cairo, 1970)

al-Mukhtasar — al-Kafiyaji, Muhyi ad-Din Muhammad b. Sulayman, *al-Mukhtasar fi 'Ilm at-Ta'rikh* in Rosenthal, *Historiography*, Arabic text, pp. 547-80

Muqaddimah — Ibn Khaldun, *The Muqaddimah: An Introduction to History*, tr. by Franz Rosenthal, 3 vols. (New York, 1958)

Muruj — al-Mas'udi, Ali b. Husayn, *Muruj adh-Dhahabi wa-l-Ma'adin al-Jawah*, (ed.) Charles Pellat (Beirut, 1966-74), 5 vols

Mushkalat — al-Ya'qubi, Abu al-Abbas Ahmad b. Abi Ya'qub Ishaq b. Ja'far b. Wahb b. Wadih al-Katib al-Abbasi, *Mushkalat an-Nas li Zamanihim*, (ed.) William Millward (Beirut, 1962)
Muzhir — as-Suyuti, 'Abd ar-Rahman Jalal ad-Din, *al-Muzhir fi 'Ulum al-Lughah wa Anwa'iha* (Bulaq, 1865), 2 vols. in 1; more recent edition (Cairo, 1945)
Ta'rikh — at-Tabari, Abu Ja'far Muhammad b. al-Jarir, *Ta'rikh ar-Rusul wa-l Muluk* (Leiden, 1879-1901), 15 vols.; recent edition (Cairo, 1960-77), 11 vols
Tuhfah — al-Iji, Muhammad Ibrahim, *Tuhfah al-Faqir ila Sahib as-Sarir* in Rosenthal, *Historiography*, 201-44

Notes

In order to enable the reader to complete a whole thought or to allow the flow of his own responses to this text uninterrupted by constant references to sources, I have clustered all the notes to this chapter in a single comprehensive reference at the end. For the reader who cares, guidance to specific citations to sources are related to particular parts of the narrative by reference to relevant pages of the text. Full citations of sources used are given in the list of abbreviations preceding the notes.

The hypothesis for a theory of Islamic history offered on p. 24 and the section immediately following evolved out of discussions over a three year period with my late good friend and colleague Dr Abdul Hamid el-Zein, Associate Professor of Anthropology at Temple University. These exchanges continued until his untimely death in August 1979. So intermixed did our thoughts become, that it is difficult to differentiate my thoughts from his except to say that I know now his influence was greater on me than mine on him. Many of the ideas generated were published in his article 'Beyond Ideology and Theology: The Search for the Anthropology of Islam', *Annual Review of Anthropology*, no. 6, 1977, pp. 227-54. My own thoughts in a less refined form were already sketched when he completed that article, but it is not mere cant to say that whatever is of value in the foregoing analysis of the nature of history in Islamic thought owes more than I can measure to Professor el-Zein.

(pp. 24–6) On the relationship of history, religion, and law, Kafiyaji/Rosenthal, *al-Mukhtasar*, pp. 554-8 (Arabic); al-Ghumri/Rosenthal, *Dakhirah*, 546 (Arabic); Ibn al-Athir, *Kamil*, I, 4-9; al-Mas'udi, *Muruj*, I, 12; al-Ghazali, *Ihya'*, I, 15, 199; al-Maqrizi, *Khitat*, I, 3-4ff; at-Tabari, *Ta'rikh*, I, 3ff, 18; Ibn Khaldun, *Muqaddimah*, I, 63ff; as-Sakhawi/Rosenthal, *I'lan*, 263-99; Iji/Rosenthal, *Tuhfah*, 205-13, 223; Qur'ān, II: 62, 189, 247; XI: 120; XII: 3, 7, 111; XXVI: 84; XXXI: 20; XLIII: 44 (these are exemplary of the verses cited by almost all the foregoing historians).

(p. 25) On *ijma'*, al-Bukhari, Abdul-Aziz, *Kashf al-Asrar 'ala Usul al-Buzdawi*, Cairo, 1889, III, 947; as-Subki, Taj ad-Din, *Jam al-Jawami*, Cairo, 1935, III, 295; Amidi, Sayf ad-Din, *al-Ahkam fi Usul al-Ahkam*, Cairo, 1929, I, 112, 150; al-Ghazali, Abu Ahmad, *al-Mustasfa'min 'Ilm al-Usul*, Cairo, 1970, I, 115-21.

(p. 26) '. . . metaphysical necessity', G.E. von Grunebaum, *Islam*, London, 1955, 11.

(pp. 27–8) '. . . historical moment of its use', Zein, 'Beyond Ideology', 240; on the necessity to give the historical process definition and shape, based on the notion that all that happens in the world is God's will, see, e.g., al-Ya'qubi, *Mushkalat*, 5-35; Kafiyali/Rosenthal, *al-Mukhtasar*, 547-8, 554, 557-8, 558-61 (Arabic) — see especially 547-8 and 557-8 for definitions and categories of historical knowledge and writing; al-Sakhawi/Rosenthal, *I'lan*, 297, 329-35 — al-Sakhawi states that any category of historical study where no moral purpose is served is forbidden; al-Jahiz, Amr b. Bakr, *Kitab al-Taj*, 112-25, 189-234; Ibn Khaldun, *Muqaddimah*, I, 63 on the historical particularity of societies; for some contemporary interpretations on how the process of history shapes social orders in Islam, see, in addition to Zein, 'Beyond Ideology', 229-47, C. Geertz, 'Ideology as a Cultural System', *Ideology and Discontent*, (ed.) D.E. Apter, New York, 1964, 47-76, especially 62, 'Common Sense as a Cultural System', *Antioch Review* 33, 5-26, *Islam Observed, Religious Development in Morocco and Indonesia*, New Haven, Conn. 1968, 94-5; D. Eickelman, *Moroccan Islam*, Austin, 1976, 63-4, 126; A.S. Bujra, *The Politics of Stratification: A Study of Political Change in a South Arabian Town*, Oxford, 1971, 112ff; on social structures and social relations see E.K. Nottingham, *Religion and Society*, Doubleday, New York, 1954, 1-81; F. Frey, 'The Analysis of Social Structure' (unpublished paper, courtesy of the author), 1-86; C. Levi-Strauss, *Structural Anthropology*, New York, 1963, 206-31; T.B. Bottomore, 'Structure and History', in P.M. Blau, (ed.) *Approaches to the Study of Social Structure*, New York, 1975, 159-71; compare these approaches with M. Weber, *The Methodology of the Social Sciences*, tr. and (ed.) E.A. Shils and H.A. Finch, Glencoe, Free Press, 1949, 111 and R. Levy, *The Social Structure of Islam*, Cambridge, 1969, 53-90, 192-270. I am obliged to my colleague, Professor George Makdisi for reminding me that Islam possesses no structural elements for reform similar to those in Christianity.

(pp. 31–2) On the study of history as a moral imperative, the Prophet Muḥammad's use of history, the importance of accuracy in historiography, and the didacticism of history, see Abu Hayyan at-Tawhidi, *Kitab al-Imta'wa al-Mu'anasa*, Cairo, 1939-44, III, 150ff; Subki Taj ad-Din, *Tabaqat ash-Shafi'iya*, Cairo, 1905-6, I, 180-5; as-Suyuti, Jalal ad-Din 'Abd ar-Rahman b. Abi Bakr, *Ta'rikh al-Khulafa'*, Cairo, 1964, 3-26; Iji/Rosenthal, *Tuhfah*, 209; Ibn al-Athir, *Kamil*, I, 4-6; as-Sakhawi/Rosenthal, *I'lan*, 273-4, 279-80, 326, 358-78 (Arabic); on Muḥammad's use of history, Ibn Kathir, *Bidayah*, I, 6ff; as-Sakhawi/Rosenthal, *I'lan*, 288, 494-5; Qur'ān, XX: 99; on the oral tradition and sources of history, al Mas'udi, *Akhbar az-Zaman*, Cairo, 1958, 200ff; at-Tabari, *Ta'rikh*, II, 123-5, 279, 376, 410-14ff, 479; as-Suyuti, *Muzhir*, I, 248-50, II, 355; al-Jahiz, *Bayan*, III, 360-8. See also, B. Lewis and P.M. Holt (eds.), *Historians of the Middle East*, London, 1962, 35-54; L.V. Thomas, *A Study of Naima*, (ed.) N. Irzkowitz, New York, 1972, 70-1, 82, 93, 110-11; H.A.R. Gibb, *Modern Trends in Islam*, New York, 1972, 1-38; A.H. Hourani, 'Islam and the Philosophers of History', *Middle East Studies*, III, 1967, 206-68.

3 THE IDEOLOGISATION OF ISLAM IN THE CONTEMPORARY MUSLIM WORLD

Ali Merad

Preliminary Remarks

The ideologisation process of religion in the Muslim world takes place in a wider context, which has allowed contemporary Muslim thought to make decisive shifts from the traditional theological field to the sociological one, and to formulate the content of 'Islam' in terms of norms and values of socio-political order. As a result, this may relativise Islam, if not relegate it to the background, or to definitely conceal the specific values of the religion.

A second remark relates to the acceptance of the concept of ideology which will be our main concern here. We use the term in its most accepted usage, that is to say, a set of political and social ideas which guide the policies of a government or a party, and which tends to constitute a dominant doctrine in as much as it becomes the ideological expression of a ruling power. From this perspective the concept of ideology presumes not only a structured body of ideas centred around a vision of society, but also a political power or at least the will of a political authority (Ibn Khaldun would have called it *asabiyya*), aspiring to realise that vision. In general, an ideology is the doctrinal expression of power.

This chapter represents only an introduction to the subject. It outlines the themes and problems of contemporary Islamic ideology. Islamic debates nowadays refer mainly to the concept of ideology in order to define the role of Islam in the political, social and cultural life of the Muslim peoples. It is beyond our interest here to provide an exhaustive list of the many essays and publications which refer explicitly or implicitly to the affirmation of this ideological option and which clearly testify to the ideologisation of Islam.[1]

Theoretical Foundations of the Ideologisation

The ideological orientation of Muslim contemporary thought seems to derive its main justification from the concept of Islam being belief and law (*aqida wa sharī'a*), religion and state (*din wa dawla*) and a system of values for spiritual and temporal affairs (*din wa dunya*);[2] in one word it is the fundamental principle of a total ideology.[3]

Such a concept leads naturally to the formulation of doctrines of power in modern Muslim societies whose primary frame of reference is Islam. Here the meaning of Islam as a fundamental ideological frame of reference must be explicitly explained. By 'Islam' it is essentially understood that it is not only a system of religious beliefs, but also a set of principles which should guide the general organisation of the community.

The understanding of the sources of 'Islam' as the foundation of an ideology is not uniform throughout the Muslim world. To take into account the diversity of schools, tendencies and personal views of researchers and well-informed scholars, we will refer to the following definitions which correspond, *grosso modo*, to the arguments of fundamentalists and reformists on one side, and to the orthodox modernists and the radical modernist schools on the other:

(1) The 'two sources', the revealed Qur'ān and the tradition of the prophet, *hadith*, to which one may add a third source, 'the tradition of *salaf*', are the most morally and religiously distinguished sources of original Islam.[4]
(2) The Qur'ān is complemented by the unquestioned elements of the *sunna*. The latter is taken as an explicative source and not having the same authority as Qur'ān.
(3) Qur'ānic revelation is an exclusive source but interpreted according to rationalist methods.[5]

The 'return to sources' as defined earlier refers in the final analysis to the argument of religious authorities. It tends to sacralise the values of loyalty to the tradition and reinforce the link of the community with its origins. In contrast, appeals to progress, innovation, creativity, liberation of women and liberation of the human conscience of all taboos and of all traditional alienations, invoke the legitimate resort to *Ijitihad* which provides the religious basis to the application of rational efforts to the methods of interpreting the sources.

No matter what the subjects of research done or th
of ideas in Muslim countries, the main problem ren
cases, a problem of legitimacy and legitimation, either
reference to the sources or indirectly by the use of *Ijitihad*

The Themes of Ideological Debate

It is beyond our interest in this brief essay to address in detail the themes, or problems, of contemporary Islamic ideology which is frequently confused with Arab ideology.[6]

The identification of these themes can be rendered possible to a great extent by making an inventory of the socio-political vocabulary of legitimacy; mainly because ideological discussions aim in fact at legitimising, in Islamic terms, the socio-economic and political options of different regimes in the Muslim countries, or expressing the aspiration of the elites in more popular language.

As we can see, ideological debates in Islamic countries centre most often around the leading concepts of contemporary political culture and thought, especially in third world countries. These include concepts related to secular and materialistic ideologies, such as the notions of socialism (*ishtirakiyya*) and of revolution (*thawra*). These express in the language of modern times something essential in terms of the Qur'ānic message itself.

The Ideological Argument of Authenticity

If there is a dominant theme in contemporary Islamic-Arabic literature, it is the one of authenticity (*asala*). The ideologists of theocratic and traditional regimes refer to it with predilection as frequently as the so-called revolutionary regimes. The various literary and political writings on the subject appeal to religious feelings, to the nostalgia of a past golden age of Islam when the community had presumably lived the Qur'ānic message in its completeness and truth. But this kind of literature is likely also to excite the imagination of the impatient youth and to create enthusiasm and deep sentiments for the old times, closely associated with the ideal images of their roots and great ancestors.

In many Muslim countries the appeal to authenticity is more likely to continue ceaselessly.[8] This talisman-like word aims at preserving the sanctuary of the Muslim personality threatened by external aggressions, essentially those of Western cultural models. It also underlines loyalty to the origins, attachment to national cultural heritage and rejection of all foreign influences considered incompatible with the traditional and socio-cultural values of the community.

The ideological implications of *asala* are considerable. Authenticity could not only legitimise the rejection of Western moral and cultural values, but also help construct a political and social order which influences young Muslims or inspires in them critical tendencies towards the established order.

Cultural Models of the West

Contemporary Islamic ideology exalts authentic Islamic values as it systematically criticises foreign ones, especially those of the West. In the ideological and apologetic literature which we find in most Islamic countries nowadays, the terms 'West' (*Gharb*) and 'Westernisation' (*Taghrib*) are frequently associated with the ideas of neo-colonialism and anti-Muslim crusades.[9] Parallel to the study of the political vocabulary of legitimacy,[10] the socio-cultural terminology which carries the values and cultural models of the West deserves special attention. More specifically, it would be interesting to make a survey of all these concepts and terms. These concepts represent an anathema to the traditionalists and invite their strong refutation. Simultaneously, they fascinate to a great extent those Muslim youths who transcend traditional loyalties and aspire to modernity, progress and social and cultural freedom by means and methods which have been proven successful in the history of Western civilisation since the end of the eighteenth century.

From these magic words, which are the subject of endless writings and controversies throughout the Islamic world, we will refer to some which appear today as polarising the feelings and ideas of some and inviting attacks and angry criticism of others. The appearance of these words, which are frequently used by different ideological discussions, is explained by the fact that they refer to great moral and philosophical concepts closely associated with a halo of idealism such as: progress, democracy, socialism, liberation and revolution. These *slogans* inspire the force of ideas and cultivate a deep sense of enthusiasm among the greatest number of speakers and listeners.

The various usages of these *slogans* deserve to be the subject of a detailed investigation. These terms are used differently according to the nature of the debate and the orientation of the author. For instance, a case study of Islamic references to the notion of democracy (*dimuqratiyya*) reveals its central position in contemporary Islamic ethical and political thought. One can also conclude that in most cases the use of the term rarely reflects a philosophical concern with democracy *per se*, but rather most analyses are either a critique or an apology of Islamic democracy.[11]

Hence, when some authors defend the establishment of an authentic democratic system in the Muslim world, that is to say, a system conceived in purely political terms without reference to the holy book or traditional legitimacy, others hastily rush to demonstrate the compatibility of the ethical dispositions of the Qur'ān and political practice of early Islam with the democratic ideal of the Greek tradition and of political institutions in liberal democratic countries. For others, in contrast, authentic democracy refers to a political system that must conform to the values of Islam. In fact, they argue, Islam and only Islam is capable of providing the world with a true democratic model.[12]

Finally, others advocate a total reversal of the values defended by those in favour of democracy, liberation and progress (referring to cultural models of the West). According to them, those who support Western values are in fact the enemies of the values whose ideal conception cannot but be in conformity with the teachings of the Qur'ān and the Traditions of the prophet. In this regard, no one can be more explicit than the rapporteur of the International Supreme Council of Mosques in the following statement: 'Those who defend democracy are the enemies of democracy, those who raise banners of liberation are the enemies of liberation, those who defend progressivism are (in fact) the enemies of progress.'[13]

The logic of such an attitude of rejection towards the values and cultural models of the West (and modern civilisation in general) renders Islamic modernists suspect. They are accused of being either unconsciously agents of the enemies of Islam or of slavishly following anti-Islamic ideologies such as neo-colonialism, the propaganda of Christian missionaries, Zionism and Communism.[14]

There seem to be two primary objectives of the advocates of the Islamic ideology. They reject the West and provide a systematic critique of the social and cultural values of Western nations. They further demonstrate the moral failure of these values and predict the decline of the civilisation they represent. At the same time they reinforce the Muslim personality through an ardent apologetic effort and intensive work of education and indoctrination. In this regard, ideological debates, whether for internal or external use, invoke the argument of Islam in all circumstances and cases; since Islam is the only argument capable of addressing all the consciences and of rallying the maximum number of voters.

An Argument with Universal Usage: Islam

The reference to Islam (motivated by different reasons which are not always innocent) is the most important striking constant of ideological debates in the Muslim world.[15] Constitutions, official proclamations and political and social debates rarely fail to refer to Islam — which seems able, in its own right, to provide an important claim to legitimacy.

Furthermore, in a number of Islamic countries, the definition of national character presumes to a great extent the affirmation of Islamic identity.[16] History-writing devotes an important part to Islam as an essential determinant in the historic development of each national community. Sociological analysis also, tends to consider Islam as a source of cohesion and social dynamics. Political ideologies, specially those of governments, attempt as much as possible to give evidence of the conformity of their policies with the eternal principles of Islam.[17]

But what should we exactly understand by 'Islam'? The great diversity and contexts in which the reference to Islam occurs does not allow us to decide with precision the meaning, or meanings, intended by each author. At first, Islam appears chiefly as a kind of mythical representation in which every one believes. By virtue of being a postulate, the conscience of the community, in its totality, contributes, more or less directly and with more or less intensity, in this mythical reality. Hence the conviction that reference to Islam will elicit a response from every Muslim because it is a reference to something to which Muslims attach a great value, something of a nature that stirs in each Muslim the most live and profound memories.

This aura of ambiguity which surrounds the meaning of Islam is not deplored by everybody. In social debates, and often in political debates, each one tends to give credence to his own religious views, philosophy of history, views of his party on socio-economic or cultural matters by using the 'label' of Islam, however distant these ideas may be from the objectives of the original sources of Islam (Qur'ān and *sunna*).[18]

Similarly, a number of political and ethical concepts which were popularised by modern culture are said to be derived from Islam. Here the objective is to support the political, socio-economic and cultural options of the dominant ideology. Those authors talk enthusiastically about Islamic socialism, Islamic humanism,[19] Islamic democracy and social justice, all of which conform to the ideals of Islam.[20] Not only do they try to reconcile the basic principles of belief and the general teachings of Islam with reason, but also they present Islam as being the religion of reason par excellence.[21]

Apologetics and Ideological Debates

The previous analysis demonstrates to what extent apologia and ideological debates are tied together, whether they are in agreement or conflict, because the two are used for the same objectives. In some cases the objective, or alibi, is the defence of Islam and the concern over its greatness as a religion, culture and civilisation. In other cases the overriding concern is the affirmation of the dominant ideology and the strengthening of the ruling elite.

This dialectic is evident to the extent that enthusiastic proclamations in the name of religion, and in the name of God, are in most cases but disguised expressions of power. To invoke the name of God in the service of human causes is a frequent practice in all human societies and in all religious communities. But this tendency undoubtedly appears more forcefully in the Muslim world, which over the centuries has become accustomed to intermingle political and religious debates.

If the principles of Muslim apologetics are relatively stable and represent a reformulation of classical arguments, ideological debates use different theses according to the subject of the debate, and whether they are of the progressive, traditional or fundamentalist type. The progressive (or revolutionary) ideologisation of Islam emphasises the values of liberation, community and distribution, whose adherents attempt to find its corresponding concepts in the ethics of original Islam. In the ideologisation of the traditional type, its advocates insist on the values of piety and obedience, which are most compatible with authoritarian and conservative regimes.[22]

Conclusion

This set of phenomena characterises a process of evolution common to most Arab-Muslim regimes whether they are revolutionary or traditional. In such a process, where differences between one regime and another are demonstrated,[23] it is possible to discern a dual reality.

On one side, there is a noticeable retreat of Islam as the 'principle of movement' in Muslim societies in favour of political dynamics which tend to become the driving force *par excellence* at all levels of national life. Politics constitute the dominant fact of our present time, largely served by all media and propaganda techniques. It captures the attention of public opinion and directs it to the actions and policies of governments. It centres the life of people around the 'historical' speeches of their presidents, whose legitimacy is of a charismatic type, or purely founded on the fact of being in power. Political expression acquires pre-eminence over other literary, religious, etc. forms of expression, and impregnates them with its concepts. In most cases religious debates appear as a simple transposition of political official debates: new forces such as state and party have become the prime actors in political life.

On the other side, there is the integration of the religious factor into the official ideology. The objective is to confer on the government a strong legitimacy from the perspective of collective conscience and, at the same time, to allow it to emphasise more effectively and comprehensively the freedom of its 'national orientation'.[24] Religion, which is being increasingly ideologised by political authorities, thus finds itself implicated in a fight, if not a revolution, whose objectives are beyond its abilities.

Traditional religious elements such as *muftīs*, *imāms* and *'ulamā* can hardly constitute, as they did in the past, an independent group in the formulation and practice of their doctrines (for example in the area of political ethics) in the name of the Islamic ideal. They are equally incapable of abstracting an ideology of power.

If governments resort to the argument of religion, it is most often as a secondary resource in their political strategy, especially in view of the expansion of civic education of the masses and the sacralisation of the principle of national cohesion around ruling authorities (such as head of the state, revolutionary council, party leadership, etc.). Thus, Islam may be invoked and exalted where needed[25] in order to reinforce official ideology and not because of the specific values it represents.

Notes

This chapter has been translated from the original French version — *eds.*

1. It is sufficient to mention the following references as evidence of this growing ideological orientation among contemporary writers, see: Abdul Hakim Khalifa (the former director of the Institute of Islamic Research of Lahore, Pakistan) *Islamic Ideology* (Lahore, 1953); A series of articles of clear ideological nature in the areas of politics, economy, culture, education, etc. in the organ of the World Muslim League in Mecca in the Journal: *Rabitat al Alam al-Islami* and its Arabic edition: *Madjallat Rabitat al Alam al-Islami*; Publications of the former minister of education in Algeria, in particular the proceedings of the 'Seminars of Islamic Thought' which are held annually; All the literature of religious inspiration published by the Algerian magazine *Al-Moudjahid*; In the area of our interest one finds various references in the 'Abstracta Islamica' of thc *Revue des Etudes Islamiques* (Paris), and in the *Index Islamicus* of J.D. Pearson.

2. Cf. for example: Mahmud Shaltut, *Al-Islam aqida wa-sharia* (Cairo, n.d.); Uthman Raghib, *Al-Islam din wa dunya* (Damascus, 1367/1948).

3. Ahmed Aroua (Algeria), in *Actes du Seminaire pour la Connaissance de la Pensée Islamique* (Constantine, 1972), vol. V, p. 65. This formulation is quite identical to the one of Amar Samb (Senegal) who suggests that 'Islam is a religion, a state and a whole social system suitable for all times and all societies', *Actes du Sem. pour la Conn. de la Pensée Islamique* (1972), vol. V, p. 151.

4. See a summary of the different arguments in my article 'Islah' in the *Encyclopédie de l'Islam*, vol. IV (1973), pp. 146-70; and in the English edition: *The Encyclopedia of Islam*, vol. IV (1973), pp. 141-63.

5. This argument was defended in 1906 by Mohamed Tawfiq Sidqi (an old disciple of Rashid Rida) in his well-known article: 'Al Islam huwa al-Quran wahda-hu' (Islam is the Quran only) in *Al Manar*, vol. 9 (Cairo, 1906), pp. 515-25 and 906-925. See also the position of Ghulam Ahmad Parwiz (1903) in his fundamental essay *Ideology of Islam* (Lahore, n.d.). In this systematic rationalisation of Quranic Islam, Parwiz made a novel effort, unprecedented in the history of modern Islamic culture.

6. See, among other, Abdallah Laroui, *L'Ideologie Arabe Contemporaine. Essai Critique* (Paris: Maspero, 1977), p. 258. A similar effort on Islamic ideology is yet to be done. One notices that 'Arab ideology' is frequently identified with 'Islamic ideology' or, at least, leans heavily upon it. See in this regard the example of the Baathist ideology (which is basically secular) of Arab Renaissance. Its principal theoretician, Michel Aflaq, refers explicitly to Islam. Cf. his interview in *Afaq Arabiyya* (Arab Horizons), no. 8 (Baghdad, April 1976), pp. 4-9. In the same line of ideas cf. Bichara Khader, 'L'Islam, Soubassement Ideologique de la Renaissance Arabe', *Maghreb-Machrek*, no. 6 (1974), pp. 45-64; Elie Salem, 'Nationalism and Islam', *The Muslim World*, vol. LII, no. 4 (1962), pp. 277-87. (There is an interdependence between Arab nationalism and Islam. Nationalist ideology subjects Islam to its own logic so as to reassure its masses.)

7. We refer here to the following studies: Michel Camu, 'Le Discours Politique de Légitimite des Elites Tunisiennes', *A.A.N.* (1971), pp. 25-68; Bruno Etienne, 'Le Vocabulaire Politique de Legitimite en Algerie', *A.A.N.* (1971), pp. 69-101; Octave Marais, 'Thèmes et Vocabulaire de la Propagande des Elites Politiques au Maroc', *A.A.N.* (1968), pp. 57-78. Studies of this sort deserve to be widely publicised in the rest of the Arab world, as well as the whole of the Islamic world.

8. Cf. the journal *al-Asala* (Constantine), organ of the Algerian Ministry of Education and Religious Affairs. See also: The important series of the proceedings of the seminars of Islamic thought (note 1); Mahmoud Ariba, *L'Enseignement Originel en Algérie*, Thèse de 3e cycle (Grenoble, 1977). In this important work the question of the ideological use of Islam is posed clearly. See in particular the chapter entitled 'The search for authenticity', p. 271f.

9. It would be tedious to provide a complete list of publications for this trend which is very much represented by the publications of the World Muslim League of Mecca. Some authors of this trend refer to the Western world only by the term *Al-Gharb al-Salibi* (The Crusading West).

10. See note 7 above.

11. F. Niyaz Ahmad Zikriya (Afghanistan), *Les Principes de l'Islam et la Democratie* (Paris, 1958); and 'Les Sens de la Democratie en Islam', *La Pensée*, vol. 1, no. 2 (Rabat, 1962), pp. 34-42.

12. Cf. for instance: S.M. Iqbal, 'Governmental Pattern in Saudi Arabia', *The Journal of Muslim World League* (March 1977), pp. 20-7. In the third part entitled 'Democracy vs. Saudi System', the author criticises the Western theories and terminology on the subject, essentially because 'These theories and terms do not mean what they ought to' (p. 23), and that the so-called modern democratic leaders in the West are not true representaives of their peoples (p. 24).

13. Cf. *Akhbar al-Alam al-Islami*, no. 620 (Mecca, 19 March 1979), p. 6. See also the analyses of Nizam Ajmir Mohamed, 'The Impact of the West on Muslims', *Journal of Rabetat al-Alam al-Islami* (Mecca, April 1978), pp. 40-4. Here we quote the following important passage:

> 'Beneath the polished and glittering surface of its fantastic achievements, modern Western civilization threatens to plunge the world into the nightmare of horrors so well predicted by the English novelists Aldous Huxley in *The Brave New World* and George Orwell in his work entitled *1984*. Western civilization excels in deceiving the people by its high-sounding slogans. It speaks of liberty and equality, yet its world-wide imperialism promoted more oppression and tyranny over subject peoples than any other civilization in human history. It speaks of peace and justice, yet it originated the most devastating wars of all time. It claims to emancipate woman only to exploit her as the means for destroying the home and family' (p. 43), and further: 'Western civilization claims to the only avenue to enlightenment and progress while it actually leads straight down the road to moral ruin and spiritual suicide' (p. 44.)

14. Cf. Muhammad al-Bahi, *Al-Fikr Al-Islami al-Hadith wa Silatuku bi' l-Istimar al Gharbi* (Modern Muslim Thought and its Relation to Western Colonialism) (Cairo: Dar al-Qalam. 2nd edn, 1960). See also among others the various articles (specially those written by Anwar al-Jundi) published by the organ of the World Muslim League of Mecca, on the theme of the contamination of Muslim thought by destructive ideologies and doctrines (*al Madhahib al Haddama*) which include: Colonialism, propaganda of Christian missionaries, Zionism, Communism, freemasonry, Bahaism, Qadiyāniyya, etc. See in this respect the following statement by Anwar al-Jundi, 'Forces of Westernism, aggression, orientalism and Communism unite together on one objective: The weakening of Islamic identity and the

assimilation of Muslim personality' in *Madjallat Rabitat al-Alam al-Islami* (August 1976), pp. 12-13.

In the same sense a number of other authors continuously denounce the slavish orientation of modernist Muslim intellectuals who view the West in a very positive manner, admire its thinkers and its cultural models, while forgetting or ignoring the wealth of Islamic heritage and the values of Islamic civilisation. A concrete example which illustrates this tendency is the denunciation of those Muslims favouring the abolition of the death penalty as 'defying God'. See *Akhbar al-Alam al-Islami*, no. 477 (1976), p. 7.

15. The following statement regarding Algeria could be applied to the rest of the Muslim countries 'Islam is always itself.' This magic word is tied to the history of Algeria. In this country it has been the expression of people's hopes. In the past it symbolised the struggle and resistance against the coloniser, today it should fight another cause, that of creating a better future. This is at least what the official ideology claims (Mahmoud Ariba, *L'Enseignement Originel en Algérie*, p. 282).

16. Visible affirmation is in the official names of certain Muslim states such as Mauritania, Iran, etc. or the similar orientation of certain regimes founded upon religious tradition such as Saudi Arabia and Morocco.

17. Even regimes which claim secular ideologies such as the Baath prove sometimes the necessity of referring to Islam as the ultimate argument for legitimacy, and in order to underline the convergence of their doctrines of government with the fundamental principles and social ethics of Islam, such as egalitarianism, social solidarity, social justice, respect for human dignity, etc.

18. Thus, one can condemn, in the name of Islam these philosophical trends, such as freemasonry and Existentialism (even if the latter doctrine can imply a spiritual or religious experience such as the Christian existentialism of Gabriel Marcel). We refer here to the resolutions taken by al-Majma' al-Fiqhi (Council of Religious Law) in its 1st session, Mecca, Sha'ban 10, 1398/July 15, 1978. *Akhbar al-Alam al-Islami*, no. 627 (April 1979), p. 3.

19. Ahmad Farradj, Abdal Aziz Kamil, Muhammad al-Ghazali, *et al.*, *Al-Islam din al-Ishtirakiyya*, Cairo, Kutub Qawmiyya, 1961; Mahmud Shibli, *Ishtirakiyyat Muhammad* (Cairo, 1962). N. Zikriya, 'L'Humanisme de l'Islam' in *La Pensee*, Rabat (1963), no. 4, pp. 6-17.

20. Ali Abu Wahid Wafi, *al-Musāwāt fi l-Islam* (Cairo, Dar al-Ma'arif, 1962). Ahmad Saqr, 'Islam Emphasizes Freedom' in *J.R.A.I.* (Nov. 1975), p. 8. The author develops here an argument largely used by apologetic Muslims since Rashid Rida, the main religious reformer in the inter-war period (see my article *Islah* referred to earlier, pp. 162-3). For Saqr, Islam aims at the elimination of physical, social and spiritual aggressiveness, the search to promote equality, defined as 'the cornerstone of Islamic Religion'.

21. Salah al-Din al-Munajjid, *Al-Islam wal-aql, 'ala daw'al-Quran al-Karim wa-l-Hadith al-Nabawi* (Beirut, 1974).

22. The great number of publications published by the World Muslim League, which is government-inspired, provide enough documentation to illustrate this point. The same tendency, though more discreet, appears throughout the essays published in the Tunisian revue *Al-Hidaya* (Cultural Islamic Revue, Tunisia).

23. In each case the regime tends to exhaust Islamic arguments in harmony with its thinking and goals. In the so-called traditional regimes, emphasis is placed on the values of piety, religiosity and strict observance of the law. In progressive or revolutionary regimes greater emphasis is put on the social values of original Islam, and on promoting interpretations (by means of *Ijitihad*) which provide legitimacy to the political and socio-economic options of the regimes.

24. In the following paragraphs we rely on the analyses in our article *Islah* referred to earlier, in particular pp. 160-1 in the *Encyclopedia of Islam*.

25. Specially on occasions of great political importance; see the following statement: 'Faithful to the great sacrifice and the memory of the martyrs of our sacred revolution, I swear by the almighty God to respect and glorify Islam' (text of the constitutional oath sworn by Houari Boumedienne at his investiture as the President of the Republic on 16 December 1976).

4 CHANGING CONCEPTS OF AUTHORITY IN THE LATE NINTH/FIFTEENTH AND EARLY TENTH/SIXTEENTH CENTURIES

Ann Lambton

The bases of Islamic government are held to have been laid down in the *sharī'a* and to be immutable for all times in all circumstances. No explicit reformulations of the theory of the jurists once established is therefore to be expected. Nevertheless, the various controversies which agitated the community and the political events which fragmented it all left their mark on the theory of government. Al-Māwardī had tried to justify the caliphate as it developed historically and, thereby, to maintain the political unity of the caliphate in spite of the usurpation of temporal power by the caliph's auxiliaries. Al-Ghazālī, impelled by the fear of civil war (*fitna*) and corruption (*fasād*) leading to disorder and anarchy, while acknowledging that government in his day was a consequence solely of military power and that that person, whosoever he might be to whom the holder of military power professed his allegiance, was the caliph,[1] attempted to incorporate the sultanate into the caliphate and thereby to maintain the religious unity of the caliphate.

It is, perhaps, too easily assumed that the caliphate had ceased to be relevant in the period between the decline of the Great Saljūqs and the Mongol invasion of the *dār al-islām*. It is true that it had ceased, broadly speaking, to exercise political power, apart from a temporary revival under the caliph al-Nāṣir (575-622/1180-1225), but in the field of theology and political theory (which cannot always be clearly distinguished) the caliphate still had revelance for the life of the community. With the overthrow of the 'Abbāsid caliphate and the disappearance of the last shreds of the outward unity of the Islamic community, the jurists were faced with a new problem: how to define the authority of rulers so that Islamic institutions might be maintained despite the extinction of the caliphate and the existence of political divisions.

Ibn Jamā'a (639-733/1241-1333) and Ibn Taymiyya (661-728/1262-1328), both of whom lived under the Mamlūk sultanate, sought new interpretations to the old juridical problems. The former accepted al-Ghazālī's theory that the caliphate included coercive power but recognised that this had, as it were, swallowed up the primary element in al-Ghazālī's theory of the caliphate, the *imām*, and was prepared to transfer to the *de facto* ruler the constitutional theories worked out by earlier jurists and to recognise him as *imām*, holding that the seizure of power itself gave authority. Ibn Taymiyya, reinterpreting the history of the community, sought a return to the example of the early ancestors, the *salaf*. He held that sovereignty on the death of the prophet devolved on all those who by their learning and virtue were the authorised interpreters of the law and charged with adapting it to new conditions of time and place. The state as envisaged by Ibn Taymiyya required from all those who belonged to it, not a mere passive obedience, but effective participation in the common life.[2]

In this chapter I shall examine the work of a third writer, in order to illustrate the way in which concepts of authority were changing in the post-'Abbāsid period in the eastern provinces of the *dār al-islām*. This work is the *Sulūk al-mulūk* of Abū 'l Khayr Faḍl Allāh b. Rūzbihān al-Khunjī al-Iṣfahānī. The title suggests that it is a mirror for princes, but it is in fact a juristic work in the line of al-Māwardī's *al-Aḥkām al-sulṭāniyya* and Ibn Jamā'a's *Taḥrīr al-aḥkām*.

Whereas Ibn Taymiyya and Ibn Jamā'a both lived under the Mamlūks fairly shortly after the overthrow of the 'Abbāsid caliphate by the Mongols, Abū'l Khayr Faḍl Allāh b. Rūzbihān al-Khunjī al-Iṣfahānī lived somewhat later and spent most of his life in the eastern provinces of the *dār al-islām*. These had been temporarily united by Tīmūr (771-807/1369-1404) only to fragment eventually into three major regions, the Ottoman Empire in the west and the Uzbeg kingdom in Central Asia, both of which were Sunni, and the Safawid Empire in Persia, which was Shī'i. Bitter hostilities prevailed between the latter on the one hand and the Ottoman Empire and the Uzbeg kingdom on the other. This led to a reconsideration of the theory of *jihād* and war against rebels, but it is not this aspect of Islamic political theory with which I shall be concerned here.

Faḍl Allāh b. Rūzbihān's family on his father's side came from Khunj[3] in Fārs and on his mother's side from Iṣfahān. His father, Jamāl al-Dīn, was one of the leading *'ulamā* of Iṣfahān. After the rebellion of Ḥājjī Beg was put down, a number of the leading figures of 'Irāq-i 'Ajam, including Jamāl al-Dīn, were summoned to

Tabrīz. There he was treated with favour by Ya'qūb b. Uzun Ḥasan, the Aq Qoyunlū ruler. Faḍl Allāh was born in Shīrāz. He studied the Qur'ān and *'arabiyyāt* and at the age of seventeen went on the pilgrimage. He was away for some two years, during which time he also visited Karbalā, Cairo, Jerusalem and Hebron. Among his teachers in Shīrāz were 'Amīd al-Dīn Shīrāzī and Jalāl al-Dīn Dawānī, to whom he refers as 'our master' (*'ustād-i mā*).[4] He made the pilgrimage a second time at the age of 25, and while in the Ḥijāz on this occasion studied the *Minhāj al-'ābidīn* and the *Iḥyā 'ulūm al-dīn* of al-Ghazālī and the *Rawḍat al-'awārif* of Shaykh Suhrawardī. He then lived for a while in Egypt and spent some time at the court of the Mamlūk sultan, Qayt Bay (873-901/1468-95). In 887/1482 he was again in Madīna, where he studied the *Saḥīḥ* of al-Bukhārī and the *Saḥīḥ* of Muslim under, among others, Muḥammad al-Sakhāwī. He returned to Shīrāz where he wrote commentaries on commentaries of various standard works on *fiqh* and composed in Persian the *Kitāb badī' al-zamān fī qiṣṣat Ḥayy b. Yaqzān*. He then set out a third time for the Ḥijāz. He went by way of Ādharbāyjān where he offered his allegiance to Ya'qūb b. Uzun Ḥasan and presented to him the *Badī' al-zamān* in 892/1487 at his summer camp on Mt Sahand. Instead of proceeding to the Ḥijāz, Faḍl Allāh became, like his father before him, attached to the court of Ya'qūb, with whom he remained for four years. During this period he began his history, the *Tārīkh-i 'ālam-ārā-yi amīnī*, but did not finish this until after Ya'qūb's death in 896/1490. Bāysonghor, Ya'qūb's infant son, who succeeded, was deposed almost immediately and with the disintegration of the Aq Qoyunlū kingdom, Faḍl Allāh left Adharbāyjān. It appears that he was in Kāshān in 909/1503 on the eve of the reoccupation of 'Irāq by Shāh Ismā'īl: his anti-Shī'i treatise, the *Kitāb ibṭāl nahj al-bāṭil wa iḥmāl kashf al-'āṭil*, a polemic work against the *Nahj al-ḥaqq* of Ḥasan b. al-Mu'ayyad b. Yūsuf b. al-Muṭahhar al-Ḥillī (d. 726/1325), is dated Kāshān 3 Jumādī II 909/3 December 1503.

In the following year Faḍl Allāh came to Khurāsān and joined the court of Ḥusayn Bāyqarā in Harāt. After the Uzbeg, Abū'l Fatḥ Muḥammad Shaybānī Khān, conquered Khurāsān, Faḍl Allāh joined his court. In the *Mihmān-nāma-i Bukhārā*, which Faḍl Allāh wrote for Muḥammad Shaybānī Khān, he gives an eye witness account of the latter's campaigns against the Qazaqs in 914/1508. After Muḥammad Shaybānī Khān was killed in battle with Shāh Ismā'īl in 916/1510, the Uzbegs withdrew to Turkistān and Bābar, the future ruler of Hindustān, took Transoxania with Ṣafawid help. Faḍl Allāh returned to Khurāsān but in 918/1512 after 'Ubayd Allāh, the nephew of Muḥammad Shaybānī Khān, had driven Bābar out of Samarqand, Faḍl Allāh came with him to Bukhārā and remained there until his death in 927/1521. In 920/1514 he wrote the *Sulūk al-mulūk* for 'Ubayd Allāh.[5]

The *Sulūk al-mulūk*, like the *Taḥrīr al-aḥkām* of Ibn Jamā'a, recalls al-Māwardī's *al-Aḥkām al-sulṭāniyya*, both in its contents and in its concern not only with the theory of government but also with its practicalities in the circumstances of the time.[6] Like al-Māwardī and al-Ghazālī, Faḍl Allāh b. Rūzbihān's overriding concern is for the legitimacy of government, but whereas al-Ghazālī was able to associate the sultan and the caliph in the government of Islam, Faḍl Allāh could not do this because the caliphate had been physically destroyed. Like Abū Yūsuf and others after him, he models the conduct of the ideal ruler on that of the prophet and the orthodox caliphs and seeks thereby to give legitimacy to his rule as being in the succession to the prophet. Like al-Māwardī and al-Ghazālī he accepts that no public function is legal unless emanating from the *imām* and that all subordinate officials held delegated authority only, but he differs from them in that he acknowledges that the bearer of power *is* the caliph. He was, perhaps, influenced in this by his master Jalāl al-Dīn Dawānī who, continuing in the line of earlier writers such as Fakhr al-Dīn Rāzī (d. 606/1209), recognised any righteous ruler as the Shadow of God upon earth, as His vicegerent and as the deputy of the prophet, and who had addressed his own patron, Uzun Ḥasan, as caliph.[7] Faḍl Allāh goes beyond his master and accepts the bearer of power, whether he was righteous or unrighteous, as the *imām*, though ideally he requires him to be righteous.[8]

Faḍl Allāh while recognising that the sultan, who was the source of all authority, held power by usurpation (or seizure), sought, by accepting him as caliph, to give a valid title to all subordinate authority. Like Ibn Jamā'a, he accepts al-Ghazālī's theory that the caliphate included coercive power, and with him recognises that this element in the caliphate had swallowed up the primary element in al-Ghazālī's caliphate, the *imām*: the sultan had become not only the holder of coercive power but also the symbol of the supremacy of the *sharī'a*. Whereas in al-Ghazālī's theory of the caliphate there had been three elements, the caliph, the sultan and the *'ulamā*, these were reduced to two in Faḍl Allāh's theory, the *imām*/sultan and the *'ulamā*.[9]

Like Sunni thinkers before him, Faḍl Allāh regarded the imāmate as the vicegerency of the prophet and held that its purpose was to carry out the *sharī'a* and to defend Islamic territory. In much of his exposition he merely restates the views of his predecessors. The interest of his work lies in the new interpretations which he gives to the old formulas and doctrines. He states that it was incumbent upon all men to follow the *imām*, whose functions were to execute the decrees of the *sharī'a* among the community which had accepted the *sharī'a* and whose members were Muslims, and to defend religion, i.e. to repel infidels from the sacred things of Islam. A prerequisite to the fulfilment of both these functions was a knowledge of *shar'ī* sciences. The *imām* must, therefore, defend these sciences and in order for him to do so it was necessary for him to have a knowledge of the *sharī'a*. Accordingly Faḍl Allāh sets out what the *sharī'a* was and the functions of the ruler under the *sharī'a*, supporting his views by numerous quotations from the writings of the *fuqahā'*.[10] In his familiarity with what his predecessors had written, he bears witness to the continuous intellectual tradition which is characteristic of medieval Islamic thought.

Faḍl Allāh accepts the traditional Sunni view that it was a *farḍ kifāya* upon the community to confer the imamate upon a suitably qualified candidate, unless there was a uniquely qualified candidate, in which case it became a *fard 'ayn* upon that candidate to take office.[11] He cites Najm al-Dīn Abū Ḥafṣ 'Umar al-Nasafī (d. 537/1142–3), the Māturīdī, on the qualifications of the *imām*. These were that he should:

(1) belong to the Quraysh;
(2) be a *mujtahid*;
(3) have good judgement and administrative talent;
(4) have financial capability;
(5) be brave so that he could defend Islamic territory against infidels;
(6) be just;
(7) be of age;
(8) be intelligent;
(9) be of free status;
(10) be male;
(11) be sound in hearing and sight, and
(12) be sound in speech.[12]

These were the standard qualities demanded of an *imām* by the Sunnis. If there was no suitable candidate from the Quraysh, Faḍl Allah states that the Imām Baghawī was prepared to dispense with this condition and had stated in his *Tahdhīb* that if none of the sons of Ismā'īl (i.e. the Arabs) possessed the necessary qualities, an *'ajam*, i.e. a non-Arab (and Faḍl Allāh points out that the term *'ajam* included Turks), who had the necessary qualities, should be appointed. Rejecting the claims of the Shī'īs, Faḍl Allāh states that it was not a condition that the *imām* should be immune from sin or that he should be a Hāshimī. Quoting al-Nasafī, he states that the latter held that the *imām* must be manifest (*ẓāhir*) and a Qurayshī; it was not permitted for him to be of any other tribe, but the office was not assigned exclusively to either the sons of Hāshim or of 'Alī. Further according to al-Nasafī it was not a condition that the *imām* should be immune from sin or the most excellent of his time, but it was a condition that he should be a man possessing authority (*ahl-i wilāyat*), a good administrator (*sā'is*), and able to put into effect decrees, defend Islamic territory and exact justice for the oppressed from the tyrannical. He did not forfeit the imamate on account of sin (*fisq*).[13]

The imamate, Faḍl Allāh states, could be contracted in one of four ways. The first three were in accordance with traditional Sunnī theory and derived their authority from the early history of the community. The first way, sanctioned by the example of the election of the caliph Abū Bakr, was for the *imām* to be elected by the consensus of the Muslims and the *bay'a* of the *ahl al-ḥall wa'l-'aqd*. Faḍl Allāh, like Ibn Jamā'a, includes among the *ahl al-ḥall wa'l-'aqd* not only the *'ulamā* and the *qāḍīs*, but also the *ru'asā'* and other leading persons (*wujūh-i mardum*), but he requires only those who could easily be present to take part in the *bay'a*. He does not consider the agreement of the *ahl al-ḥall wa'l-'aqd* in outlying regions as a necessary condition for the valid contraction of the imamate. Whenever news reached the people in a distant region that the imamate had been contracted, it was necessary for them to agree and to conform with the consensus arrived at. Further, it was not necessary for a specific number of persons to give the *bay'a* for the contraction of the imamate to be valid: Faḍl Allāh accepts al-Māwardī's view that the *bay'a* of one person from among the *ahl al-ḥall wa'l-'aqd*, who commanded obedience among the people, was sufficient. Those who gave the *bay'a* must have the quality of *shuhūd* and acceptance of the *bay'a* by him to whom it was given was also a condition; if he refused to accept it he could not be compelled to do so unless he was a uniquely qualified candidate. The second way was by nomination by the preceding *imām* of someone who had the necessary qualifications. Sanction for this method was found in the elevation of 'Umar to the caliphate. In such a case the 'less excellent' could not be nominated. The third way was by election by a council (*shawrā*), for which sanction was found in the election of 'Uthmān. In none of these cases, however, was the appointment of the *imām* valid until the *ahl al-ḥall wa'l-'aqd* had given him the *bay'a*. Faḍl Allāh repeats the traditional view that it was not permissible to appoint two *imāms* at the same time because this, he states, would lead to war. He is prepared, however, to permit it if they were in areas separated by sea.[14]

It is in the fourth method that Faḍl Allāh's exposition is of special interest. He states, 'usurpation (*istīlā*) and power (*shawkat*) are among the ways of contracting kingship (*pādishāhī*) and the imamate. The *'ulamā* have said that when an *imām* dies and a powerful person becomes *imām* without a *bay'a* and without anyone having made him caliph and subdues the people by his power (*shawkat*) and military force (*lashkar*), his imamate is confirmed (*muta'aqqid*) without a *bay'a* whether he is a Qurayshī or not, an Arab, Persian, or Turk, and whether he possesses the qualities demanded of an *imām* (or not), whether he is of bad character (*fāsiq*) or ignorant (*jāhil*) (or not). Although the usurper (*mustawlī*) by this action becomes a rebel (*'āṣī*) since he has taken the place of the *imām* by force and by usurpation, he is called sultan and (the title of) *imām* and *khalīfa* can be applied to him.'[15] Faḍl Allāh would appear to have had some doubts as to the propriety of this method of contracting the imamate for he adds 'and God knows best'.

Whereas al-Māwardī had sought to bring the independent or semi-independent ruler within the scheme of caliphal government by recognition of the amirate of seizure, Faḍl Allāh was under no such compulsion. There was in his day no caliph to whom was due the submission, albeit nominal, of all Muslim rulers. Accordingly he recognises usurpers as rightful rulers and accords to them the title of sultan and *imām*. By implication, therefore, he does not insist upon the requirement that there should be only one *imām* at any one time.

Discussing the meaning of the term *sulṭān*, Faḍl Allāh states, 'in *shar'ī* parlance (the sultan) is he who exercises dominance over the Muslims by virtue of his power and military force. The *'ulamā* have said that obedience to the *imām*/sultan[16] is incumbent in whatever he commands and forbids as long as it is not contrary to the *sharī'a*, whether he is just or tyrannical. It is incumbent to give him council (*naṣīḥat*) as far as possible. It is permissible to call him *khalīfa*, *imām*, *amīr al-mu'minīn* (or) *khalīfa* of the prophet of God, but it is not permissible to call him *khalīfat allāh*.'[17] In fact, however, Faḍl Allāh addresses his patron Abū'l Fatḥ Muḥammad Shaybānī Khān, as *imām al-zamān* and *khalīfat al-raḥmān*.[18]

Faḍl Allāh, basing himself upon the practice of the orthodox caliphs, states that it was permissible for the *imām*/sultan to provide for his sustenance from the public treasury. Whereas, he states, men had feared the orthodox caliphs because of the aura which still attached to them from the days of the prophet, in his time things had changed and if the *imām* did not surround himself with ceremony and provide himself with trappings, horses and military slaves (*ghulāmān*), people would not obey him and the affairs of the Muslims would be neglected.[19]

Discussing the duties of the *imām*/sultan in respect of the imamate/sultanate, Faḍl Allāh states that when someone became dominant over the regions of Islam by power — one of the ways, he reminds his readers, by which the imamate might be contracted — and was called, in the parlance of the *fuqahā*, sultan, ten things were incumbent upon him in respect of his being *imām*/sultan. These were in fact the same duties which al-Māwardī demands of the *imām*. They were that he should:

(1) protect religion according to fixed principles and what had been established by the consensus of the early ancestors;
(2) execute decrees between litigants and settle disputes between contestants so that justice might be universal among Muslims;
(3) drive away enemies from the borders (*ḥarīm*) of Islamic countries so that it might be easy for the Muslims to earn their livelihood and travel to and fro safely;
(4) apply the legal penalties so that the prohibitions of God were not violated;
(5) strengthen the frontiers and appoint strong persons over regions where infidels might enter Islamic territory;
(6) undertake *jihād* against those who refused to embrace Islam after they had been invited to do so until they surrendered or made peace;
(7) collect the taxes, *ṣadaqa* and *khums* from booty;

(8) fix the stipends of those who were entitled to them without prodigality or parsimony;
(9) demand that those to whom he entrusted the affairs of the kingdom should acquit themselves of their duties in a fit and proper way and entrust *shar'ī* affairs, such as the wazirate, the amirate, the office of *qāḍī* and *muḥtasib*, to persons whom he considered to be good counsellors and trustworthy; and
(10) personally oversee affairs and enquire into how all groups (*ṭawā'if*) were conducting themselves.[20]

In short, it was incumbent upon the ruler to protect the *sharī'a* and to fulfil its requirements so that its decrees might be observed in the community and so that he, by reason of his protection of the *sharī'a*, might be called just (*'ādil*) because he had protected the laws of God (*nawāmīs-i illāhī*) and watched over its decrees. If he failed to defend the *sharī'a* he became a rebel and a sinner.[21]

Faḍl Allāh reinforces his argument by justifying kingship in terms similar to those used by the philosophers. 'Man is by nature sociable (*madanī al-tab'*),' he states, 'and in gaining his livelihood he needs the society of his own kind (*ijtimā'-i banī naw'*) to co-operate with him and to be his partners, but since the power of lust and passion stimulates men to violence and discord, there must be a just man who will abate violence — and the just man is he who finds what is congruous and equal among things which are incongruous and justice is achieved for him who has knowledge of "the mean" and that which defines the mean is the divine law. Justice is, therefore, laid down by the *sharī'a*; and for the execution of its ordinances and the protection of all its laws, to which are due the continued existence of the human race, there is need of a person singled out by divine support, who is endowed with ability to manage affairs and with power and authority so that he is obeyed, and who will protect the laws of the *sharī'a*. Such a person is the king. It is not necessary for someone in every age and century to bring a law[22] because the general legislation (*waḍ'*) carried out under divine inspiration by the bringer of the law (*ṣāḥib sharī'at*) suffices for the people for many eras, but an administrator (*mudabbir*) is required every day to accomplish some affair or other for the generality of men, because if administration ceases order departs and the continued existence of the human race is not achieved in the most perfect way.'[23]

Defining the king as the administrator of the world (*mudabbir-i 'ālam*), Faḍl Allāh states that his prime duty was to protect the *sharīʿa* and to lay upon the people the performance of the duties imposed by the *sharīʿa*. The sanctions, however, were purely moral: 'If he (the king) failed in this, God would punish him for the sins of the whole world because if he had taken steps to defend the *sharīʿa* justice would have reigned among mankind.'[24]

In addition to the special position which Faḍl Allāh, in company with most other jurists, accords to that group of the *ʿulamā* who belonged to the *ahl al-ḥall wa'l-ʿaqd*, he appears to envisage a limitation on the absolute power of the ruler by submitting religious affairs to the judgement of the most learned of the *ʿulamā* of the kingdom (who, he states, was called in his day the *shaykh al-islām*) and by removing religious affairs from the competence of the ruler, except so far as the appointment of the main religious officials and the execution of their decisions was in his hands. Once the ruler had been established in the seat of the *imām* (*masnad-i imāmat*), Faḍl Allāh states that it was his prime duty to follow the practice of the orthodox caliphs. He must seek out the most learned of the *ʿulamā* in his kingdom and entrust to his judgement the affairs of Islam. If there were several persons who, by general agreement, were equally well versed and competent in the *sharʿī* sciences, then piety (*warʿ*), knowledge (*khubrat*) in matters of *ʿurf* (customary law), perspicacity, maturity, courage, energy and compassion were successively to be taken into account until someone was found having pre-eminence over all his fellows. Faḍl Allāh was, however, a realist and he remarks that a person having such qualities was rare, or even, like the *ʿanqā*, non-existent. He deplores the fact that most of the *ʿulamā* in his time were inclined towards philosophy (*falsafī ṭabīʿat shuda and*), the study of which gave them a facility in disputation to the detriment of the true scholar of the *sharʿī* sciences.[25]

While apparently wishing, through the appointment of the *shaykh al-islām*, to reassert the authority of the religious institution *vis-à-vis* the political institution — and in this he was in the line of al-Bāqillānī rather than al-Māwardī — Faḍl Allāh recognises the dangers of royal appointment both to the integrity of the man appointed and to his reputation. Accordingly, he insists that once the *shaykh al-islām* had been appointed the king must not force him to be continually in his retinue and service 'because the continued company and service of kings destroys the prestige of the *ʿulamā* and distracts them'.[26] The king, however, needed someone to act as an intermediary between him and the *ʿulamā*, for without such he could not know which of the *ʿulamā* were worthy of *sharʿī* office.

This function was to be performed by the *ṣadr*, who was in effect, Faḍl Allāh states, the *naqīb al-'ulamā*.

The king was to accord full respect to the *shaykh al-islām*. He was not to fail for one instant to honour him. Once he had tested him, he was to consider him as having complete control in all *shar'ī* affairs (*ūrā ba'd az āzmūdan bar jamī'-i umūr shar' amīn-i muṭlaq dānad*) and he was on no account to delay the execution of any matter concerned with Islam which the *shaykh al-islām* submitted to him. He was to charge the military and those in charge of the affairs of the kingdom to execute the decisions (*ra'ī*) of the *shaykh al-islām*, and if one of the 'pillars of the state' transgressed his command he was to be severely punished: and in order that respect for the power (*shawkat*) of the *shaykh al-islām* might be firmly implanted in the hearts of men, on no account might negligence be shown in the carrying out of such punishments.[27]

Faḍl Allāh was aware of the importance of financial independence for the *shaykh al-islām* if he was to carry out his functions, and so he states that his livelihood should be assured from a source such that it would reach him without trouble or waste of time and without recourse to the officials of the diwan or wazirs. He should have no cause to refer to the pillars of the state or the wazirs in financial affairs; when the *'ulamā* were in need (for their livelihood) they practised hypocrisy (*mudāhina*), but if their wants were provided for the reason for hypocrisy was removed. The *'ulamā* play an important part in Faḍl Allāh's theory: it was the ruler's duty to defend the *shar'ī* sciences but it was through the *'ulamā* that knowledge of these sciences was preserved. Thus Faḍl Allāh states that a pious *'ālim*, one who wanted nothing of the king, would have great authority in this matter and the king in referring to him and in acting according to what he considered right would fulfil his obligations in respect of the preservation of the *shar'ī* sciences.[28]

Faḍl Allāh then discusses the appointment and qualifications of the *muftī* at some length. The consensus of his own day was, he states, that kings were not *mujtahids*. The kings of Transoxania, who were Ḥanafīs, therefore had to act upon *fatwās*. If the *imām*/sultan had the qualifications of a *mujtahid* there was no need for a *muftī*, but kings who were *mujtahids* were few and far between. If the king was not a *mujtahid*, it was incumbent upon him to appoint a *muftī*. If he found someone whom he considered worthy of office, he was to decide, in the presence of the *'ulamā*, whether such a person had the qualifications necessary for a *mujtahid*. If he had, and it was confirmed that he possessed the quality of justice (*'adālat*), the king must appoint him to the office of *muftī* and when some happening occurred refer to him for a *fatwā* and act thereon.[29]

The *muftī*, like the *shaykh al-islām*, was to be freed from the need of earning his living, but in his case means for his subsistence were to be assigned by the sultan on the public treasury. The appointment of the *muftī* was a *farḍ kifāya* and if the king failed to appoint a *muftī* and some region of the world remained without one, all the people would be sinners in this respect.[30]

Faḍl Allāh's discussion of the appointment of *qāḍīs* by the ruler reflects his concern for the validity of the authority of subordinate officials. What was for him important was the valid delegation of authority, not the qualifications of the person by whom that authority was delegated. At the same time, by his recognition that the pious were reluctant to accept office, he underlines the fact that the holders of power (even if their appointment was valid) were unrighteous. He seems, however, to believe that this reluctance on the part of the pious to accept the office of *qāḍī* should be modified by the fact that it was a *farḍ kifāya* for a fully qualified person to accept this office, since it concerned the welfare of the Muslims generally, and also because it was concerned with enjoining the good and forbidding evil.

Basing himself upon the example of the prophet and the orthodox caliphs, who themselves exercised judgement personally, Faḍl Allāh states that it was permissible for the *imām*/sultan to judge. But it was the custom of the prophet to appoint *qāḍī*s and he was followed in this by the orthodox caliphs, their general practice being to appoint *qāḍīs*. It was, therefore, incumbent upon the king, if he could not personally give judgement, to appoint *qāḍīs*; without such it was not feasible for him to execute the ordinances of the *sharī'a*. Faḍl Allāh mentions that there was a difference of opinion among the Ḥanafī *'ulamā* as to whether it was permissible for the sultan to give judgement. Some held that since the judgements of the *qāḍī* who exercised power delegated to him by the sultan were valid (*nāfidh*), a judgement issued by the sultan must also be valid. Faḍl Allāh does not express his own view on this matter but merely states that since time did not suffice for the sultan to decide disputes himself the appointment of *qāḍīs* was incumbent upon him.[31]

After discussing the views of various Ḥanafī authorities on whether it was permissible to seek the office of *qāḍī* and the qualifications needed for this office, Faḍl Allāh states that no one who felt himself equal to carrying out the duties of the office need fear to undertake it since he would be following the example of the *ṣaḥāba* and also because the office of *qāḍī* was concerned with enjoining the good and forbidding evil. The office of *qāḍī* was not, however, to be deliberately sought.[32]

Faḍl Allāh then states that it was clear to him after studying the works of the Ḥanafī *imāms* that it was incumbent upon the *imām*/sultan to appoint someone to the office of *qāḍī* and proceeds to a discussion of who was to be appointed and whether the one chosen should be forced to take office or not. He mentions three possible cases. (i) If there was in a town only one qualified person, his appointment was obligatory to ensure the protection of the rights of the people (*jihat-i ṣiyānat-i ḥuqūq-i bandagān*) and the execution of the ordinances of the *sharī'a*, so much so that if he refused, he must, according to some authorities, be forced to accept. (ii) If a number of persons in a town were qualified, if one of them refused he was not a sinner (*athīm*) and if they all refused, similarly they were not all sinners provided the sultan could personally judge cases, but if this was not so then they were all sinners. If all those who were qualified refused office and an ignorant person was appointed they all shared in sin (*gunāh*). From this Faḍl Allāh deduced that if the sultan could decide cases personally it was not incumbent upon him to appoint a *qāḍī*, but, he continues, following the custom of the orthodox caliphs and the early ancestors, the tradition (*sunnat*) was that he should appoint a *qāḍī*. This being so, if there was in a town a number of persons who were qualified, it was fitting that the sultan should select the most capable, most learned and most pious among them. Faḍl Allāh then asks the question could the sultan force such a person if he refused office, there being others qualified, to accept office, and answers that he apparently could do so — though he adds the caveat 'God knows best' — because the choice of the most capable was in accordance with the interest (*ṣalāḥ*) of the Muslims and it was for the ruler (*ḥākim*) to act upon what was in the public interest (*ṣalāḥ-i 'āmma*). It was disapproved of (*makrūh*) for anyone, even if he was not the most learned and the most pious to seek the office of *qāḍī* and according to the *Hidāya*[33] many of the *'ulamā* considered it unlawful to accept office except under constraint. (iii) If in a town there was a person qualified to hold the office of *qāḍī*, the sultan must on no account appoint someone who used bribery to obtain office or who was of bad character, but, according to the *Hidāya*, once a person of bad character had been appointed, his exercise of office was valid. Therefore, Faḍl Allāh states, if the sultan could not find a person of good character to appoint to the office of *qāḍī* and put a person of bad character in charge, his exercise of office was valid (*nāfidh*). After mentioning various views on the problems of whether a *qāḍī* who became of bad character after his appointment ought to be dismissed or not, Faḍl Allāh states that it was clear that the appointment of a person of bad character was valid and that a *qāḍī* did not forfeit office on account of bad character (*fisq*).[34]

Faḍl Allāh also quotes the views of various Shafi'ī scholars. In their view if he who was qualified for the office of *qāḍī* was manifest, there being no other qualified person, he was to make himself known to the sultan and if selected must accept office; if he refused the sultan must force him to take office: he was not excused on the grounds that he feared (that the government would commit) extortion and peculation.[35]

The propriety of the *qāḍī*'s acceptance of office was a problem which had exercised the minds of the pious for centuries. Discussing this matter Faḍl Allāh appears to make a distinction between the *imām* and the sultan, for he writes that if an *imām* having the requisite qualities for his office existed in the community and he appointed *qāḍīs* in the regions, all the rites (*madhāhib*) agreed that the *imām*'s knowledge and justice having been confirmed, it was permissible to accept the office of *qāḍī* at his hands. If there was no *imām* but there was a just sultan, it was also permissible to accept the office of *qāḍī* at his hands. If the sultan was not just, there were two possibilities: either he was a tyrant (*jābir*) or he was a rebel (*bāghī*) against the true *imām*. Faḍl Allāh states that, in the former case acceptance of the office of *qāḍī* from him was, according to the Ḥanafīs, permissible, while according to the Shafi'īs, he who had taken possession of the regions of Islam by force was sultan; his writ ran whether he was just or tyrannical and it was permissible to accept from him the office of *qāḍī*.[36]

It was also incumbent upon the *imām*/sultan to appoint someone with the requisite qualifications to the office of *muḥtasib*, because *iḥtisab*, enjoining the good and forbidding evil, was a *farḍ kifāya*. As such it was incumbent upon all Muslims, but it was for the *imām*/sultan to see that it was undertaken so that he should not be the cause of the suspension of the ordinances of the *sharī'a* by reason of the fact that the members of the community had left the duty of *iḥtisāb* to each other to perform, each one relying on the other to carry it out, so that it remained undone.[37]

The *imām*/sultan by delegating his authority in respect of *shar'ī* matters to these various officials of the religious institution fulfilled one part of his functions. The other part was concerned with the execution of the ordinances of the *sharī'a* among the people living in his kingdom, and for this he required coercive power. Since it was not possible for him personally to protect all the provinces in his possession, he required for the fulfilment of his functions in this connection another series of officials, amirs and governors (*wālīs*),[38] to whom he could delegate his power. Faḍl Allāh seeks sanction for their appointment also in the practice of the prophet and the orthodox caliphs.[39] It was, he states, the established practice of the caliphs to appoint amirs in the regions (*bilād*), and since the exercise of government had devolved upon the sultan, and since it was difficult — indeed impossible — for him to exercise this personally in all regions, it was incumbent upon him to appoint in every region a governor (*ḥākim*) to be his deputy in the exercise of coercive power (*siyāsat*) and justice and in strengthening the weak (against the strong), just as it was necessary for him to appoint *qāḍīs* to maintain the regulations (*qawā'id*) of the *sharī'a*.[40] It was fitting that these amirs should be endowed with such of the qualities of the sultan as would enable them to protect the territories entrusted to them. These qualities included justice, bravery, good judgement and administrative ability and competence in matters of war and what concerned the protection of the frontiers.[41]

In his discussion of the validity of the appointment of provincial governors, Faḍl Allāh is clearly influenced by the need to maintain the authority of the governor. He states that if a sultan who was a tyrant appointed a man of bad character amir of a town, his amirate was nevertheless effective, although the sultan in appointing him would have failed to observe what was right (*ra'āyat-i ḥaqq nakarda bāshad*). If an amir was of good character when he was appointed and later became of bad character and tyrannical, there was a difference of opinion as to whether he forfeited his office or not. Faḍl Allāh considers that the general sense was that he merited dismissal.[42]

Once he had appointed an amir over a town or region, the sultan must always be aware of how the amir was conducting himself. If someone from the town complained against him, and it was established that the complaint was justified, the sultan was to summon the amir. If this was not feasible because of fear of disturbances in the town if the amir left the district, the sultan should write to him, commanding him to abstain from such action and if this had no effect, he should dismiss him and appoint someone in his stead.[43] Faḍl Allāh had no illusions about the conduct of amirs. He insists that 'the sultan must act in such a way towards the amirs of the regions that they are always in fear of dismissal and of his anger; they must know that the sultan will dismiss them at the slightest complaint of the subjects. When they are thus fearful and apprehensive, they will not treat the subjects with tyranny and the country (*mamlakat*) will be safe from their evil and the sultan will hold undisputed sway over the city. But if the amir of a city knows that the sultan will not listen to the complaints of the subjects against him and will not call him to account, he will become independent and the management of the people of that city will depart from the sultan's hands. God will call him to account for the actions of that amir who is his deputy.'[44] Defence of the frontier regions was also incumbent upon the *imām*/sultan and those nominated to protect the frontiers should always be vigilant and in a state of preparedness to resist attack.[45]

Redress of grievances was the prerogative of the *imām*/sultan. Faḍl Allāh quotes al-Māwardī to the effect that the *khalīfa* or sultan, or a person whom the *khalīfa* or sultan had entrusted with affairs (such as the amir or the wazir of delegation), could undertake the redress of grievances and that it was not necessary to appoint someone especially to undertake this charge. This was, however, not always the case and if such persons were unable to undertake the redress of grievances it was necessary to appoint someone especially for the purpose, who was called *wālī-i maẓālim*.[46]

Through these two series of delegations, the one to officials of the religious institution — the *shaykh al-islām* to protect *shar'ī* sciences, *muftīs* to answer such problems as might arise, *qāḍīs* to execute the ordinances of the *sharī'a* and *muḥtasibs* to enjoin the good and forbid evil — and the other to officials possessing coercive power — amirs to administer the outlying provinces, *wulāt-i maẓālim* to redress grievances and wardens of the frontiers — Faḍl Allāh provided for the fulfilment by the sultan of his responsibilities for the protection of the *sharī'a* in its theoretical and in its practical aspects (*ḥifẓ-i 'ulūm wa a'māl-i sharī'a*) so that caliphal government might continue, even though the caliph as such no longer existed. He then turns to the practical details of how these various officials were to be paid. This leads him to a discussion of the taxes and rules pertaining to them according to the traditional Sunnī theory.[47] He discusses *ṣadaqa*, *zakāt*, *'ushr* and *kharāj*, giving the views especially of Ḥanafīs and Shafi'īs. Regarding *kharāj* he states that it was obligatory upon the *imām*/sultan to take *kharāj* from the owners of land and to expend it on its *shar'ī* purposes — many people had a right in the *kharāj* and the livelihood of the army was provided by it. If the sultan in taking *kharāj* showed negligence, he became a sinner because such negligence would result in the army being deprived of their livelihood, which would result in corruption (*fasād*) in the territory of Islam. For the *imām*/sultan to show such negligence as would inevitably result in corruption in the territory of Islam was the essence of sin and rebellion against God. Therefore, it was incumbent upon the *imām*/sultan to know first who must pay *kharāj* and who it was from whom it must not be taken.[48]

Faḍl Allāh emphasises repeatedly that *kharāj* was to be expended upon the army. Quoting the standard tag about agriculture being the basis of prosperity in an adapted form, he states, 'know that the support and allowances of the people of Islam are from the proceeds of *kharāj*, because the livelihood of the inhabitants of the regions of Islam comes from agriculture, the good order and preservation of which depends upon the army; and the stability of the army depends upon its wages and its wages come from *kharāj*. Therefore, if the sultan shows negligence in the collection of *kharāj* or abandons it, disorder will occur in the livelihood of the people of Islam and the regions of Islam will be disturbed (*mukhtall*) because of that disorder.'[49]

The concern of Faḍl Allāh for the practicalities of government is shown especially in his discussion of *nawā'ib*, i.e. what was demanded of the people, not on account of *kharāj*, *'ushr* and other *shar'ī* taxes, but on account of new taxes such as kings customarily imposed upon the subjects in the public interest for the military (*lashkariān*). He alleges that the prophet ordered the *aṣḥāb* to dig a canal in Madīna and allocated wages for this purpose and states that the sultan was permitted to act in the same way. 'Our *shaykhs*,' he writes, 'have said that whatever the *imām* lays upon the subjects for the public interest is right, and this also applies to the pay (*ujrat*) of those who protect the roads and preserve public order.' He mentions various definitions of *nawā'ib*, most of which were concerned in one way or another with the pay of the military. He contrasts them with *ḍarbiyya* or *ḍarā'ib*, defining the latter as what the king imposes upon the Muslims by way of tyranny and in breach of trust without the existence of a general need touching the interests of all Muslims. Such taxes were null and void (*bāṭila*) and were taken from the subjects unjustly (*bi nā-ḥaqq*).[50] According to one definition the *nawā'ib* were the support or allowances (*ma'ūnat*) which a group of people made to the men they were required to furnish as their quota to the army, while some said that they were the wages of guards, and others that they were levied by the sultan for the mobilisation of the army to fight infidels and to provide for the ransom of Muslim captives.[51] 'Therefore,' Faḍl Allāh states, relating the levy of *nawā'ib* specifically to his own day and local conditions, 'what is taken in Khwārazm from the generality of men for the repair of dams on the Oxus or for the building of walls round the kingdom (*sūr-i mamlakat*) or other such matters of public interest is a loan which is incumbent (*daynī wājib*) and a right which is due (*ḥaqqī mustaḥaqq*), and refusal to pay is not permissible; such (taxes) are not unjust.'[52] *Nawā'ib* were thus taxes levied because of some emergency affecting the welfare of the Muslims. For example, if an infidel attacked Muslim territory and there was need of soldiers or support, once the sultan had issued a call, it was incumbent upon all who could take part in the military operations to do so, and if anyone could not do so, it was his duty to equip someone else in his stead. This was one kind of *nawā'ib*. Another was the making of dams on the great rivers. All these *nawā'ib*, Faḍl Allāh states, were legal (*ḥaqq ast*) and the Ḥanafī *'ulamā* considered each of them a *farḍ kifāya* and their payment an incumbent duty.[53]

Faḍl Allāh analyses the various sources of the sultan's revenue. These were:

(1) inherited property, of which the sultan could dispose as he wished;

(2) what he had acquired by trade and from agriculture in his private estates and on which he paid *'ushr* and *kharāj*, or from flocks, or from a canal (*nahr*) which he had made with his own money, or from the revivification of land by means of his own men (*rijāl*) or money, all of which could be disposed of as he pleased, and which, together with inherited property, went to his legal heirs in the event of his death;

(3) money which he had taken from the public treasury surplus to his needs to maintain the dignity of kingship; this included money drawn on the *kharāj* of the preceding year for the pay

of the army, any part of which remaining unspent if the sultan died before the year was up passed as an inheritance to his heirs;

(4) *zakāt*;
(5) *khums* on booty, mines and treasure trove;
(6) lost property and escheats;
(7) unclaimed property;
(8) property left by former sultans;
(9) money from *nawā'ib* and *ḍarā'ib*;
(10) presents sent from infidel territory;
(11) presents from Muslims;
(12) bribes, which were, however, like *ḍarā'ib-i bāṭila*, illegal.

It was incumbent upon the sultan to know the rules for each and to apply the revenue accordingly. 'If the sultan acts thus and devotes the taxes of which God has made him the collector (*ḍābiṭ*) to their proper purposes and makes the military (*lashkarīān*) and those who have a right to stipends happy (because they receive a share) of the public revenue (*amwāl-i maṣāliḥ*), he will have fulfilled his responsibility as sultan from the point of view of the revenue, and if he makes a vow that every kingly action which issues from him and every order which he gives shall be in accordance with the *sharī'a*, he will have fulfilled one part of his kingly functions, namely the collection of taxes according to the *sharī'a*.'[54]

Like al-Ghazālī, Faḍl Allāh recognises that the actions of sultans fell far short of the ideal and that the legality of their wealth was open to question. No sultan could be termed just unless he had four treasuries for the different types of tax[55] and spent the income of each on its proper purposes; unless this was the case the money in his treasury would be mostly unlawful.[56] Faḍl Allāh recognises that the pious might well have scruples about accepting money which came from illegal sources. Discussing the unlawfulness or otherwise of the taxes and the legal and illegal uses to which they were put, he records al-Ghazālī's recommendation that the *'ulamā* should not take money from sultans because it was likely to have been acquired illegally.[57]

It was for the sultan to exact the legal penalties (*ḥudūd*), because this was the right of the *imām*/sultan.[58] Also, by virtue of the fact that he was learned and exercised sole power (*'ālim wa qādir 'alā'l-iṭlāq*), he had special responsibilities with regard to the *furūḍ-i kifāya*. In the event of no-one undertaking them, he would be a sinner if he did not step in to undertake them. Therefore, he should inquire diligently into the performance of the *furūḍ-i kifāya*, including those which concerned the sacred observances of Islam. One of these concerned the pilgrimage. The caliphs, when they did not go on the pilgrimage, appointed an *amīr ḥajj* who acted as the caliph's deputy in the performance of the pilgrimage. Faḍl Allāh states that in his time the great amir of the *ḥajj* (*ṣāḥib-i imārat-i kubrā dar ḥajj*) was the amir of the Egyptian pilgrim train (*qāfila*) because the 'Abbasid caliphs in the region of Egypt had an independent caliphate, the sultans of Egypt being their deputies (*wukalā*). But, he states, it was fitting that the sultan of every kingdom (*mamlakat*) should appoint an *amīr ḥajj* for the performance of the *ḥajj* so that the people of the region would set out for the *ka'ba* under the shadow of his protection.[59]

While thus conceding the primacy of the 'Abbāsid caliph of Egypt in the matter of the pilgrimage, Faḍl Allāh does not recognise him as the only caliph of the *dār al-islām*, though clearly his position was rather different from that of the *imām*/sultan with whom Faḍl Allāh's exposition is mainly concerned, in that there was in Egypt a caliph and a sultan.

It was also, Faḍl Allāh states, the right of the *imām*/sultan to lead the Friday prayers in Islamic countries; if he fell short in this he would be a sinner. According to the Ḥanafī rite, the Friday prayers without him or his deputy (*nā'ib*) were not valid. It was, therefore, incumbent upon him to lead the prayers so that the Muslims would not become sinners through the abandonment of that which was incumbent upon them.[60]

In this brief examination of the *Sulūk al-mulūk* I have attempted to show how Faḍl Allāh b. Rūzbihān adapted the theory of his predecessors to the circumstances of the late ninth/fifteenth and early tenth/sixteenth centuries. He postulates an unbroken continuity between his day and the day of the prophet. He insists also that the purpose of the rule of the *imām*/sultan was the defence of the *sharī'a* and the implementation of its ordinances and that his functions were defined and limited by the *sharī'a*. He seeks to institutionalise this limitation on the absolutism of the *imām*/sultan by the appointment of a *shaykh al-islām*, but since the only sanctions against the sultan were moral sanctions this limitation was entirely theoretical and the *imām*/sultan's acceptance of the advice and guidance of the *shaykh al-islām* and the officials of the religious institution purely voluntary. The specific contributions which Faḍl

Allāh makes to the development of Islamic political theory are his unequivocal recognition, in his concern to preserve continuity with the past, that the bearer of political power was the *imām*, and in his equally unequivocal recognition, in his concern for the effective exercise of government, of the legality of non-*shar'ī* taxes which the *imām*/sultan levied to provide himself with the revenue needed to carry out his functions. He thus removed the permanent illegality into which the pious had pushed the ruler by their persistent refusal to enlarge the scope of lawful taxation.

Notes

1. *Iḥyā' ulūm al-dīn*, quoted by H.A.R. Gibb in 'Constitutional Organization' in Majid Khadduri and J. Liebesny (eds.), *Law in the Middle East* (Washington, DC, 1955), p. 19.

2. See further H. Laoust, *Essai sur les doctrines sociales et politiques de Ibn Taimiya* (Cairo, 1939).

3. The inhabitants of Khunj retained their allegiance to Sunnism until the twelfth/eighteenth century.

4. Faḍl Allāh b. Rūzbihān, *Mihmān-nāma-i Bukhārā*, (ed.) M. Sotoodeh (Tehran, 1341/1962), p. 335.

5. See further Ursula Ott, *Transoxanien und Turkestan zu Beginn des 16. Jahrhunderts: das Mihmān-nāma-yi Buḫārā des Faḍlallāh b. Rūzbihān Ḫunǧī. Übersetzung und Kommentar* (Freiburg, 1974); U. Haarman, 'Staat und religion in Transoxanien im frühen 16. Jahrhundert' in *ZDMG*, cxxiv/2 (1974), pp. 332-69; V. Minorsky, *Persia in A.D. 1478-1490* (London, 1957); Faḍl Allāh b. Rūzbihān, *Mihmān-nāma-i Bukhārā*, introduction by M. Sotoodeh; ; Muḥammad Amīn Khunjī, 'Faḍl Allāh b. Rūzbihān Khunjī' in *Farhang-i īrān-zamīn*, iv (1335/1956), pp. 173-84; and Muḥammad Aslam, 'Faḍl-ullāh bin Rūzbihan al-Iṣfahānī' in *JAS of Pakistan*, x/2 (December 1965).

6. I have used the B.M. ms. Or. 253. The ms. is not paginated. References are to a microfilm of the ms. The printed edition of the *Sulūk al-mulūk* (ed.) Muḥammad Nizāmuddīn and Muḥammad Ghouse, Hyderabad (Deccan), 1386/1966), was not available to me.

7. Cf. *Akhlāq-i jalālī*, lith., undated, p. 236. Jalāl al-Dīn appears also to have been willing to accord the title of *imām* to Ya'qūb b. Ḥasan. Nūr Allāh Shūshtarī relates that in reply to a question put to Jalāl al-Dīn as to who should be regarded as *imām*, he answered 'for the Shī'is it is Muḥammad b. Ḥasan and for the Sunnis Ya'qūb b. Ḥasan Beg' (*Majālis al-mu'minīn*, quoted by Minorsky, *Persia in A.D. 1478-1490*, p. 3, n. 2.) The attribution of the title of Shadow of God upon earth to the caliph and the sultan had already by the ninth/fifteenth century a long history especially in 'Mirrors for princes'.

8. Cf. Faḍl Allāh's own account of the interpretation which he gave to the *ḥadīth*, 'there are seven persons to whom God will give shade on the day when there is no shade but His' when preaching in a mosque in Harāt in 914/1508. In his address he stated that the first of these seven persons would be the just *imām*, the king of Islam, who fulfilled the conditions demanded of the *imām* and was called *imām* 'because he had brought the world under the shadow of his justice, made men secure from calamities and safe from the violence of khans and the tyrannical actions of

rebels . . . (He) is the just *imām* whom the prophet made the first of the seven saved persons to be under the shadow of God's wing, because he, the just *imām*, is the Shadow of God, and, in this world and the next, king by right and the vicegerent of the prophet; and the sign of the king's fear of God (*murāqabat*), which causes him to reach this rank, is that he is never negligent of the conditions of his subjects — for God most high and holy will hardly accept the excuse of the king who is negligent and will punish any lack of awareness of the condition of his subjects with every kind of retribution. It is not sufficient for him to say to God (when he is called to account) "I gave the government of such and such a province to so and so and I am not responsible for his actions", because it is incumbent upon the *khalīfa* to look into the actions of that amir . . . the king must be personally aware of the condition of each and every one of his subjects and provide for his condition in a fitting way. If he does not do so he will be visited with retribution.' (*Mihmān-nāma-i Bukhārā*, 32ff.)

9. For a discussion of al-Ghazālī's theory see further L. Binder, 'al-Ghazālī's theory of Islamic government', *The Muslim World*, XLV/3 (July 1955), pp. 229-41.

10. Usually Faḍl Allāh mentions his sources by name, but sometimes he simply uses some phrase such as 'the *fuqahā'* have said'. It is not always absolutely clear where a quotation begins or ends, though sometimes after quoting the views of some authority Faḍl Allāh states 'and this is the view of . . .'

11. *Sulūk al-mulūk*, pp. 15, 19.

12. Ibid., p. 15.

13. Ibid., pp. 15-16.

14. Ibid., p. 16.

15. Ibid., p. 17.

16. In his exposition Faḍl Allāh frequently uses the phrase *imām wa sulṭān*, in which *wa* could be translated as 'and' or 'or', but his meaning in most cases may perhaps best be rendered by '*imām*/sultan'.

17. *Sulūk al-mulūk*, p. 17.

18. Ibid., p. 110; cf. also *Mihmān-nāma-i Bukhārā*, p. 1 and passim.

19. *Sulūk al-mulūk*, pp. 17-18.

20. Ibid., p. 19.

21. Ibid., p. 20.

22. The text has no negative, but this is clearly an error.

23. *Sulūk al-mulūk*, pp. 20-1.

24. Ibid., p. 21.

25. Ibid.

26. Ibid., pp. 21-2.

27. Ibid., p. 22.

28. Ibid.

29. Ibid., pp. 23ff.

30. Ibid., p. 28.

31. Ibid., p. 33.

32. Ibid., p. 34.

33. The *Hidāya* of Burhān al-Dīn al-Marghīnānī (d. 594/1196) is frequently quoted by Faḍl Allāh.

34. Ibid., pp. 34-6.

35. Ibid., p. 38.

36. Ibid., pp. 38-9.

37. Ibid., pp. 55ff.

38. Faḍl Allāh stated that the *wālīs* were called *dārūghagān*. This, if he is right, was a Central Asian usage. See further E.I. (2), art. *dārūgha* on the functions of the *dārūgha*.

39. *Sulūk al-mulūk*, pp. 65ff.

40. Ibid., p. 67.

41. Ibid., pp. 67-8.
42. Ibid.
43. Ibid., p. 69.
44. Ibid., pp. 69-70.
45. Ibid., p. 78.
46. Ibid., p. 72.
47. Ibid., pp. 78-9.
48. Ibid., p. 99.
49. Ibid., p. 111.
50. Ibid., p. 118.
51. Ibid., p. 119.
52. Ibid.
53. Ibid.
54. Ibid., p. 120.
55. These were for (i) *zakāt*, *'ushr* and *kafārāt*; (ii) *kharāj*, *jizya* and *ṣadaqāt*; (iii) *khums*; and (iv) *luqṭāt* and *tarakāt*.
56. Ibid., p. 121.
57. Ibid., pp. 121-2.
58. Ibid., p. 122.
59. Ibid., pp. 137-8.
60. Ibid., p. 143.

PART TWO:

ASPECTS OF POWER IN HETERODOX ISLAM

5 AYATOLLAH KHOMEINI'S CONCEPT OF ISLAMIC GOVERNMENT

Abbas Kelidar

This chapter is based primarily on Ayatollah Rouhallah Khomeini's treatise entitled 'Islamic Government', and subtitled variously as *Durus fiqhiyya* (Lessons in Jurisprudence), or *Wilayat al-faqih* (The Guardianship of the Jurist). Two versions have been translated into Arabic.[1] One states that the treatise is made up of three lectures while the other claims twelve lectures given by Ayatollah Khomeini to his students in the holy city, Najaf in Iraq, where he was living in exile between 1963 and 1979. Najaf serves as the main teaching centre for the theology and jurisprudence of the Islamic Shī'i Twelver sect. The book is written in a rather discursive style which tends to be repetitious; and it is likely that either a student or a group of them collected the lectures of their master as they were given, i.e. made a verbatim record of them which was offered for publication later. There is little difference between the two versions. In essence they are the same; the only divergence seems to have been caused by the translators, neither of whom is named. However, they indicate that in *Durus* the translator is familiar with the terminology of the social sciences, while in *Wilayat* he is much more of a theologian.

The remarkable fact about Khomeini's thesis is that he does not seem to have been touched or affected by any of the modernising influences which led many of the Muslim reformers in the last two centuries to write about Islam, its relation with the West, and the compatibility of Islam with modern science and technology. Unlike many of his predecessors and his own contemporaries he completely dismisses the manifestations of Western culture as irrelevant, and proclaims them as useless to Islam and the Muslims. They are to him no more than false images that have to be eradicated. He has a healthy respect for the technological achievement of the West, but this could be borrowed without the necessary concomitants of wholesale Westernisation. Khomeini looks at concepts not so much in terms of their evolution in the Western philosophical and scientific traditions but in their more tangible form and end product. By ignoring the means, he can easily argue that Islam seeks the same end, and therefore there is no need for Westernisation or modernisation as the Shah tried in Iran.

What has characterised the movement led by the Iranian religious divine more than any other factor is political activism. Khomeini has succeeded like no other Islamic religious campaigner in modern times to imbue Iranian politics with the kind of religious zeal that has lain dormant for many years. Many observers have expressed surprise that in the second half of the twentieth century, and after more than a century of modernisation, this should be so. Others have come to see Khomeini as a latter-day modernist and reformer. They expected him to continue the march towards the ultimate objective of Islamic liberalism, whereby religion would be divorced from politics to produce a system of government which could serve as a model for the other Islamic countries; and at the same time would be favourably contrasted with those of the West. Only a few have seen Khomeini in his traditional role of a Shī'i *mujtahid*, a learned religious jurist, who is capable of interpreting the intentions of the missing Imam of the Shī'i Twelvers through his own vast knowledge and experience of Islamic traditions. As such he could easily engage in activist, seditious and even revolutionary politics, because of the prevailing social conditions, their inequity and deprivation suffered by the poor in a society undergoing rapid economic transformation. And fewer still have taken Khomeini as a religious bigot who seeks the purification of his own society irrespective of the consequences.

Islam ordains the establishment of a theocracy, a community of believers governed by the prophet Muḥammad in accordance with the divine revelations of the Qur'ān which has become the holy writ. The state in Islam therefore is one of perfect order, sacred and immutable. However, since the source of legislation was the revelations to the Prophet, this perfect order could be sustained for as long as Muḥammad was alive. After his death the community has had to devise alternative arrangements for government, symbolised in the institution of the caliphate. The Shī'is, those Muslims who could be distinguished from the others by their devotion to and their conviction that Ali, the Prophet's cousin and his son-in-law, was the best and most qualified person to succeed, have continually questioned the legitimacy of Muslim rule when their candidate was passed over. They have considered the Imamate, the leadership of the Muslim community, as the God-given right of Ali and his descendants after him as ordained to them by the Almighty. The Imams, according to

Shī'i doctrine, were the only people who inherited the Prophet's authority to govern after him; a power they have been denied from exercising formally, a fact which served to reinforce their rejection of existing government as unjust and iniquitous. Thus the essence of Shī'i doctrine has remained an objective to be sought, and the existing order a reality to be suffered, lamented and, occasionally, violently resisted.

It is the discrepancy between the real and the ideal coupled with new socio-religious factors, particularly as the non-Arab population entered the world of Islam, that has contributed in no small measure, to the development of the messianic nature of Shī'i Islam. It has spurred on the believers to renew their effort in pursuing the activist approach in the quest to attain the desired millennium. The notion was fortified when the twelfth Imam of the Shī'i Twelvers went missing in mysterious circumstances in the ninth century. He has remained hidden ever since. His reappearance will mark the inauguration of an age of eternal peace, absolute justice and complete righteousness. So long as the twelfth Imam is invisible, there can be no binding interpretation of the Qur'ān which holds true for all times and all places.

Until the reappearance of the Imam, the community would have to resort to its religious *mujtahid*s who, by their knowledge of Islamic rules and regulations, traditions and precedents, are qualified to interpret the current purposes of holy writ. In this capacity the *mujtahid*s of the Shī'i community can exercise considerable authority over the community. They attain prominence not by virtue of appointment or election but simply when their followers as well as their peers defer to them on the grounds of piety and extensive knowledge of religious matters. Their emergence as *marji' al-taqlid*, which simply means an authority to be followed, would bestow on them eminence, influence and, at times, vast income from the alms tax paid voluntarily to the *mujtahid*s to be spent for charitable purposes. An alliance between the mercantile elements and the religious establishment could wreak havoc as it did in Iran when the two groups become disenchanted with a particular government. This is particularly so as in Shī'i Islam temporal rule could be rendered tolerable by its deference to religious advice and injunctions from the *mujtahid*s, but it could not be pronounced legitimate since only the Imam's rule is so endowed. It is for this reason that the Iranian constitution of 1906 provided for a religious college of five *mujtahid*s, whose function was to examine all legislation and reject or repudiate any bill deemed to be incompatible with the Islamic *Sharī'a*. The provision was never put into effect.

However, while the first three Imams of the Twelvers, namely Ali and his two sons Hassan and Husain, campaigned actively for their right to be acknowledged as the legitimate successors to the Prophet, the fourth Imam Ali Ibn al-Husain, better known as Zain al-Abidin (who acquired the title for his extreme piety and religious devotion) was so shocked by the massacre at Karbala which claimed the life of his father and the 72 members of the household and followers whose life was spared because of his ill-health, decided to abandon the struggle. He became extremely quiescent in his claim to the succession. His own successors followed an equivocal approach to their legitimist claims, an approach which became a characteristic of the Shī'i profession of faith. The ambivalence was transformed into a practice known as *taqiyya* or dissimulation. *Taqiyya* remained a natural corollary of the prevalent conditions; a necessity imposed by the danger of holding religious and political views contrary to the official establishment. The Imams could not proclaim themselves as the avatars of divinity, and therefore the sole object of obedience, since that posed a direct challenge to the temporal and religious sovereignty of the 'Abbāsid Caliphs. *Taqiyya* became an article of the faith. It has led Imams as well as *mujtahid*s to refrain from a direct challenge to the established order.

Ayatollah Khomeini's treatise on Islamic government constitutes a radical departure from these accepted norms of Shī'i traditions of faith. The breach with the Twelvers' conventions becomes total as he seeks to restore the original activist drive of early Islam by overlooking the position of the later Imams and citing the example of the Prophet and the first three Imams as his examples. There are references to the other Imams in the text but only when they indicated their legitimist claims against the incumbent rulers of the 'Abbāsid dynasty. He is not concerned with the caliphate; nor is he bothered with any modernist notion of Islam and government. He condemns the modern, Westernised system of government in the Islamic world as nothing but a sham, and no more than an aberration. His is an adulterated Islamic concept. It is as if the last two hundred years of political and institutional changes had not taken place at all.

Iran is the focus of his interest, but what he has to say does not preclude other Muslim countries, especially as references are made to the necessity of Muslim unity. The very concept of the guardianship of the jurist seems to be an adaptation from Sunni jurisprudence which may suggest that Khomeini does not want the introduction of his notion of Islamic government to be confined to Iran as a predominantly Shī'i society. He charges the government with the obligation of striving to maintain the unity of the Muslims. However if such unity is to be achieved it would be strictly under the Shī'i traditions of the Imamate since he quotes Fatima, daughter of the prophet, wife of the first and mother of the second and third Imams, to the effect that obedience to their household is the rule of the community and their leadership is immunity from (a safeguard against) division: 'ta'tuna nizaman lil-milla, wa Imāmatunā amānan min al-firqa'. His call for unity which may fall on receptive ears is given political expression as he makes virulent remarks about the evils of imperialism in dividing and exploiting the natural resources of the Islamic world. He also condemns Zionism, and asserts the need for the liberation of Palestine, though this emanates from a religious rather than a national concern with the problem.

There is little doubt that Islam to Ayatollah Khomeini is the noble warriors' religion; it is of those who seek justice and righteousness; it is of those who demand independence and liberty; but above all it is of those who struggle to prevent the infidel as well as the presumptuous tyrant (*tāghūt*) from exercising power over the Muslim. His message is pure and rather simple if not simplistic. Islam is not just a code which governs the moral conduct of the individual, but the corpus of rules and regulations which provide for every need and all requirements. He refuses to believe that Islam is merely concerned with the rules of menstruation and childbirth, *Ihkam al-hayd wa al-nifās*.[3] He has little doubt that it is the orientalists and their modernist followers who have portrayed Islam as such in order to distort its face and obliterate its original message. He considers the introduction of modern education, the adoption of constitutional parliamentary systems of government, the promulgation of Westernised penal codes, as nothing but deliberate means to undermine Islam by encouraging the faithful to abandon their religion.

In order to deal with these threats, and to redress the prevailing injustice in the Muslim world and especially in Iran, Khomeini calls on the Muslims, through his theological students in the Najaf schools, to emulate the example of the Prophet and the first three Imams. He demands their transformation into holy warriors to save Islam from the dangers confronting the religion. It is rather significant that he overlooks the quiescent Imams, only to state that they would have undertaken the same path had circumstances allowed.[4] However, he enjoins his students, as the new soldiers — *Junūd al-Islam* — to believe that theirs is a total system and to reject the notion that there is a similarity between Islam and Christianity, or that there is little difference between mosque and church.[5]

When outlining his case for the establishment of Islamic government, Khomeini follows in the tradition of the Muslim jurists, albeit a Shīʿi one. Since Islam is threatened and in constant danger, only the jurist can save it from its plight. It is his duty to do so through the establishment of an Islamic administration whose precedent was that of the Prophet himself. Muḥammad was not simply a messenger of the divine revelations. He was not just a preacher but a ruler and an administrator as well. Imam Ali was exactly the same. Government, therefore, was of the essence to Islam, and has remained imperative for the well being of the community. Khomeini states clearly that he believes in the *wilaya*, or succession, which ensured the continuity of government. He indicates his belief in the necessity of appointing a successor to the Prophet, and he has no qualms in reminding his students that this was done in accordance with God's instructions. Thus the Prophet's successor must be a preacher, a jurist who will rule over the community in order to maintain and protect the achievement of the predecessors and guarantee the security of the Muslim realm. The successor could not legislate but he would execute and carry out the rules and regulations. He would ensure the obedience of the community to the holy writ. And it is for this reason that the institutional framework of good government would have to be set up and maintained. Khomeini invites his students to take forth the following clarion: 'And tell them (the public) we believe in the succession, and that the Prophet appointed him in accordance with God's instruction; that we believe in the necessity of establishing Islamic government, so that the divine regulations may be applied, a government to administer the people, lead and care for them. The struggle for the formation of such a government is the twin of belief in the succession'.[6]

There is no doubt in Khomeini's mind that after the death of the Prophet, government had to continue. The difference that existed, which led to the great schism in Islam he states, was not about the continuation of Islamic administration, but about the person best qualified to be in charge of it. However, as the Prophet was not simply a legislator but gave the Revelations an executive dimension — since he personally punished offenders, chopped off the thieves' hands, flogged and stoned adulterers and adulteresses respectively in order to ensure the prevalence of his just rule — the successors are charged with the same obligations. They have to secure obedience to the laws of Islam. It is this reasoning that leads Khomeini to conclude that the laws of the *Sharī'a* stipulate that there must be a state based on Muslim jurisprudence; a state that can provide for all the exigencies of a living community. Such a state has to be able to deal with all kinds of problems ranging from matters of personal status to questions of international relations. A brief sketch of what could serve as the model of such a structure is offered. It would derive its economic policy and financial administration from the Qur'ān and the Sunna. He cites such institutions as *al-khums*; *al-zakat*, and *al-jizziya* as well as *al-kharaj* as the foundation for this administration.[7]

Having established that Islamic government is a divine commandment and therefore cannot be abandoned or suspended following the disappearance of the twelfth Imam, Khomeini proceeds to make the case for the government, or the guardianship, of the *faqih*, i.e. the jurist. He argues for instance that what was required at the time of the Prophet is more than needed at the present. It has been more than a thousand years since the twelfth Imam went missing, and his absence may last another thousand before his reappearance. Thus Khomeini argues that the affairs of the muslim community could not be allowed to degenerate into chaos. If that were to happen Islam would wither away and die. In the absence of the Imam the faithful have no alternative but to obey those in command over them. God has demanded obedience unto Him, his prophet, and the guardians from amongst the followers. Those guardians to Khomeini could not be any other than the jurists, the *faqih*s. He quotes the eighth Imam to the effect that Muslim communities at all ages need the Imams to maintain law and order, and prevent the spread of anarchy. Government would be essential at all times and in all places, merely as a means to an end in this respect, the end being the continued application of the religious law. 'It would prevent people from encroaching upon God's limitations, and from seeking their own personal pleasure; it would eliminate corruption on earth, and protect the rights of the weak'.[8]

There is no hesitation in the treatise that it is the duty of the learned and just jurist to take on the task of government after the

Imam. God did not limit the rule of the religious law to two hundred years, and therefore it must be a duty of the jurist to assume these tasks entrusted to them by the Prophet through the Imams, and on to the *faqih* since they have been meant to rule over the community.[9] This statement is qualified by the reservation that the jurist could not enjoy the same rank; he would not be impeccable for instance, but he will have to bear the same responsibilities. There is no doubt that this conclusion is the product of Khomeini's own reasoning, since he declares that it is jurisprudence — *Shar'* as well as reason, *'Aql* — that call upon the Muslims not to leave the business of government to people ignorant of the religious laws. When that happens, he contends, then *shirk*, or heresy, would prevail, and the ruler would be a presumptuous tyrant — a *tāghūt*. He exhorts his students to create suitable conditions to facilitate the emergence of a generation of believers who would destroy the thrones of the despots, just as Imam Husain attempted to do at Karbala in 680.[10]

The jurist-governor would enjoy the same powers as the Prophet or Imam but could not enjoy the same position of eminence since the latter were especially privileged to be impeccable.[11] But he insists that when a just and a learned jurist rises to form a government, he would inherit all the authority to enable him to give the community the same consideration as the Prophet had done; and the people will be obliged to listen and obey. He describes the position of the *faqih*-ruler in the following terms: 'He will have to assume what the Prophet assumed, no more and no less. He will establish the limitations as the Prophet set them out, and will govern in accordance with the divine revelations. He will collect the dues on the people's wealth just as practised under the rule of the Prophet, he will organize the treasury — *bayt al-mal*, and act as a trustee over it'.[12]

It is not surprising when Khomeini declares that such a government would be unlike any other. It is not despotic but constitutional! The limitations imposed on it are not in the form of representative or parliamentary checks, but by the body of the *sharī'a* or the revealed law. It is a government by divine law where the legislative process is confined to God, and no other source. In it there is no legislature because there will not be a need for one, but there will be a planning board to oversee the organisation of government departments, and the application of the holy laws. In short it is a theocracy where sovereignty does not rest with the people but with a power beyond them, namely, God.

The assertion in Khomeini's thesis is clear that the succession does not end with the missing Imam, but passes on to the *faqih* or jurist, provided he is knowledgeable and just, who is charged to establish God's rule on earth. The reason for the choice of the jurist is rather obvious. Islamic government requires extensive knowledge of jurisprudence, and it is the jurist who possesses it. In addition Khomeini cites several traditions from the Prophet as well as the Imams in support of his case. These may be erroneous, tendentious and tenuous, but that is not important so far as this chapter is concerned. He insists that the just *faqih* alone is qualified to implement Islamic rules and regulations, to establish a righteous administration, to impose God's limitations and safeguard the security of the Muslims.[13] His case is mainly based on such traditions as 'the *faqih*s are the shield of Islam', and that they are 'the trustees of the prophets'.[14] Moreover, he contends that the jurists take precedence over other rulers when they become the actual governors, when he cites the tradition 'the *faqih*s are the judges of kings',[15] and that they have been appointed to rule.[16] Even when they do not, Khomeini states, the God-fearing rulers would defer to the jurists, thus allowing God's government to be proclaimed and be effective.

Khomeini is not content to fundamentally radicalise the role of the Shīʻi jurists in the politics of a modernising society like that of Iran. He is also intent upon waging a relentless war on the traditionalist *mujtahid*s. He urges them to renounce their quiescent posture which they have assumed in the absence of the Imam. He calls upon them to take much more of an activist involvement in the affairs of their people for the sake of Islam. He inveighs on the necessity of saving the deprived and the oppressed and to defend them against the injustices of the modern world.[17] His invitation is nothing short of a populist campaign to gather support for his cause. If the *faqih* is true to himself and his faith, if he is to be truly the Shield of Islam, then he must work for the restoration of religious values and Islamic practices to justify that designation. He makes it clear that the religious establishment must mobilise all its capabilities to meet the challenge of modernism so that the doctrine of Islam, its rules and regulations could be safeguarded.[18] This duty assigned to the *faqih* is so important that Khomeini compares it with such basic tenets of Islam as daily prayers and fasting during the month of Ramadan, and once again he invites the *mujtahids* to emulate the ultimate sacrifice which the third Imam Husain had made in the quest for legitimate Islamic government.[19]

Ayatollah Khomeini is completely resolute that the Shī'S, *faqih*s or not, should not spend their years in prayerful waiting for the coming of the Mahdi, the missing twelfth Imam. He wants his students to assume the role of militants. In rhetorical manner he asked them what they had done for their religion when they shirked every responsibility to see that Muslim rules were implemented, and concludes rather sarcastically what kind of a shield will they be when there is practically nothing left of the original structure to protect.[20] He proceeds to inform them that they are the successors to the Prophet. And as they would not abandon their daily prayers because the Mahdi has not returned, the cause of Islamic government should not be forsaken in the absence of the Imam. 'You should not say that the Imam will not come until the earth is full of corruption. Learn the real purpose of your religion, and go out and strive for it'.[21]

This campaign should be aimed at the students and the teachers and those who work in government. The purpose should be to undermine the existing order from within, and then attempt to sweep the establishment away in a frontal attack. He calls upon his supporters to co-operate with all political groups and forces, especially those opposed to imperialism, Zionism and atheistic materialism, which he characterises as being bent on distorting and emasculating Islam from its true mission. There is also the intention to promulgate annual Islamic congresses at the time of the pilgrimage, where Muslims from various parts of the world could discuss their common problems and propose uniform resolutions for them. Moreover, the Ayatollah seems anxious to utilise the Friday prayers as an integrative process for the Muslims to familiarise themselves with current questions, and what the *mujtahid*s propose to do about them. It is all part of his populist campaign to attract support for his cause.[22] He wants to renew the rising of *Ashura* which is commemorated annually by the Shī'i Muslims in order to mobilise the masses and exploit their grievances so that they could be triumphant against the forces of evil and darkness.[23]

Towards the end of his treatise, Ayatollah Khomeini delivers a passionate appeal to save Islam from the mortal dangers it faces. He informs his students: 'Today you do not have a state or an army, but you have the ability to propagate, inform and guide the populace. Your concern should not be just the spiritual aspects of their life.

You have to explain to them the political dimension of Islam, its principles, the rule of its laws, its penal, economic, and social codes. These dimensions must become the focus of your work'.[24] He concludes his text with what could only be described as a vitriolic attack on the quiescent religious establishment of the Shī'i community in Najaf, Qum and Khurasan, and demands a drastic purge of its ranks. He accuses many of them of being agents of the state, working for the intelligence services or the secret police. The purge would weed out what he termed pejoratively as the sultan's *faqih*s — '*fuqaha al-salatin*'. Their practice of dissimulation — *taqiyya* — and of shunning temporal political questions is denounced as dangerous to the well-being of Islam. He rejects their argument that they should not assume the role of the missing Imam in the following manner: 'The Imams charged the *faqih*s with certain obligations. They called upon them to be their trustees. We should not abide by *taqiyya* in all matters, however small or insignificant. *Taqiyya* was introduced to afford the person protection under certain conditions; but when Islam itself is threatened there is no room for *taqiyya* or silence'.[25]

His rejection of *taqiyya* is total, and therefore he feels the need to justify it. He points out Jạafar al-Sadiq, the sixth Imam, who codified the jurisprudence of the Shī'i Twelvers, and declares that al-Sadiq paid but scant regard to *taqiyya* when he set out the broad outlines of Islamic government. He appointed jurists and judges for the community despite the existence of an Abbasid caliph. Al-Sadiq, according to Khomeini, did that when the formal exercise of power was denied to him, thus exposing himself to the dangers of an Abbasid state. He did it because he had the religious authority, and he calls on the leading *mujtahid*s to follow the example of their Imams.[26]

It is clear that what Khomeini seeks in the propagation of his concept of Islamic government is to theocratise the state and politics, and at the same time politicise Islam and the religious establishment. For a Muslim who believes in the indivisibility of politics and religion this is not really surprising. It has, however, some serious implications for both, particularly in the Iranian national context as well as within the hierarchy of the religious divines. These two elements are so intertwined that the twofold objectives of the Khomeini thesis may become impossible to achieve for, despite his emphasis that Islam knows no distinction between the spiritual and the temporal realms, and that the clergy should busy themselves with the affairs of the mosque leaving politics to what he has designated as the *taghut*, or the despot, politics and religion, state and mosque have been drifting apart for years.

Iran in particular has been undergoing a process of modernisation and secularisation for almost two centuries. Riza Shah and his son Muḥammad pushed this process forward at a merciless pace between 1925 and 1979, the years of the Pahlavi dynasty. They were able for a long period of time not only to control but also to manipulate the religious establishment for their own purposes. However, the White Revolution of the last Shah, which was launched in the early 1960s, posed an agonising dilemma for the regime. Genuine changes in the power structure of the Iranian state would have inevitably ended the Shah's powers and reduced his prerogatives as new social forces are accommodated to partake in the decision-making procedure. On the other hand, superficial tinkering with some aspects of the Iranian social and political life served to heighten tension and arouse the antagonism of thc religious leadership, particularly as some of the Shah's measures adversely affected the *mujtahid*s' and their *mullah*'s role and position in society.

The quadrupling of the oil prices in 1974, and the huge increase in revenue from oil prompted the Shah to embark on an enormous economic development programme with the direct consequences of dislocations in every sector of the economy and the disruption of the social fabric of a traditional and semi-tribal society. The programme, which began to run out of steam as early as 1976, only served to add fuel to the simmering resentment. The displacement of traditional institutions was accompanied by the creation of political alternatives which could not provide for and accommodate the changes that occurred. The changes proved to be a futile exercise, and an empty gesture to obtain the support of the new social elements among the merchants and the intelligentsia, the direct benefactors of the new economic boom. The extravagant expenditure undertaken by the Shah to make Iran the Japan of the Middle East, meant that power became more centralised, and the administrative channels seized up. Inefficient and stilted bureaucracy enjoyed corruption on an unprecedented scale.

While the governmental institutions were marked by immobility, the people of Iran were anything but static. Education and such sectors of the economy as those of services as well as the construction industry enjoyed a boom which violently disturbed the habits of the conservative inhabitants, especially those in the rural areas, and radicalised their attitude. The Shah continued to rely on his courtiers and maintained his personal supervision of the transformation of Iran from an imperially proclaimed two-party state in 1963, to the equally royal one-party regime in 1978. No meaningful political accommodation for the newly emergent social forces, the professional groups, the intelligentsia, the merchants and the small businessmen, was attempted. Thus no lasting and legitimate political institutions could be acknowledged and allowed to function. All these groups gravitated towards the opposition as the offers to buy their support in exchange for limited participation in the political process were spurned by the majority of them.

Discontent was not confined to these social elements but extended beyond them. It engulfed the urban poor, especially those who flocked from the countryside, from the rural areas to the urban conurbations like Tehran and Isfahan, to be immediately absorbed in the construction and services industries. In their new urban environment, these basically conservative people have shown a marked reluctance to change their traditional values and outlook or abandon their religious belief in a rapidly changing society. Many of them became so alienated and disoriented that keen native observers of the Iranian social scene have characterised them variously as the 'lost souls' and 'people of the cave', or simply as the 'children of a new age of ignorance — *Jahiliyya*', a reference which bears definite religious connotations. In the absence of political or social institutions which could organise, represent and articulate their interests they found themselves almost subconsciously drifting back to the only institution they knew and was familiar to them: the mosque. In the mosques, the *mullah*s and *mujtahid*s, charged with the zeal of the missing Imam, offered solace and comfort. They had a mutual interest in the quest for the millennium. The *mullah*s became their spokesmen and the *mujtahid*s their leaders as they could not produce leaders from their own ranks. Moreover, the well-off elements, the so-called middle class, seem to have spurned those people and despised them as uncouth illiterates. The urban poor themselves did not look to the intelligentsia for leadership because of the cultural gap which had developed between them. Thus the Khomeini syndrome, with its populist tendencies to adopt the grievances of the oppressed, became a marked feature of Iranian politics.

Khomeini's opposition to the Shah is of long standing, but both he and his supporters adeptly manipulated the phenomenon of the urban poor to press their campaign against the Shah. In Iran the *mullah*s constitute a nation-wide network controlled by a number of prominent *mujtahid*s known as *ayatollah*s. The more eminent the *mujtahid*, the greater the following he would enjoy. The *mullah*s, those who ran the local mosques in towns and villages throughout the country, depend on the *ayatollah*s for their appointment, promotion and financial rewards, especially as members of the community may call on an *ayatollah* they have resolved to follow, because of his extensive knowledge of the holy writ, to send them a *mullah* to lead in the performance of their religious rites. The *ayatollah*s are not elected or appointed, but they literally emerge. They attract a wide following by the example of their good work, setting up charitable institutions for example, and for their piety. People pay them the alms tax to serve the religious purposes of the community. In this sense they are inclined to be populist, but not necessarily democratic, in their concern for their flock.

The politics of the Iranian revolution of 1979 are of no concern here. However, the repercussions of Khomeini's dramatic success in toppling the regime of the Shah, and whether his campaign to theocratise the state and politicise religion could be achieved, are relevant consequences of his concept of Islamic government which he outlines in *Wilayat al-faqih*. There are indications that Khomeini will be opposed by forces from both camps, from the religious establishment and the political groupings of various ideological orientations. A theocracy in Iran will not be acceptable to all the political parties, including those who derive their ideological notions from the late Ali Shariati, who managed to devise a synthesis between certain Islamic and Marxist social objectives. The role of political parties would be nullified by the proclamation of a theocratic state. It is for this reason that these groupings like the Fidaiyin Khalq or Mujahidin Khalq, or even the more liberal and secularist National Democratic Front, as well as the Communist and the Kurdistan Democratic parties, have been driven underground. It is for the same reason that wrangling amongst members of the 'Council of Experts' continued when examining the draft constitution about Article 5 which provides for the appointment of an eminent *faqih* as head of state.

After almost two centuries of modernisation, the clock cannot be put back painlessly two hundred years or fourteen centuries. Khomeini's rejection of the designation 'democratic' of his new Islamic Republic in Iran on the grounds that the term democratic is Western-inspired when in fact a 'republic' is no less Western, proved ominous for the secularist political groupings as well as for an important segment of the *mujtahid* leadership. Ayatollahs Shariat Madari and the late Mahmud Taleghani, who died in September 1979, are among many who disagreed fundamentally with Khomeini's concept of Islamic government and the rule of the *mujtahid*s in it. Shariat Madari, a respectable conventionalist, declared that *mullah*s and *mujtahid*s should not have an overt role in politics, thus upholding the traditional stand of the Shī'i Twelvers position on this question. In considering the draft constitution, he stated his preference for the old one of 1906 when suitable amendments have been made deleting all references to the Shah in the text. Thus he called for a boycott of the elections for the 'council of experts' and left the capital for Mashhad as a gesture of his displeasure.

Ayatollah Kazim Shariat Madari, considered by many to be more learned than Khomeini, made poignant remarks upon the triumphant return of Khomeini to Tehran, when he warned the faithful that the long awaited twelfth Imam did not return to earth on a chartered Air France jumbo jet. The late Ayatollah Mahmud Taleghani, who was in close touch with modern ideas, and presented to left-wing intellectuals the acceptable face of Islam because of his belief in freedom and a plural society, expressed similar dissatisfaction with the course the revolution had taken. The position of Taleghani has been taken up by many revolutionary leaders, who reject the imposition of a *faqih* — a jurist — as head of the state, as it would create dual authorities with the inevitability of a clash between them. They see the guardianship of the *faqih* as being dangerous to Islam. An ordinary government could be removed if and when it made mistakes, but the people would lose their faith if the *faqih*-ruler made the same mistakes. No doubt the opposition of Dr Mehdi Bazargan, Khomeini's hand-picked prime minister, and a man known to be familiar with religious traditions, is based on similar grounds, and represent the attitude of many of the religious modernists on this question.

The former prime minister's apprehensions extend to graver prospects than the issue of the headship of state or that of freedom of expression and political organisation, which Khomeini seems intent to deny since his retort to those who seek such latitudes is that they want nothing short of 'bars, brothels, drugs, and casinoes' which he would not countenance. Bazargan was concerned about the unity and the territorial integrity of Iran. The ethnic, linguistic and sectarian composition of Iranian society tends to threaten a breakup which could be caused by Khomeini's concept of Islamic government. The non-Shīʿi elements like the Kurds and the Turcomans as well as the non-Persian communities like the Arabs, the Azerbaijanis, the Kurds, Turcomans and the Baluchis who, because of their ethnicity or religious sect have expressed their disaffection at the prospects of Khomeini's government. Their disenchantment, expressed in periodic violent action, has led to the emergence of what could only be described as *mujtahid* warlords of the Khomeini variety. The claims for autonomy on the part of the various communities have been given a fresh impetus by Khomeini's quest for political power. These communities are led, it seems, not by political or tribal leaders but by religious figures, as in the case of the Kurdish Shaykh Izzudin Hussaini, and the Arab Shaykh Tahir Khaqani. It is not inconceivable that the prominent Shīʿi *mujtahid* Ayatollah Shariat Madari, who is from the most populous province of Iran, Azerbaijan, would assume the role of a spokesman for the Azerbaijanis if his disagreement with Khomeini is to continue.

The disaffection of eminent *mujtahid*s with Ayatollah Khomeini's campaign to establish the guardianship of the jurist in Iran may provide a pointer to the more esoteric nature of the Twelvers' religious establishment. The leading *mujtahid*s normally compete with each other for acknowledgement by their peers as well as their followers as the paramount authority in religious matters, a position that has become known as *marjiʿ al-taqlid al-aʿla or al-akbar*. Shīʿi Twelvers *mujtahid*s aspire to attain this rank more than any other ephemeral distinction, whether in politics or any other profession. In the absence of the Imam, the authority of the *marjiʿ*, his knowledge of holy writ and traditions qualify him to pronounce an opinion on all matters pertaining to the affairs of Shīʿi Islam.

If Khomeini is to be pronounced as the *faqih*-ruler, i.e., if he is to succeed in theocratising the state, he would have to receive the acknowledgement of the other leading *ayatollah*s that he is the most learned, an honour which he is likely to be denied. The present holder of this prestigious and highly influential position is Ayatollah Sayyid Abu-al-Qasim Khu'i, a religious divine of Iranian origin, resident in the holy city of Najaf in Iraq. Khu'i, a sick old man over 80 years old, has maintained a silence on recent events in Iran, characteristic of his quiescent predecessors who refrained from interference in politics. Khomeini is obviously aware of the importance of this position to enhance his claim as the *faqih* who is the official head of the Iranian republic. He will do his best to be proclaimed the paramount authority in religious matters as it would automatically entitle him to the headship of the state. After that, the transition to the rule of the *faqih* would be smooth and simple. Conversely, he may have to assume the headship of the state in order to be proclaimed as the *de facto marji'*.

Thus his attempt to politicise the religious establishment, his campaign for activist Islam and the abandonment of *taqiyya*, his denunciation of its practitioners as the 'Sultan's *faqih*s' and therefore 'the enemies of Islam',[27] as well as his departure from the capital Tehran, the centre of political activity, to the holy city of Qum in the summer of 1979, may be taken as indications of his desire to assert that he is primarily a *mujtahid*, who has the welfare of Islam uppermost in his mind, and not simply a politician. It is beyond question that the radicalisation of the rank and file of the *mujtahid*s would make his accession to the highly-coveted position of *marji'* much easier.

However, the mark of distinction for the holder of the *marji' al-a'la* has been piety and religious knowledge rather than political activities. Devotion to religious matters has been the fundamental qualification for the position. In his pursuit to be acknowledged the paramount authority of the Shī'i community in Islam, Khomeini will have to maintain a paradoxical position of dominating the politics of Iran, a role which will irritate, and may alienate, the religious establishment. The *mujtahid*s do not constitute a cohesive political organisation. Khomeini seems to be aware, concerned and rather wary of his rivals. Under these difficult circumstances, Khomeini has had no alternative but to accept the designation of 'the supreme guide' of the Islamic Republic of Iran which has been accorded to him. A college of religious guardians has also been appointed as provided by the new constitution. Its function is to oversee the work of the Iranian parliament and government. Both institutions constitute political innovations as there are no precedents for either of them in the historical development of Islam. As such they are likely to aggravate the persistent tension, and sharpen the divisions which have characterized the politics of Iran since the overthrow of the monarchy.

Notes

1. The two versions are: Ayatollah al-Khomeini: *al-Hukuma al-Islamiyya: Durus fiqhiyya*, Dal al-Talia, Beirut 1979; and Ayatollah al-Uzma al-Imam al Khomeini: *al-Hukuma al-Islamiyya, Wilayat al-faqih*, Dar al-Quds with an introduction by Sheikh Jaafar al-Muhajir, Beirut, no date.
2. Khomeini, *al-Hukuma al-Islamiyya: Durus fiqhiyya*, p. 35.
3. Ibid., p. 11.
4. Ibid., p. 16.
5. Ibid., p. 5.
6. Ibid., p. 20.
7. Ibid., pp. 29-30.
8. Ibid., pp. 38-9.
9. Ibid., pp. 88-90.
10. Ibid., pp. 33-4.
11. Ibid., p. 49.
12. Ibid., p. 70.
13. Ibid., p. 70.
14. Ibid., pp. 67-72.
15. Ibid., p. 46.
16. Ibid., p. 88.
17. Ibid., p. 36.
18. Ibid., p. 65.
19. Ibid., p. 66.
20. Ibid., pp. 63-4.
21. Ibid., p. 66.
22. Ibid., p. 126.
23. Ibid., p. 127.
24. Ibid., p. 120.
25. Ibid., p. 142.
26. Ibid., pp. 130-49.
27. Ibid., p. 143.

PART THREE:

RELIGIOUS ORDERS AND MOVEMENTS IN ISLAM

6 OFFICIAL ISLAM AND SUFI BROTHERHOODS IN THE SOVIET UNION TODAY

Alexandre Bennigsen

This chapter concerns 'forgotten Islam' — the Muslim community separated more or less completely from the rest of the Muslim world. This community resides in the Communist world. It is numerally important, numbering some 75 million believers: 45 to 50 million in USSR; 15 to 20 million in China; 3 to 4 million in Yugoslavia; 1.5 million in Albania with smaller Muslim colonies in Bulgaria, Rumania and Poland.

These communities live under regimes which are seen as either 'alien' (non-Muslim) or 'godless', or both alien and godless. In all Communist countries a more or less thorough secularisation has been imposed on the Muslim community and religion has been reduced to a 'private affair'.

Some of these forgotten communities have lived under alien rule for more than 500 years (the Kazan Tatars for instance) and under Communist rule for 30 to 60 years. Their experience is unique in the entire Muslim world. All have survived as 'Islamic communities'. How? Why? And what are their attitudes toward the alien power? These are the issues which I am trying to discuss in this chapter devoted to the Muslim community in the Soviet Union.

Until recently, our knowledge of Soviet Islam has been limited to two fields: first, the demographic aspect; and second, the character of the Muslim intelligentsia.

The demographic problem is the best known. In brief, the Soviet Muslim community consists of some 45 to 50 million people. It is a fast growing group, with one of the highest birth rates in the world (above 2,000 per cent for the Uzbeks and the Tajiks). By the turn of this century, the number of Muslims in the USSR will be between 80 and 100 million. One in every three Soviet citizens will be a Muslim (and one in every four, a Turk), and it will be a young community in contrast to the ageing Russian or Slavic ones.

The character of the Muslim elite (party and Soviet bureaucrats, technicians, engineers, faculty members) is indeed less known, but may be analysed through a careful study of Soviet sources. This elite is a dynamic and aggressive group, competing with Russians for the posts in administration of their republics. It is closely tied to the masses unlike its Russian counterpart which is isolated from them. It is strongly attached to and proud of its national culture and history rediscovered since 1964 (in the process of *Mirasism*). It is certainly more interested in, and more respectful of the Muslim religion than the generation of their fathers. It is cautiously xenophobic and keeps itself segregated from the Russians, as is evidenced by the fact that there are relatively no more mixed marriages with Russians in the native elite than in the native masses. Members of this group are potential nationalists, but our knowledge of their nationalism, of its aims and expressions is still embryonic; not because we lack reliable sources but because there are not enough qualified specialists in the West capable of undertaking the study of this difficult subject.

Soviet Muslims (elite and masses) experience a curious sense of security (an unusual attitude in the USSR) founded on the strong belief that 'the future belongs to them'. They are indeed conscious both that their population growth is higher than that of the Russians, and that they have survived half a century of very hard pressures aimed at their assimilation by the Russians. This sense of security may explain, partly at least, why in spite of its anti-Russian xenophobia, the Muslim community has not yet reached the point of exasperation which characterises other more threatened groups, like the Lithuanians or Georgians. It may also explain the absence of a Muslim *Samizdat* (except the well known case of the Crimean Tatars and the Meskhetian Turks), of appeals to the world abroad, or of protests against religious discrimination. (The only recent mention of an organised Muslim *Samizdat* comes from a Chechen source, but it concerns the reproduction and dissemination of purely religious literature).

How did Muslims succeed in resisting assimilation? The answer is easy and everybody in the Soviet Union knows it: by remaining attached to Islam. That means by remaining attached to a corpus of customs, habits, social traditions and psychological attitudes which constitute the 'Muslim way of life', including the observance of some important religious rites such as circumcision, religious marriages and burials, fasting during the month of Ramadan and observance of great religious festivals, which make the biological or cultural symbiosis with the Russians difficult or even impossible.

In explaining the survival of this 'Muslim way of life', Soviet specialists confuse the 'national' with the 'religious'. For them,

Islam is a simple element of the national culture, deprived of any spiritual meaning. Personally, however, I find it difficult to accept this oversimplified explanation.

It is true that the Muslim religious establishment has been more hardly pressed over many years than any other religion in the USSR, and as a result it has been reduced — in appearance at least — to almost nothing. In 1978, it was in control of probably less than 300 'working mosques' (less than 150 in Central Asia, 16 in Azerbayjan, 27 in Daghestan, two in the Chechen-Ingush ASSR), less than 1000 official 'clerics', two *madrassas*,[1] and one quarterly religious publication.

Official Islam

Official Islam alone would be perfectly unable to satisfy the religious needs of the believers and to resist the anti-religious propaganda. But at the same time, in spite (or because) of the hard anti-religious pressure, Soviet Muslims remain relatively more 'religious' than the members of any other community. In the Muslim territories, the average percentage of those who declare themselves 'atheists' (but who however perform some essential religious rites and observe some customs of religious origin) has been estimated at 20 per cent (80 per cent among the Russians).[2] The remaining 80 per cent represent various levels of belief: by conviction, by tradition or under the pressure of the 'milieu'. Moreover, even the official non-believers, including the militant atheists, follow to a certain degree the 'Muslim way of life', with its sex segregation, its high sexual morality, early marriages of girls, the payment of *Kalym*, polygamy (camouflaged of course), the exaggerated respect for the elders (*aqsaqalism*), circumcision and, above all, religious burials.

Finally, and this is the important point, Islam is still the common denominator, the bond of unity for believers and *non-believers*. 'A non-Muslim cannot be an Uzbek' (or a Turkmen, or an Azeri . . .) as the saying goes and the corollary is also true: 'An Uzbek must be a Muslim'. In the USSR, a 'Muslim' is popularly deemed to be a person who belongs or who wishes (in the secret of his heart) to belong to a community of Islamic background (and this is the modern expression of the *Shahada*, the most important in the Soviet Union and finally the only important of the five *Arkanud-Din*.[3] It is frequent to find in Soviet sources the expression 'non-believing Muslim'.

The paradoxical survival of Islam as a faith and as a way of life[4] in the Soviet Union is due to the conjunction of two opposite trends: official liberal Islam and non-official or 'parallel' Islam. (Soviet specialists also use the expressions of 'mosque trend' and the 'Communautarian trend'.)[5]

The first, by far the weakest, is represented by the officials of the four Muslim spiritual directorates (or Muftiats) — Tashkent, Ufa, Makhach-Kala, Baku — controlling the few working mosques and the officially appointed and remunerated clerics. It is a remnant of the once powerful Muslim 'establishment' (24,000 mosques in 1917) which has been almost entirely destroyed by a half a century-long anti-religious drive (1928-64). But present-day official Islam is also the inheritor of the brilliant pre-revolutionary *jadid* movement which had dominated entirely the intellectual life of Russian Islam and had exercised a deep influence on the entire Muslim world, and whose influence is not completely forgotten.

Toward this weak but hereditarily still prestigious official Islam, Soviet authorities have an ambiguous attitude. A religious modernist adversary is or was deemed to be more dangerous than a conservative fanatic. Consequently, the Soviet regime has tried to weaken the official Islam to the utmost, succeeding only partly without however destroying it completely.

Two main reasons explain the survival of official Islam: firstly, the Soviet government utilises it in a cautious way both in the USSR (hoping that the religious leadership would guarantee the loyalty of the believers) and abroad for propaganda purposes; secondly, Soviet authorities (as recently as 1976) understood that the total destruction of official Islam would not favour the progress of atheism but would rather reinforce 'parallel Islam'. As a consequence, a strange limited co-operation between the atheist regime and the religious Muslim leadership, established in 1943, is still in existence today.

The attitude of the religious Muslim leaders toward the regime is also ambiguous. They are loyal to the Soviet governments as their forerunners, the pre-revolutionary *jadids*, were (in their majority) loyal to the Tsarist regime. They never protest against, or even mention, the anti-religious pressures and are helping Soviet propaganda by violently attacking all those abroad who criticise the anti-Islamic character of the Soviet regime. But at the same time they have taken advantage of their co-operation with the Soviet regime to create around the four muftiats (especially around Tashkent and Ufa) a kind of 'general staff' of highly intellectual and well-educated Muslim *'ulamās*, consisting of former graduates of the *madrassas* of Mir-iArab and Imam al-Bukhari, a number of whom had undertaken further studies at the universities of Al-Azhar (Cairo), Qarawyin (Fez) and al-Baydha (Libya). This group of liberal scholars would be able to counterbalance (partly at least) the influence of the conservatives, and guarantee the future of Soviet Islam by preserving its purity and its high intellectual level.

Official Islam has but an insignificant influence on the masses and cannot contribute to the preservation of the religious feelings of the masses. It has no mass media through which it could disseminate its liberal modernistic 'ideology', except through some specific channels which cannot reach the greater part of the masses, such as the editorials of the unique religious quarterly *The Muslims of the Soviet East* of Tashkent,[6] the Friday preachings of the *Imam-Kalībs* of the few surviving mosques, or the *fatwas* published by the muftis. Therefore, the discussions concerning the compatibility of Marxism and Islam which are going on in the Tashkent Muftiat, especially in its quarterly organ, and to which Soviet specialists attribute such a great importance, remain purely platonic and do not reach the masses of believers.

The manoeuvring capacity of the official Muslim religious leaders is limited; by pushing the co-operation with the Soviet authorities too far and making their submission to the regime too obvious they would antagonise an important part of the believers and provoke a rift which both trends of Islam, the official and the parallel, are anxious to avoid. Both belong to the same realm and until now there was no serious conflict between the two. In spite of the continuous efforts of Soviet authorities to oblige the *muftīs* to condemn parallel Islam as illegal (except a few *fatwas* concerning the practice of *zikr* and the pilgrimages to the holy places)[7] and in spite of their political differences, the leaders of *parallel* Islam have never, to our knowledge, attacked the leaders of *official* Islam.

When talking about official Islam we must avoid the classical error of treating its representatives as simple 'agents of the Soviet power' (as many foreign Muslim visitors do). The reality is more complex. While serving the regime as propagandists abroad and as 'moderators' in the Soviet territories, Soviet *muftīs* are struggling to preserve the existence of a skeletal but necessary religious establishment without which conservative underground Islam would relapse into ignorance, superstition and Shamanism.

Parallel Islam

'Parallel' Islam, represented essentially by the followers of the Sufi brotherhoods and by the most conservative elements among the believers is, according to all the Soviet sources, much more powerful.[8] It is a popular 'establishment' deeply rooted in the rural and urban communities,[9] but with a growing number of intellectuals joining it or expressing their sympathy. It is intolerant (Soviet sources use the expressions of 'fanatic'), conservative, anti-socialist, anti-modernistic, anti-Western, violently anti-Russian and anti-Communist. Soviet sources talk about its 'criminal anti-Soviet activities'. Communism is regarded by the conservatives as a new form of 'Unbelief' (*Kufr*) or as a heresy (*Shirk*), but certainly not as a rival ideology.

For 50 years, Soviet authorities have underestimated the dynamism and the vitality of the conservative trend, and it is only recently in the mid-1970s (judging by the changes in the anti-religious propaganda) that they became aware of its potential danger.

Parallel Islam is a dynamic and well-disciplined organisation controlling a large network of clandestine mosques (in Azerbayjan there are 16 official mosques and more than 1000 clandestine houses of prayer) and of underground religious schools and probably more than 1000 places of pilgrimage (300 in Azerbayjan alone). According to recent Soviet sources it is this parallel Islam which is responsible for the existence of a 'conservative public opinion' among Muslims,[10] without which religious beliefs would have disappeared long ago.

Conservative Islam is deprived of all official mass media (press, radio broadcasting), but its influence infiltrates the masses of believers and unbelievers through numerous channels represented by various traditional institutions or organisations which, up to now, have escaped all efforts of Soviet authorities to destroy or to control them.

The most important of these channels is represented by the *Sufi Orders*, more numerous today than in the 1920s, and as violently anti-Russian as ever. Outlawed by Soviet legislation, the brotherhoods are secret or semi-secret but mass organisations. (In the

Chechen-Ingush ASSR, according to a 1975 survey by one of the leading Soviet sociologists, 'more than half of the believers' belong to a Sufi Order which would represent a minimum of 150,000 to 200,000 followers — certainly more than members of the Communist Party.)[11]

North Caucasus (Chechnia, Daghestan) remains the bastion of Sufism, but the brotherhoods are also expanding elsewhere in Central Asia, especially since the deportation of the Chechens-Ingushes, and particularly in the areas where tribal clan systems still persist (Kazakhstan, Kirghiziya, Turkmenistan) the Sufi brotherhood being often superimposed on the clan system.

A second channel, through which the influence of conservative Islam infiltrates the masses is traditional social organisations — extended families, clans, tribes — that still survive in the North-east Caucasus and in former nomadic areas. A third channel is provided by a number of related traditional institutions such as the Muslim guilds (based on initiation and often absorbed by the Sufi brotherhoods); the clan or village assemblies (*Jama'at*); the village councils of elders; the holy places of pilgrimage (which tend to become the real centres of popular religious life), etc.

Conservative Islam

With all its capacity to mobilise masses, conservative Islam had, until now at least, no political ideology (and even less a political programme) except a vague but powerful desire to build a world based entirely on Islam, where Muslims would be entirely liberated from the domination of the hated godless or infidel aliens. For the time being, its recognised leaders (or 'portes paroles') — the Murshids and the Shaykhs of the Sufi brotherhoods — show no interest in politics (or so it seems). Their main effort, and a victorious one, is centred on purely religious affairs. It is due to the unrelenting and missionary activity of all Sufi followers that the religious feeling is still running high among Soviet Muslims. Even Soviet specialists have finally understood that the 'religiosity' of a community does not depend on the number of 'working' mosques, nor on the theological competence of the believers, and that a 'corrupted' form of Islam more or less contaminated by various Shamanistic rites and beliefs can be as 'fanatic', if not more so, as unadulterated official Islam (in the Checheno-Ingush Republic, the real bastion of Muslim conservatism, there was not a single working mosque between 1943 and 1978).

In Soviet Islam, however, the 'religious' and the 'political' are always closely related to each other and it is unavoidable that sooner or later conservative public opinion would begin to advance some re-vindication of the political character, especially in the North Caucasus where the anti-Russian feelings are more violent than in other parts, and where there exists a tradition of political unrest (the *abrek* tradition). In this connection, the example of nearby Iran may become inspiring.

For the time being, with the exception of vague references to 'bandit groups' in the mountains generally linked to one specific Sufi *tariqa* (the Battal Haji brotherhood),[12] conservative Islam exerts only a passive influence on Soviet domestic affairs, an influence which none the less, even in its present form, is already highly disturbing to the authorities. Its impact may be summarised as follows:

(1) By maintaining, or helping to maintain, a 'conservative public opinion' and by preserving various traditional customs and rites (especially the marital custom) it makes very difficult any *rapprochement* between Muslims and Russians;
(2) It gives to political local nationalism a definitely religious colour by reinforcing among the believers (and also the unbelievers) the consciousness of belonging to a Muslim *umma*;
(3) It makes impossible a new frontal attack against the official Muslim establishment;
(4) It helps to maintain a climate of general xenophobia, 'us' versus 'them'.

Given the impact of the Iranian revolution, the general progress of fundamentalist trends in the entire Muslim world, and the fact that no Iron Curtain could nowadays protect completely Soviet Islam from the 'contamination' from abroad, one may wonder what policy or policies the Soviet government could devise to keep its Islam under control.

In this connection, I see the following possibilities. With regard to official Islam, the Soviet government might pursue a programme of spectacular but limited concessions, a policy which has already been applied in Central Asia in 1977-8 and which will probably be continued and even strengthened. New mosques have been built (or old ones re-opened?). In the Chechen Republic where all the mosques had been destroyed in 1943, two were rebuilt in 1978. Such favours will probably remain limited, however, both because of their obvious potential danger and because Soviet authorities are beginning to realise that they might have overestimated the prestige and the influence that official Islam may exert over the believers.[13] None the less, a counterpart of such a policy would be to make greater use of the official Islamic hierarchy abroad and in the Soviet Union in an effort to condemn the 'illegal' character of Sufism. However, the success of such measures remains doubtful since even the most loyal among the representatives of the Muslim hierarchy appear reluctant to engage themselves too far on the side of Soviet authority. The psychological unity of the Muslim community remains for them an essential condition. It may be also that Muslim religious leaders feel themselves in a stronger bargaining position with the Soviet government than the Russian Orthodox Church.

With regard to parallel Islam, there could be neither concessions nor compromise. In any case, the unsuccessful conservatives would not accept them and, so far, the underground Muslim organisations (Sufi brotherhoods especially) have defeated all attempts to infiltrate or to destroy them. So there remains only one solution which Soviet authorities are already employing against the conservatives, namely to re-inforce (in quantity but not in quality) the anti-religious propaganda directed essentially against conservative Islam, and to attempt (as is already being done in the North Caucasus) to use the traditional channels (*Jama'ats* and Councils of elders) to fight the influence of the conservatives from within.[14]

This measure is inefficient and may easily become counter-productive. It is therefore possible to predict the following evolution of Soviet Islam during the next ten years:

(1) A general increase of the religious feeling[15] and a steady strengthening of the conservative trend (including among the intelligentsia) and, as its corollary, the growth of anti-Russian xenophobia (Russians being supposedly responsible for secularisation);

(2) A greater competition for jobs between native and Russian cadres and, as its corollary, the growth of local nationalism. In this respect there might grow a greater *rapprochement* between the native elite (often officially atheistic) and the native masses still deeply attached to Islam;

(3) A steady growth both of an Islamic consciousness among all levels of the Muslim society and of the feeling of brotherhood with foreign Muslim countries (this being the case for both the believers and the non-believers);
(4) An increased activity on the part of the official spiritual directorate (particularly of the Mufti of Tashkent) with a clamorous and spectacular pro-Soviet propaganda in the Muslim world abroad in a steady, but disguised, effort to reinforce its own position in the Soviet Muslim territories, and especially to bridge the gap between Islam and the new generation of young Soviet intellectuals;
(5) Finally, an increasing reluctance on the part of republican and local Party and Soviet authorities to attack Islam (either official or parallel).[16]

Conclusion

It is necessary to place the double conflict agitating Soviet Islam (religion versus power; and official Islam versus parallel Islam) in an historical perspective. Soviet Islam had lived and *is still* living an almost unique, 60 year-long, historical experience: a systematic attempt by an alien power to destroy completely the religious roots of the community. This experience may be compared to the first years of the Chagatay Khanate in Central Asia, whose Mongol rulers had in the beginning a strong anti-Islamic attitude.

In both cases, Islam survived the pressures because of the intense activity of popular Sufi brotherhoods. In both cases, the survival exacted a heavy price. Today, the traditional conservative Islam of Central Asia or North Caucasus represents — from the intellectual standpoint — at least a step backward if we compare it to the brilliant *jadid* reformist movement of the early twentieth century. As under the Mongols, Islam had to hide deeply in the popular masses. Without the Sufi *tariqats*, the official Islamic establishment in the USSR would be a head without a body. This is the historical truth and the justification of the existing conservatism, but it is also true that without this head the body would relapse into ignorance, shamanism and unbelief.

Notes

1. Mir-i Arab of Bukhara (medium level) opened in 1945 and Imam Ismaīl al-Bukhari of Tashkent (high level), opened in 1971, called 'Baraq Khan' until 1974.

2. Among the most important recent works analysing the level of the religiosity in the Muslim community, cf: Yu A. Aidaev and V.G. Pivovarov, 'Problemy konkretnykh issledovanii religii', *Sotsiologiia, Ateizm, Religiia* (Groznyi, 1972), pp. 3-23; Avksent'ev, *Islam na Severnom Kawkaze* (Stavropol, 1976); V.G. Pivovarov, 'Sotsiologicheskie Issledovanie problem byta natsional'nykh traditsee i verovanii v Checheno-Ingushskoi ASSR', *Voprosy Nauchnogo Ateizma*, XVII (1975), pp. 310-20 and *Na etapakh Sotsiologicheskogo Issledovaniia* (Groznyi, 1974); Krianev, 'Tiopologiia religioznykh ob'edinenii i differensiiatsiia ateistichekogo vospitaniia', *Voprosy Nauchnogo Ateizma*, III (1967), pp. 40-64; O.A. Sukhareva, *Islam v Uzbekistane* (Tashkent, 1960); Bazarbaev, *Sekuliarizatsiia naseleniia Sotsialisticheskoi Karakalpakii* (Nukhus, 1973); A. Makatov, *Islam, Veruiuschii, Sovremennost' — opyt Konkretno-Sotsial'nogo Izucheniia Musul'-manstva* (Makhach-Kahr, 1974); N. Ashirov, *Evolutsiia Islama v SSSR* (Moscow, 1973), and *Islam i Natsii* (Moscow, 1975); T. Izimbetov, *Islam i Sovremennost'* (Nukhus, 1963); Filimonov, 'Sotsiologicheskie issledovanie protsessa preodoleniia religii v sel'skoi mestnosti-Itogi, problemy, perspektivy', *Voprosy Nauchnogo Ateizma*, XVI (1974), pp. 71-89.

3. T. Izimbetov in his excellent work, *Islam i Sovremennost'* (Nukhus, 1963), p. 101, writes: 'Muslim clerics in their preachings and in private talks explain that if your heart is attached to Islam, then your apparent atheism and your verbal godlessness would not be obstacles to your Muslim quality.' You can even openly deny the existence of God and oppose Islam. Your body and your tongue may be 'Kafir' (infidel), but your soul must remain Muslim; there will be no sin and God is all-forgiving and all merciful. It seems thus that the Shia traditions of the *taqiya* (the legal right to apostasy) had penetrated a purely *Sunni* milieu.

4. About 1972, Soviet islamologists introduced a new idea. Instead of simple 'survival', they are talking today of 'revival' of religiosity. M.A. Abdullaev, Professor at the University of Daghestan, writes in his article 'Za glubokoe kriticheskoe izuchenie Islama', *Sotsiologiia, Ateizm, Religiia* (Groznyi, 1972), p. 33: 'The level of productivity and the material life of the Daghestanis is today much higher than before the War, and in spite of that, the level of religiosity is higher in many areas than before the War . . .' The author rejects such simple explanations for this phenomenon as the hardship of the war or 'the influence of the bourgeois world', but does not give his own explanations.

5. Cf. L. Klimovich, 'Bor'ba ortodoksov i medernistov v. Islame', *Voprosy Nauchnogo Ateizma*, II (1966), p. 66.

6. Appeared from 1969 to 1979 in Arabic and Uzbek (in arabic script) under the title of *Al-Muslimun fi ash-Sharq as-Sufiati*. In January 1979, two new editions in English and in French were added (*The Muslims of the Soviet East* and *Les Musulmans de l'Orient Soviétique*).

7. Published in *Muslims of the Soviet East*.

8. Cf. Klimovich, 'Bor'ba ortodoksov', p. 67.

9. Cf. M.A. Vagabov, 'Za glubokoe izuchenie ideologii Islama', *Sotsiologiia, Ateizm, Religiia* (Groznyi, 1972), p. 30: 'The conservatives are tightly bound to the believers — they live among them and their influence is much stronger than that of the modernists. They influence the public opinion not only of the believers, but in many areas of entire villages. In some cases, members of the intelligentsia do not dare to criticise religion being afraid to face the public opinion of the community.'

10. Pivovarov, *Sotsiologicheskie Issledovanie*, p. 318, discovered during a survey carried out in 1970-2 in the Chechen-Ingushe ASSR, that 'local atheists were obliged

to hide their anti-religious ideas because of a 'collective conservative religious public opinion'.

11. Pivovarov, *Sotsiologicheskie Issledovanie*, p. 316. V.A. Aidaev and V.G. Pivovarov, 'Problemy konkretnykh issledovanii religii', *Sotsiologiia, Ateizm, Religiia* (Groznyi, 1972), pp. 12-13, write: 'Today there are no professional clerics left in the Checheno-Ingushe Republic who could influence the believers with their religious ideology because there is not a single working mosque left in the Republic. But Muslim propaganda is still going on thanks to the murid (Sufi) societies.'

12. Cf. M.A. Abdullaev and N.V. Vagabov, *Aktual'nye problemy kritiki i preodoleniya Islama* (Makhach-Kala, 1975), p. 183: 'these groups (Sufi Orders) . . . are dangerous. They can provoke an explosion of religious fanaticism among the masses which would lead to criminal activities.' Krianev, 'Tipologiia', p. 59, classifies the Sufi Orders of North Caucasus among the declared adversaries of Soviet authority, such as the Adventists, the Spritual Molokans (the 'Jumpers') and various 'God's People' (*Khlysty*).

13. Abdullaev, 'Za glubokoe kriticheschoe izuchenie Islama', p. 25: 'We have a tendency to overestimate the influence of the modernists on the believers . . .'

14. Abdullaev and Vagabov, *Aktual'nye problemy kritiki i preodoleniia Islama*, p. 209, mention the activity of the councils of elders, the assemblies (*Jama'at*), the councils of *mahalli* (city quarters) mobilised by Soviet authorities in order to fight the 'obnoxious religious survivals'. On page 211, they insist on the role of the 'elders', whose authority must be used in the struggle against Islam. Pivovarov, 'Sotsiologicheskie Issledovanie', p. 314, also insists on the potential importance of the *Jama'ats* to canalise the public opinion and the use of them as platforms for anti-religious action,

15. Makatov, *Islam, Veruiushchii, Sovremennost*, p. 100, makes this astonishing acknowledgement: 'Some external facts, such as the greater number of persons who assist at the ceremonies in the mosque and who perform religious rites may give a wrong idea about a general increase of the religious feeling among masses. Certainly we must not exclude the possibility of an active religious agitation which may have as a result the increase — in some areas — of the participation of the citizens in the Muslim rituals and rites.' And Makatov concludes on an optimistic note: 'But such a phenomenon cannot be longlasting.'

16. Ashirov, *Islam i Natsii* (Moscow, 1975), pp. 69-70, notes that 'Members of the older generations, including the atheists pretend that religion is harmless and that it is even useful and necessary. It provides people with a discipline, it protects them against bad things, alcohol, tobacco, dirty words; it helps to preserve the originality of the nation, and it protects its national language. As a shepherd, it protects its flock, while the young generation of atheists is forgetting its mother tongue and has lost its national heritage.' And Ashirov concludes that 'A conciliatory attitude toward religion by some representatives of the older generations, especially when they are former Communist Party militants, who enjoy great authority, facilitates the growth of the religious feeling among the youths.'

7 THE RESURGENCE OF ISLAMIC ORGANISATIONS IN EGYPT: AN INTERPRETATION

Ali E. Hillal Dessouki

The revival of Islam and Islamic organisations has become the focus of a great deal of attention in the West.[1] Popular magazines such as *Time*, *Newsweek* and *L'Express* have devoted special issues to different aspects of contemporary Islam. The manifestations of 'Islamic revival' in Iran, Turkey, Afghanistan, Pakistan, Egypt and other Islamic countries provide credence and justification for this concern.

The purpose of this chapter is to analyse the reasons behind the revival of Islamic organisations in Egypt since 1967. One interpretation is the old-standing argument by Sir Hamilton Gibb to the effect that, since the collapse of the Ottoman Empire, there has been a tendency among the Arabs to work for a revival of Mahdism, a form of millennialism.[2] Another general interpretation is to argue that the emergence of these groups is a reaction to the process of modernisation. These interpretations are too broad and general to explain why Islamic groups flourish at a particular point in time.

Before dealing specifically with the Egyptian case, three remarks are in order at the outset. First, the resurgence of Islamic organisations in a number of Arab and Islamic countries must not be treated as a singular phenomenon. The universality of manifestations and symptoms should not tempt observers to seek a uniform causation or diagnosis. What is lumped together as 'Islamic revival' is in fact diverse sets of phenomena which have different sources and lead to different conclusions.

Secondly, a serious discussion of 'Islamic resurgence' should not underestimate the multiplicity of Islamic organisations and movements. No monolithic revival is to be found in most cases. In almost every Islamic country, there are numerous Islamic groups, each presenting its teachings as the true Islam. Relations between these groups are not always cordial. They differ in their understanding of religion, the analysis of the social problems and how to handle them. While some confine their activities to preaching and persuasion, others move to the realm of politics, militant agitation and military action.

The third and last remark has to do with the distinction between the reaction against some aspects of Western lifestyle and the reaction against modernisation and/or development. John A. Williams made the very perceptive remark that the wearing of *Zayy Shar'i* (Islamic attire) by an increasing number of Egyptian young women is not 'a return to some costume worn by one's grandmother, it is a modern, urban and middle class phenomenon'.[3]

In theory, fundamentalism, which is our focus here, is 'the affirmation, in a radically changed environment, of traditional modes of understanding and behavior'.[4] In contrast to other views, which assume 'that things can and should go on much as they have for generations past, fundamentalism recognises and tries to speak to a changed milieu, an altered atmosphere of expectations. Fundamentalism is by no means a blind opponent of all social change, but it insists that change must be governed by traditional values and modes of understanding'.[5] Fundamentalism is an outlook which primarily appeals to the educated strata of population who are aware and proud of their Islamic heritage. It is not a popular religion of the illiterates, but can be an effective instrument for their mobilisation. Further, it appeals to those social groups whose positions and roles are undermined by the process of social change.[6]

In Egypt, the manifestations of Islamic resurgence are numerous in the political and behavioural spheres. In the universities, for example, Islamic associations have obtained a visible presence and a felt influence. They enjoy a tight hierarchical structure, starting downwards from each faculty or college to the general federation of Islamic associations. In the 1970s these associations emerged as the most cohesive and organised force in the Egyptian universities and controlled most of their student unions. The results of the Alexandria University student union elections of 1978 indicate the degree of their influence. The candidates of Islamic associations won in the various faculties as follows: Medicine 60 out of 60, Engineering 60 out of 60, Agriculture 47 out of 48, Pharmacy 42 out of 48, Science 43 out of 60 and Law 44 out of 48.[7] Their growing influence invited a *décret-loi* (decree), issued by the President, using his exceptional constitutional power to issue laws in the absence of the parliament, in July 1979, concerning universities' student unions. According to the new law, student unions are brought under the control of the faculty staff, and the activities of religious associations are considered illegal in the universities.[8]

Outside the universities, a major important development has been the re-emergence of the Muslim Brethren Association's activities. Its journal, *al-Da'wah*, began publication in June 1976. The cover of its first issue carried one of the Brethren slogans 'The Koran is above the constitution'. The editors made a point of designating this issue as no. 1 of the 25th year of its publication; a reference to the fact that it was a continuation of the old *Da'wah* and not a new venture. The two-page editorial reflected the same sentiment.[9] The Brethren organised a mass meeting in April 1977 in commemoration of Abdel Kader Auda, one of their prominent leaders who was hanged in 1954.

Though the Brethren have not been legally reinstated, they were politically recognised by the regime when Omar al-Telmesani, the managing editor of *al-Da'wah*, was invited to attend a meeting of the President with Muslim religious leaders. Al-Telmesani was one of four speakers who made an opening statement and his speech was reported in the newspapers as representing the Muslim Brethren Association.[10] Actually the greater part of the meeting was taken up by a discussion between al-Telmesani and the President on the political activities of the Brethren.

In addition to the familiar issues advocated by Islamic associations in Egypt, such as the rehabilitation of the Muslim Brethren Association, the application of *sharī'a* (Islamic law) and the implementation of *al-hudud*, *al-Da'wah* delved into political and social issues as well. It took a highly critical position against the peace treaty with Israel, thus becoming the major platform of public opposition.[11]

In addition to the Muslim Brethren, who are keen on projecting an image of legality and who may appear as old hats to the younger generation, there exist a number of extreme, militant, clandestine organisations. The best known of them is *al-Takfir wa al-Higra* group which was held responsible for the assassination of the Minister of Endowments in July 1977. A military court tried several of its members and four of its leaders were hanged. Another militant organisation, *Shabab Muhamed*, stormed the Technical Military College in April 1974 to seize arms and ammunition. The attempt ended in failure and two of its leaders were eventually executed. Other associations include a group related to *Hizb al-Tahrir al-Islami* (Islamic Liberation Party), *al-Jihād* (Holy war) and *Gund al-Allah* (God's Soldiers) groups.[12]

Islamic revival has not been the work of opposition groups alone.

The government has contributed its share. The resort to religious symbolism, or whatever Weber calls traditional calling codes, is a characteristic feature of President Sadat's style. An ideological document issued in 1978 on democratic socialism relied heavily on Islam as a source of legitimation. Shaykh al-Azhar (The Rector of the Azhar) was promoted, in terms of protocol and salary, to the rank of prime minister. The Speaker of the Parliament, Dr Sufi Abu Taleb, activated the work to codify the *sharī'a*[13] and to draft a constitutional amendment making the principles of *sharī'a* the *main* source of legislation, and not merely *a* source of it (Article 2 of the 1971 constitution).[14] This new amendment was approved in May 1980.

In an attempt to interpret the revival of Islamic associations in Egypt, two kinds of argument may be invoked: The historical-cultural argument and the politico-social argument. The first is general, the second more specific and particular. Together, they help to understand the phenomenon under investigation.

The Historico-cultural Argument: the Absence of a Synthesis

This argument refers to the failure of Egyptian intellectuals to formulate a functioning synthesis between Islam and modernism or to define the role of Islam in modern society. A continuous state of confusion surrounded this issue. This remark can be placed within the larger context of Egyptian development. A characteristic feature of this process has been the peculiar relation between the old and the new. New elements have not replaced or substituted old ones but coexisted with them, thus creating a kind of dualism. In the realm of thought, two societies continued to survive with their different intellectual universes and collective consciousness, each having its own educational system, journals, masters and symbols. The dualism can be explained by the pattern of development which took place in Egypt in the nineteenth century.

The two prominent modernisers of the last century, Mohamed Ali and Ismail, followed a strategy of establishing new structures and institutions without abolishing the old ones. Accordingly, modern legal codes and a court system were introduced alongside *sharī'a* law. New schools were established alongside the old *Kuttabs* and *madrasahs*. This strategy might have been very practical to avoid the opposition of the *ulamā* but, in Daniel Crecelius terms, 'it led to a painful cultural bifurcation in all fields. Two societies, the one modernizing around imported institutions and concepts, the other clinging tenaciously, but often in bewilderment, to traditional values and habits were now locked in constant competition.'[15]

The social, economic and political change in Egypt led to the emergence of three schools of thought. For some intellectuals, Islam was the key element of their thinking and they conceived of *al-nahdah* (renaissance) in Islamic terms. They regarded Islam as important not only for individual salvation but also as a cohesive social force and the source of moral solidarity which gave unity to the nation. Their goal was thus to strengthen religion and to prove its worth in the face of Western cultural encroachment.

Within the context of the Islamic school of thinking, there have been a number of trends. At one extreme we find those who were concerned with a passionate defence of Islamic traditions and orthodoxy. Their writings were more of a nostalgic attachment to the past than a coherent set of ideas and beliefs. Instead of attempting to understand the problems facing them and their socicty, they turned to the glorification of the past without indicating or even trying to find out why this glory had vanished or how this past could be restored.[16]

Others were more preoccupied with a reinterpretation of Islam in order to bring it more in harmony with modern ideas and realities. They tried to regenerate Islam by cleansing it of those corrupting and perverting alien accretions which had clung to it in the course of time. Mohamed Abduh, who was the main architect of this group, was concerned with the compatibility of Islam and modernity. He was struck by the Muslims' backwardness and recognised it as the problem which all Muslims had to face. For him, the cure lay in a return to the true Islam through 'the recovery of the essentials of that religion, the minimum of beliefs without which Islam would not be Islam'[17] and understanding them in the light of modern times.

A second major group of intellectuals reflected the transitional nature of the society.[18] Janus-faced, they combined in their ideas both the taditions of Islamic Arab culture and the new concepts of Western culture which 'made them vague and inconsistent and to some extent confused'.[19] Islam was, so to speak, the national cultural heritage.[20] But it could not be accepted as the source of legislation and policy in society, nor was it believed that traditional Islam was capable of meeting the problems of a modern society.

The members of this group were quite aware of the crisis taking place within themselves, of the duality of their life, ideas and general outlook. They knew they belonged to two different worlds, the old world of traditional Islam and the new world of Western civilisation. Unable to decide between the two, their contribution was primarily in the area of reconciliation between the new and the old, reason and faith, the East and the West and finally, tradition and modernity. The works of Taha Husayn, Muḥammad Husayn Haykal, Ahmad Amin, Abbas Mahmud al-Aqqad and Qasim Amin betray this duality of mind and their simultaneous belonging to two different worlds.[21]

A third group representing yet another intellectual stream was the bearer of what may be called the secular-rational trend. Their point of departure was Western culture and civilisation. Its members believed in the scientific spirit and rational reasoning and their aim was the establishment of a modern society, similar to those of Europe and North America, a society which retains tradition as long as it does not impede change and progress. This trend encompassed a multiplicity of views extending from *laissez faire* liberalism to Marxism.[22]

They viewed Western civilisation with its material and cultural elements as a well-integrated whole. Thus, the unprecedented material advancement of Europe was seen as inseparable from the cultural values that underlay it. If so, it was impossible to adopt the material achievements without adopting the cultural and intellectual foundations that accompanied them. It followed, therefore, that the immediate task was to modernise the Egyptian society in the full sense of the word, i.e. to adopt Western civilisation in its entirety.

Clearly for this group, the purpose of the introduction of Western values and structures was not to perfect tradition, but to replace it. The problem, as they saw it, was no longer how to adapt Islamic traditions to modern life, but rather how to assimilate European thought and technology. Their assumption was that Egypt could never equal the West unless it was completely Westernised. And to be effective, the process of transformation had to be total or nearly so; for it had to reach the very roots of the society and its outlook.[23] This group was spearheaded by the Syrian intellectual émigrés, such as Farah Antoun, Faris Nimr, Yacoub Sarrouf, Shibli Shumayyil and the Egyptian Salama Musa,[24] all of them, incidentally, Christians.

Each of the three trends had its limitations. Abduh's religious efforts were to end at the hands of Rashid Reda who affirmed a fundamentally orthodox social and political thought, i.e., *al-Salafiyya*. On the other hand, the representatives of the rational-secular trend were basically non-Egyptians and Christians, which posed a limitation on their influence regarding the issue of Islam. Their ideas appeared abstract and foreign. Though deeply affected by modern science and technology, they failed to grasp the scientific spirit, the critical sense and the mental discipline that accompanied them.[25] Those who attempted to reconcile the two cultural traditions also failed to produce the much needed synthesis. What most of them actually did was either to build a superficial bridge between the two cultures, or to read Western civilisation in Islamic terms. Finally, the process of modernisation of thought touched only a fragment of the population. For the majority of Egyptians Islam remained 'the widest and most effective basis for consensus'.[26]

The historical-intellectual argument, true as it may be, remains insufficient and incomplete. It tells us about a constant crisis in the life of modernised Muslims and the failure to arrive at a working synthesis, but it fails to explain why Islamic groups emerge at a particular time and what is the interplay of forces which leads to their revival.

The Politico-social Argument: the Crisis Situation

Up till now, our analysis has been operating at the intellectual ideational level which has, by definition, a number of serious limitations. Thoughts and ideas, to be properly and fully understood, must be studied within their societal context. The main hypothesis of this section is that the revival of Islamic groups and associations is invited by a particular social environment. It is a product of a *crisis* situation characterised by economic difficulties, moral and ideological confusion and political instability. The evidence for this hypothesis can be marshalled from two periods in Egyptian history, the 1930s and the 1940s which experienced an intellectual shift to Islamic subjects[27] and the ascendency of the Muslim Brethren, and the present-day situation in Egypt which is our focus in this chapter.

Since 1967 Egyptians have been going through a period of soul-searching and self-evaluation. The defeat of that year was not merely a military one, but it represented a challenge to what Nasser symbolised for Arabs and Egyptians, i.e., the semi-secular revolutionary nationalist option. It also challenged the Egyptians' self-image and their perception of their country's role in the area.

Nasser resorted to Islam to rationalise and explain the much unexpected defeat. He referred to it in his speeches as Egypt's fate, God's will and a destiny from which there could be no escape. The government encouraged religious activities as a diversionary technique. In December 1967, *al-Ahram* reported the longest march of Sufi orders ever organised in recent history. Christians were to have their share as well. The Virgin Mary allegedly continued to appear over Cairo for more than a week. People flocked from all parts of the country to Cairo and the Arab Socialist Union (the sole legitimate political organisation at the time) had the responsibility of seating and maintaining order while people awaited the 'appearance' of the Virgin Mary.

Islamic groups wasted no time, seized upon the opportunity and offered an Islamic interpretation for the defeat. Their message was simple and straightforward: we were defeated because we arc no longer good Muslims. It was imported Western ideologies, such as socialism, nationalism and secularism, which were defeated, they argued. The only solution lay in a return to Islam. It would provide Egyptians with a cause to fight and die for and cultivate a new sense of dignity and courage among them.[28] Later, they compared the performance of Egyptian soldiers in the 1967 and 1973 wars. Egyptians fought better in 1973 because, they argued, they were convinced that it was an Islamic war. It was fought in the month of *Ramadan* and its code name was *Badr*. A number of shaykhs volunteered the story that God sent his angels to fight on the side of the Muslims. Thus, the defeat of 1967 and the weakening of Nasser's position, created the objective environment for the emergence of an alternative.

The death of Nasser in 1970, the succession of Sadat and the rise of new social and economic priorities accentuated the process of social confusion. Within five years the new regime effectively reversed the country's domestic and foreign orientations from what they were under Nasser.

Internally, Sadat began to criticise Nasser's socialism and to defend private enterprise and individual initiative. In August 1979, the criticism reached its climax when Sadat informed the representatives of chambers of commerce and industry that capitalism was no longer a crime in Egypt.[29] Regionally, Sadat mocked at the distinction between progressive and conservative Arab states.

Saudi Arabia, which was perceived before as the arch-enemy of revolution and socialism, became the best friend of Sadat's Egypt, and a Cairo-Riadh axis developed during the period 1972 to 1977. Internationally, the Soviet Union which was considered for long the 'strategic ally' of Egypt was exposed as opportunist, atheist and as having imperialist objectives. The most important reversal, however, took place in relation to Israel. In November 1977 Sadat visited Isreal, and fourteen months later he signed the Camp David agreements.

The net effect of these reverses has been a mixture of shock, unbelief and a wait-and-see approach. The impact on younger generations must have been devastating. They saw their idol Nasser being attacked and criticised. Almost all the symbols of Nasser's Egypt are no longer to be found. Nasser's photos are not visible and all songs referring to him are not broadcast. What is at stake here is not the evaluation of Nasser and his policies, but the impact of these reverses upon younger people in Egypt. It cultivates a sense of cynicism and uncertainty. Further, the regime failed to provide an alternative symbol to Nasserism. The economic open door policy may be of great attraction to businessmen and entrepreneurs, but has very little to offer to young people asking questions about their identity and role in society. The result is a situation of ideological confusion, alienation and uprootedness; a situation which was described long ago as *anomie*. Youth find themselves frustrated between the old values with which they grew up and the new situation with which they have to deal. In the midst of such a confusion, Islam provides a yardstick, a compass and a comprehensive set of values and norms. It provides the certainty which younger people search for.

The resort to religion, however, was encouraged by some policies of the regime. Sadat flirts with religion and projects himself in the image of a good believer. In fact, he is introduced occasionally in public appearances as the 'believer-President'. In his pursuit of legitimacy after liquidating his opponents, in May 1971, Sadat manipulated religion for his purposes. The government encouraged Islamic associations in the universities as a counterweight to Nasserite and Marxist ones.

To these developments, we may add two more factors. One is the existence of an acute economic problem which makes life increasingly intolerable for the bulk of Egyptians. For a suffering population, religion offers solace, safety and security. Many of them find in religion what the earthly world has failed to deliver: equality, justice and the promise of a better world. The other is the probable impact of Saudi Arabia upon Islamic groups in Egypt. This factor must not be overstated. *Wahabi* puritanism is not attractive to Egyptians. It is possible, however, that Saudi Arabia has provided financial contributions to some of these groups. In their trials, some members of *Shabab Mohamed* group referred to their contacts with Libya.

In 1970, I wrote about the tendency towards polarisation or fundamentalism in the Arab world.[30] The thrust of my argument was that, in contrast to many European countries where the major issues of development were faced successively, in the Arab world, they are posed simultaneously. Thus, Egypt, for instance, faces the problems of economic development, distributive justice, democratisation, technological change and secularisation at the same time. 'Our hypothesis is, therefore, that what is probably to dominate Arab thought is a total view of the universe, a view which is both consistent and emotionally satisfying since it reduces all social ills to one cause and then proposes an overall remedy. It is a view based on a fundamental principle or concept which makes it easy to be understood by the masses. Finally, it reduces intellectual tensions and doubts since it has ready answers for almost every issue.'[31]

Conclusion

The revival of Islamic groups in Egypt is basically a social phenomenon which is interpreted against its historical background and its political context. The background is a situation of cultural dualism and intellectual confusion. The contemporary context is one of 'decline in morality and of corruption in high places. Huge fortunes have been made in few years, primarily by people engaged in import-export business or in helping the Saudis and Kuwaitis who flock to Cairo to invest their money . . . Few Egyptians have a great deal of money and they flaunt it shamelessly.'[32]

The rise of Islamic groups is in a sense a political statement. It is a cry for authenticity and egalitarianism. It reflects the sentiments of a section of the generation whose members lost faith in secular elites and ideals. The future of these groups depends on the course of Egypt's economic and social evolution and how far her leadership can provide the symbols and policies to energise the population and mobilise its resources for national development.

Notes

1. See for example: Bernard Lewis, 'The Return of Islam', *Commentary* (January 1976), pp. 47-8; Israel Altman, 'Islamic Movements in Egypt', *The Jerusalem Quarterly*, no. 10 (Winter 1979), pp. 87-105; and R.H. Dekmejian, 'The Anatomy of Islamic revival', *Middle East Journal*, vol. 34, no. 1 (Winter 1980), pp. 1-12.

2. H.A.R. Gibb, *Modern Trends in Islam* (Chicago: University of Chicago Press, 1947), pp. 106ff.

3. John Alden Williams, 'A Return to the Veil in Egypt', *Middle East Review*, vol. XI, no. 3 (Spring 1978), pp. 51, 52.

4. R. Stephen Humphreys, 'Islam and Political Values in Saudi Arabia, Egypt and Syria', *Middle East Journal*, vol. XXXIII, no. 1 (Winter 1979), p. 3.

5. Ibid.

6. Ibid., pp. 3-4.

7. *Al-Da'wah*, vol. XXVII, no. 20 (January 1978), p. 55.

8. *Al-Ahram*, 13 August 1979.

9. *Al-Da'wah*, vol. XXV, no. 1 (June 1976), pp. 2-3.

10. *Al-Ahram*, 22 August 1979.

11. *Al-Da'wah*, vol. XXVIII, no. 20 (January 1978) and no. 40 (September 1979). The other main source of opposition has been the leftist party and its newspaper *al-Ahali*. *Al-Ahali* was constantly confiscated on the charge that it contained news and analysis which threatened national unity and social peace.

12. See details about these groups in Altman, 'Islamic Movements in Egypt', pp. 97-9.

13. *Al-I'tisam*, December 1978.

14. On the discussions about the 1971 constitution see Joseph P.O. Kane, 'Islam in the new Egyptian Constitution: Some Discussion in al-Ahram', *Middle East Journal*, vol. XXXVI, no. 2 (Spring 1972), pp. 137-48.

15. Daniel Crecelius, *The Course of Secularization in Modern Egypt*, mimeo., p. 18.

16. W.C. Smith, *Islam in the Modern World* (New York: Vintage Books, 1963), p. 124.

17. Quoted in Charles C. Adams, *Islam and Modernism in Egypt* (London: Oxford University Press, 1933), p. 109.

18. The major study on this group is that of I.I. Ibrahim, *The Egyptian Intellectuals Between Tradition and Modernity A Study in Some Important Trends in Egyptian Thought: 1922-1952* (unpublished PhD dissertation submitted to the University of Oxford, 1967). This group was called by I.I. Ibrahim the *udaba* (Men of letters), ibid., pp. 18-179. See also H. Sharabi, *Arab Intellectuals and the West* (Baltimore: The Johns Hopkins Press, 1970), pp. 87-104.

19. Ibrahim, *The Egyptian Intellectuals*, p. 19.

20. Ibid., pp. 23-4.

21. For a full and lengthy analysis of the ideas of this group see ibid., pp. 18-179, and also G.E. Von Grunebaum, *Modern Islam* (New York: Vintage Books, 1964), pp. 388-9. Ibrahim argues that this duality and belonging to two worlds was always present in their thought. Thus, he contradicts Nadav Safran's view about the existence of two phases in the development of their thought: a progressive phase followed by a reactionary one. See Safran, *Egypt in Search of Political Community*

(Cambridge, Mass.: Harvard University Press, 1961), pp. 141-64, 209-28. An earlier version of Safran's view is found in C. Issawi, *Egypt, An Economic and Political Analysis* (London: Oxford University Press, 1947), p. 185.

22. Anouar Abdel Malek, *Anthologie de la Littérature Arabe Contemporaine* (Paris: Editions du Seuil, 1965), pp. 15-17.

23. Von Grunebaum, *Modern Islam*, p. 33.

24. See Ali E.H. Dessouki, 'The Views of Salama Musa on Religion and Secularism', *Islam and Modern Age*, vol. IV, no. 3 (August 1973), pp. 23-33.

25. Hisham Sharabi, 'The Burden of the Intellectuals of the Liberal Age', *Middle East Journal*, vol. XX, no. 2 (Spring 1966), p. 232.

26. Morroe Berger, *Islam in Egypt Today* (Cambridge: Cambridge University Press, 1970), p. 47.

27. Charles D. Smith, 'The Crisis of Orientation: The Shift of Egyptian Intellectuals to Islamic Subjects in the 1930's', *International Journal of Middle East Studies*, vol. 4, no. 4 (October 1973), pp. 382-410.

28. Ali E.H. Dessouki, 'Arab Intellectuals and al-Nakba: The Search for Fundamentalism', *Middle Eastern Studies*, vol. IX, no. 2 (1973), p. 190.

29. *al-Ahram*, 19 August 1979.

30. Dessouki, 'Arab Intellectuals and al-Nakba'.

31. Ibid., p. 193.

32. Williams, 'A Return to the Veil in Egypt', p. 52.

8 RELIGIOUS RESISTANCE AND STATE POWER IN ALGERIA

Jean-Claude Vatin

1. The Study of Religion in Algeria: A General View

1.1. When dealing with the history of Islam in Algeria, observers have tended to stress, most of the time, certain topics, i.e., men: *khwan* of the brotherhoods and *marabouts*, *'ulamā* and scholars, or ideas: Islamic thought and theology. Institutions have also been taken into consideration such as mosques, brotherhood centres (*zawiyas*), former pious trusts or *habous*, or Qur'anic schools. And when Islamic law has been at stake, that can be easily explained through comparison with Western law. Among those who have, more recently, indulged in writing on Algerian Islam, we notice both an explicit tendency to work and explore the same fields and a less patent propensity for following in other scholars' tracks. We are still presented with academic divisions between orthodox, maraboutic and schismatic Islam, between principles and practices, law and prophets, the *umma*, the whole community of Islamic believers, and the national Algerian society. We are constantly invited to apply a dialectical system of explanation to a country, opposing rural and urban religion, holy men and doctors, mysticism and puritanism, conservatism and reformism.

Such analyses are not at all irrelevant. They have proven their capacity to highlight some of the main differences within Islam. They have also demonstrated that orthodoxy is not only on the side of puritanism; that the latter is not concentrated only in cities. We know now that the dividing lines do not separate the good *'ulamā* from the bad marabouts, traditional orders and reformist movements, but cut through the groups themselves. For instance, within so-called popular Islam, several brotherhoods demonstrated their orthodoxy and their radicalism during the years 1830 to 1840 in Algeria. All the same, the reformist movement which took place one century later, did not produce an automatic opposition to it in all rural areas.

Can we look at societies through the same, even better adapted, glasses? Political independence, social and cultural transformation and economic development in Algeria since 1962, have deeply modified the relations between people and religion. By saying this, we are not challenging other scholars' statements, but questioning the way in which social science has been used to understand a rather complex phenomenon.

1.2. We are right in the middle of a new period of investigation, at a moment when the basic assumptions of Islamic studies, religious sociology, Muslim theology and Islamic thought are being modified. At the same time, we have (a) to face legislation which is said to be based on a new exegesis of the Qur'ān, (b) to understand how a general anthropology of Islam, of North African Islam — and more precisely of Algerian Islam — is going to be reshaped, (c) to see a new 'religious sociology of Islam' appearing (Charnay) together with books on 'contemporary Arab ideology' (Laroui), 'Islamic thought' (Arkoun), 'Arabo-Moslem personality and its future' (Djaït).

Islamology has been recently revised, with scholars from Islamic countries playing an important role. They have mentioned that most of the recent research on their own societies by foreign students, Islam has been regarded as an obvious element which needed no special treatment. Moreover, when political scientists have been dealing with Islam they have presented it as a religious ideology, thus forgetting to take into account the evident links between political philosophy, political practice and religious belief.

It is also true that there has been a growing polarisation of research on political actors, institutions and structures, on the political system as a whole. Studies have insisted upon 'functions' of modernisation, economic and national development, national integration, etc.While there has been an anthropological interest in 'Moroccan Islam' (Geertz, Gellner, Eickelman, Morsy, Rosen; but also Leveau, Waterbury, Brown) Algerian Islam has been mostly approached from the outside. Very little has been said about what the people themselves think and do, about the way in which Algerians perceive and experience their religion. Not much has ever been written on how political actors conceive foreign and internal politics as Muslims, or as members of a Muslim country.

1.3. It has even been argued that, despite the formal constitutional provisions of 1963 and 1976 declaring Islam the religion of the state, there have been signs of a falling away from religiosity — as if the extension of the sacred within the political sphere had led to a development of the profane within the social one. And, in fact, the state takeover of religion for secular ends might have produced such an apparent outcome. The Algerian community appears to be undergoing gradual clericalisation or de-confessionalisation, while its leaders proclaim their fondness for Islam and for its rules. Certainly, there is some kind of paradoxical secularisation through the recent assertion of state control over the petty 'clergy' of the mosques, over the Qur'ānic schools, checking the influence of Muslim congregations or Islamic associations over the people, and mastering cultural and theological expression or manifestations, thanks to the 'seminars on Islamic thought' among other devices.

Relations between the people and the central power have changed throughout the years. The interference of the state in private affairs, and especially with regard to people's belief in God, has increased. There is no longer a sultan, no longer a caliph or commander of the faithful. There happens to be no longer a Dey in Algiers. The 'sovereign', head of the state and the governing body do not owe their power to the divinity but to citizens going to the polls and selecting them. State religion tends to impose new political norms and structures to promote the growth of new ideological forms and social institutions.

Nevertheless, all this cannot prevent the development of social practices and underground religious observances. People growing out of one set of habits have grown into others, which are not very easy to spot. They keep to their religion according to terms and patterns about which we have still to learn. They may very well look at politics and at the 'political centre' with different eyes, and we are rather unaware of what their opinions are now.

There is some circumstantial evidence that the official interpretation of religion given through various governmental decisions has not always been met with a kindly reception. There have been clues on several occasions of resistance to the state on religious grounds. And that is not new, if we compare it with what has almost been a tradition in Algeria. In practice, religious opposition to central power has almost never ceased to function since the end of the eighteenth century, though the forms that such a resistance has taken and continues to take have varied over time. This does account for an historical analysis of religious and political relations in Algeria for about two centuries.

2. Ways and Means of an Approach

2.1. To approach the connections between Islam and the state from a conflicting — and not complementary — point of view does not oblige one to rewrite Algerian history since 1800. Not being an historian, this would have gone beyond my capacity anyway. However, as some scholars have published articles and essays which are related to the subject, we might use them as a basis.

In doing so we must keep in mind that each author or researcher has been working on a limited period of time and on a specific matter. It has thus been impossible to explain the whole series of clashes between religion and politics, when Islam (i.e., certain types of Islam) and the state (i.e., certain forms of state) have been fighting each other throughout the decades.

In the meantime, there might exist some unity (if not continuity) in what has emerged from scholars' research. Although the interpretations are supposed to be different — and they are — they may be fitted together without too much forcing. We could try to establish some kind of synchronic demonstration out of this.

Perhaps we could push a bit further and carry the conclusions of various analyses of more than 150 years of the Algerian past to a more general and common level. In order to adhere to a logical line, i.e., to authors who have tried to answer the same kind of question we are asking ourselves today, I have chosen several works among them those of Augustin Berque, Fanny Colonna, Ernest Gellner, Jean Leca and Ali Merad.

This might sound a bit 'mechanical', according to the double-meaning of the word. On the one hand, this is a study of 'driving powers, of physical laws governing stability and movement', as applied to societies. We would take the state as the main *power* put into action and certain Islamic forces as resisting forces. On the other hand, to insist on the second aspect of that somewhat mixed metaphor, the word mechanical might apply to our effort to reduce other peoples' analysis and conclusions to a single, continuous observation.

2.2. When reading most of the literature devoted to Islam in Algeria, we notice the permanence of disputes between religious groups on the one hand and the central power on the other. A main characteristic, then, is the lasting opposition to central administration either based almost directly on religious arguments, or using

Islam at least as a means or a channel to contest the legitimacy of governmental authorities.

Such a statement implies that there might be antagonistic differences between two fields which are said not to be separated. It is clear enough that I have taken a possible division between politics and religion for granted. And this goes against many opinions and options. But is it not mainly because this has in fact been the case in Algeria? Until 1962, *the* power imposed upon the Algerian community was of foreign origin, and there were reactions along religious lines against such a type of illegal, illegitimate, domination.

Was religion not only the language to be used by a majority of people, and the only local political means of collective exchange and expression to be opposed to the official political system which was French or at least controlled by the French?

In other words, if there seemed to be no clear separation between religion and politics within the Algerian sphere itself (i.e., the indigenous 'periphery'), it was mostly because Islam was used to express political arguments and criticisms concerning the 'centre' in the hands of a foreign governing body. By contrast, on the colonial side, all efforts were made to gain control over the Islamic sphere. And the French did their best to achieve that. They could even imagine that they had succeeded, after the First World War, and especially when they were enjoying themselves during the feasts celebrating the centenary of the conquest, in 1930.

It was at that very moment that a new group of men found a way to use religious language again. They constructed a new code and they elaborated a new set of values. And it was certainly the *'ulamā* who were the initiators of a different kind of contestation, while remaining cultural leaders and not trying to become political leaders. The reformist movement in Algeria, though it was not directly responsible for the final French defeat thirty years later, did help to reconstruct an original 'identity' or 'personality', mostly based on Islamic principles.

After independence, the problem was that the reinforcement of the state tended to lead to a similar type of control over religious activities, as that put into practice by the French. Following the example of the colonial state, the national state tried not to allow any kind of autonomy either to local cultures or to groups (associations or organisations) based on or referring to Islamic principles. Since then, we have noticed a continuous strengthening of the government together with a nationalisation of Islamic ideology to the benefit of the state. But this does not mean at all that central authority is no longer censored and criticised and that Islam is not being called upon to argue about and blame various aspects of the general policy of the government and of particular policies and political decisions.

2.3. One remark here: According to a somewhat vulgar typology, relations between Islam and politics could be classified as follows:

(1) Islam helps to support and comfort the power in office. Thus, it makes *integration* easy. It serves the objectives of the nation-state. It also facilitates the social and cultural unification of a collectivity, which might have obtained no autonomy without such a catalyst. The prototypical example being Pakistan where a nation has been built with members sharing the same faith and possibly not much else.
(2) Islam contributes to a progressive *adaptation* to realities and problems of 'evolution', or 'modernisation'. The state appeals to Islam to acquire, then to strengthen, its own legitimacy and political base, to find arguments, to transform the country. Algeria would be a good example of modernisation brought about through or with Islam.
(3) Islam becomes a centre of *resistance* to the state. Or, another way of looking at it, there is some kind of conflict between politics and religion. The state establishes itself against religion, as it did in modern Turkey.

Such a classification does not seem to be valid as it mixes two different types of data: those related to national integration and to the part played by religion within it on the one hand and, on the other, those linked to relations between society and the state in a socio-political system.

As far as our analysis of Algeria goes, I do not think we can use it, as evidence shows that contrasts between religion and power have been modified continuously. It seems obvious that it cannot be the same contesting Islam we are talking about when we refer to 1830, 1871, 1919, 1945, 1962 or 1979, and it is not the same power either, as has already been pointed out. While there have been several 'State formations', there have also been several Islams.

3. Stages and Forms of Religious Resistance to State Power

The historical records indicate a permanent (if not continuous) religious resistance to state power. At the start, we notice revolts based on Muslim brotherhoods. Then a sort of denial or refusal to accept French rules which were imposed; popular Islam becoming some sort of a shelter. Then reformist movements, inspiring an anti-colonial struggle, developed. Finally, a new puritanism arose which harboured an even more modern form of protest, though difficult to make conspicuous.

3.1. Sufism was the first way of opposing the state, both the Turkish before 1830 and the French after, when they occupied the country. What we could call 'brotherhood Islam' had almost never stopped fighting the central authority (the Dey in the *Dar es Soltan* and the Beys in the three other provinces).

There were many cases when *shurfa* and *shuyukh* led their men against local representatives of the Dey: tax collectors, Dey's envoys or Bey's *mahalla*. An important part was also played by some of the religious families in interfering in disputes at various levels of the intricate segmentary system of alliances, in finding compromises between confederations of tribes, clans, *soff*, *ferka*.

From the end of the eighteenth century to the beginning of the twentieth century, powerful brotherhoods led several attacks, endangering the whole Turkish structure. Most of the well known *tariqa*s had taken part in alliances against Algiers. And we can say that the extension of sufism was responsible for putting an end to the possible transformation of the system of government at that time. The Sufis did not succeed in overthrowing the Dey, as they constituted coalitions which never lasted long enough to do so, but they could have achieved it as they were the only groups recruiting throughout the whole country, and not at all along ethnic lines, as the tribes or clans did. Later on, although brotherhoods could always whip up their followers and mobilise warriors against the French, they proved unable to constitute a single powerful organisation capable of sending the French back home.

Between 1804 and 1817, Rahmāniya, Taïbiya, Derkawa, Qādiriya, Tijāniyya, Senoussiya had more or less taken a hand in assailing the Turks. The Derkawa, for instance, had been leading one of the last important coalitions against the Dey. The Tidjāniya, in the west, was said to be much stronger than the Bey of Oran. Its members came and attacked Mascara after the French had landed near Algiers but had not occupied other towns yet. In both cases it was demonstrated that, because of their social basis, religious groups had competitive projects and strategies which were mutually hostile. They thus played with one another the same kind of alliance-rivalry game which interfered with their common hostility in the last resort to the 'city state' of Algiers.

In fact, there was not one religious leader capable of unifying brotherhoods and *marabtin* in his name, of defeating the French; there was no *mahdi*. There was no *shaman* (*homme fétiche*) or prophet, who could later have been recognised as the Prince, then legitimised as head of state, according to some sort of neo-Khaldunian law of tribes arising and defeating urban governments before filling the same type of functions afterwards. There was indeed some prophecy going on throughout rural areas that French soldiers would be forced to re-embark. But this symbolic announcement did not lead to a general uprising, whose normal end would have led to the formulation of the dogma of a new state.

The French manoeuvred religious orders in the same way the 'Turkish Regency' had handled them beforehand: they allied with several, opposed others, had one competing with another, etc. Within twenty years most of them were militarily defeated, bought, or condemned to reduced activity.

The only attempt to build up political structures and institutions did not in fact — despite many interpretations — arise from 'mystic' but from more orthodox Islam, that embodied by Amiz Abd al-Qādir.

3.2. In regard to Abd al-Qādir, we face problems of interpretation. According to recent works by Algerian and foreign scholars, the Amir was the first Algerian to try to create a government of his own on a territory in the years 1832-1840. For the first time an Algerian-born local leader (a member of a powerful brotherhood himself) launched a new system of power on a piece of land that Turkish administration had just left and that French troops had not yet occupied.

Abd al-Qādir, at the beginning, did not call for a holy war (*jihād*) against the French. He did not pretend to be a *mahdi* but an *imām*. His main purpose was to impose his own authority on populations between the Moroccan and Tunisian borders (if the word 'border' is not being taken as precise geographical limits). He even signed treaties with French generals on two occasions and made sure that *'ulamā* in Fez and Cairo would give *fatwas* favourable to such agreements with 'religious enemies', i.e., non-Moslems.

Though the heir of a prominent figure of an important group, as he was the son of a shaykh of the Qādiriya order, having close links with Morocco, he did not want to unite all the brotherhoods and to have them fight against the European invaders. On the contrary, he started playing all brotherhoods one against the other, doing everything possible to demolish Derkawa hegemony and to oust Tidjāniya influence from his home region. He even laid siege to the main city of the latter (Aïn Mahdi in the south-west) and occupied it. On the other hand, he recruited well known marabouts to assume administrative responsibilities in the political and judicial system to which he gave birth.

His various attempts tended to prove that he was compromising with the political conditions of his day, by signing treaties with the infidels — in order to save time and to recruit followers — as well as by recognising the formal authority of the Moroccan sultan. He was also using religion for secular ends, as he referred to Islam to collect taxes, to unify the judicial system and to open schools. In doing so he started creating a kind of a state upon a specific part of Algeria.

This is the picture that comes out of studies, for instance, not so much by Fournier, Gallissot, Ageron, or even Emerit, but certainly out of Danziger's thesis. The Algerian authors themselves could not resist hagiographical inclinations even after 1962. Some of them have so avidly searched for a founding father of the Algerian nation and state, and thus could not help choosing Abd al-Qādir. This is not to mention either the foreign chroniclers of the nineteenth century who painted the Amir as a pure hero (Roches, Churchill, Daumas, even Duff Gordon, for instance), or the biographers of the twentieth (Azan, Blunt, D'Estailleur-Chanteraine, Habart, among others) who did no better.

We may wonder whether we have not overestimated Abd al-Qādir's role, and been partly the victims of both modern concepts brought out by social scientists and of portraits of the Amir drawn before (Kateb, Sahli) or after (Benachenhou) the Algerian independence.

The picture might need some revision on different points. First, we might have passed over some 'details' in silence, for instance, over a necessary comparison with other 'reformers' of his time, with men like Abderrahman Bou Qobrin, Tidjāni, and especially Mohammed es-Senoussi of Cyrenaïca. Second, are we not insisting too much on the establishment of a 'state' of an 'independent government' which in practice lasted two years (1837-9). After the Amir went to war again, in 1840 and more precisely after the Moroccan defeat at Isly in 1844, Abd al-Qādir's 'state' went into progressive decay, before falling to pieces. Algeria reverted then to partisan or guerilla war, to brotherhoods and local leaders playing their own part again. We were back to the official central system of the state opposing the different forces to one another, with the French in command instead of the Dey and, for instance, getting the Taïbiya on their side.

Third, we tend to leave aside other insurrectionary movements at the same time as Abd al-Qādir's: the Bey Ahmed of Constantine in the East, Bou Maza in the Dahra, the Ouled Sidi Shaykh in the south, and others, brotherhoods or tribes led by *marabouts*, which resisted the French. We also forget about what was going on after the Amir's defeat and following surrender and which took place between 1847 and 1880. Perhaps there were no further attempts to develop a project of an independent region or state. Perhaps the high religious dignitaries ended their military activities while, by contrast, the petty 'clergy' intervened in the battle with the French. Bou Baghla led an insurrection in Kabylia (1850), so did Si Sadok bel Hadj (1859), and both were *shurfa* affiliated to the Rahmaniya order. So was Shaykh el Haddad, who provided crucial help for El Moqrani during what was said to be the last movement of resistance of some importance. After 1870, there was a general disintegration of the religious movements of resistance, with local blazes bursting out: in the Aurès with Bou Borma in 1879, in the south-west with Bou Amāma of the Ouled Sidi Shaykh the year after.

When looking back at that period, we tend once again to oversimplify its characteristics, by opposing orthodox and mystic Islam. During the military clash with the French, all that happened looked as if orthodox ideology (embodied in Abd al-Qādir) and Muslim mysticism (the brotherhoods) had opposed and destroyed each other for the main benefit of the colonial foreign new order. But if we could add from what we know of what happened afterwards, the clash also benefited the urban doctors and *'ulamā* of the 1920s.

In practice, the picture is too simple. Recent research of Ahmed Nadir and Peter von Sivers for example, have insisted on these points:

(1) The orthodoxy of the Amir, his spirituality and the part played by Muḥammad in his thoughts and actions. Abd al-Qādir was certainly not some sort of Machiavelli using religion for purely political purposes. Resistance to the French was not only tactical, a mere means to carve his own way to power through the Muslim orders, political adaptation or pure pragmatism in order to reassemble the greater part of the Algerian community under his leadership.

(2) A new type of differentiation, though using the old dichotomies fundamentalism/mysticism, urban/rural or classical (or orthodox)/popular Islam. According to Nadir and Sivers, the division was not between puritans and mystics, 'Muslim aristocracy' and brotherhood but among Islamic orders themselves, between *new* brotherhoods, i.e., those in favour of a return to orthodoxy to the Prophet's principles, and *old* brotherhoods, i.e., those manipulating messianism and mysticism.

This helps to explain the various conflicts which did oppose the *tariqas* at the time of the Amir. This also accounts for the different ways in which the French, while extending their control over all central North Africa, were resisted. One religious challenge relied on dominant popular Islam and was defended by some of the religious orders, occasionally manipulated from the outside, as was Bou Maza — a member of the Taïbiya who fought the French on Abd al-Qādir's side for a while and who was said to be working for the Sultan of Morocco. Another religious challenge came from more fundamentalist associations, the Qādiriya, to which the Amir belonged, the Rahmāniya, the Tijāniyya to name but the main ones. Those two groups were competitive and could not come together upon a common political project. Their conflicts were partly responsible for the impossibility of building a local state. They thus facilitated the domination of the foreign colonial state.

3.3. At the end of the nineteenth century, up to the end of the First World War, there took place a period during which colonial culture, colonial organisation, colonial law and colonial economy were imposed with very few exceptions.

From the outside, and from the French point of view, there was no more resistance. Moreover, the increasing number of Algerians attracted by and penetrating the French system (entering French schools, gaining French diplomas) seemed to demonstrate that 'assimilation' was slowly becoming an ideal for the rest of the Algerian community.

In fact, resistance was still there as one of the students of the period (Ch. R. Ageron) has very well demonstrated. Not active, but passive, resistance. That of people refusing French codes, French culture, being protected from Western influence by being kept away from the colonial market, from the economic system of exchange between the settlers (*colons*) and metropolitan tradesmen and merchants, and by being the natural victims of special laws which constituted an organised set of rules (*code de l'indigénat*).

'Maraboutism was a "shelter" for them.' The word is used here as an image, a picture of a rural community which had not much to do to preserve its identity but to hold back, to keep to traditions, to institutions (*jemaas quadis*) before the French would take control over them, to return to local *marabtin* as large brotherhoods had cried for mercy or been compelled to reduce their activities. I do not think that we can understand the rise of reformism between the two world wars, if we do not keep in mind the existence of a more or less conserved sector, of scraps of a cultural code of habits and beliefs which had survived throughout the period of expanding and triumphant colonisation.

3.4. The *ulama* were the first to articulate a policy based on the old Islamic common background, in order to build up a programme of renovation and to help the revival of Arabo-Muslim Algerian identity. They offered the whole Algerian community a new set of rules, based on the orthodox tradition. In fact, they developed a counter-strategy resting on cultural bases, which was a counter-code, applied to the colonial code. In a sense, they transformed passive into active opposition, defensive into an offensive attitude.

But the resistance to French power was by no means a direct one. They had to face the *marabtin* and the conservative movements which kept up the myth of legendary saints and unlikely *mahdis*. They had to meet with the critics of official Islam, under French control, as well as those of traditionalists who were very touchy about reformism. They had to prove that *M' Tourni* — people who had abandoned their faith to become French — had chosen a dead end.

Despite difficulties, they built a policy of confrontation with Western ideals based on a trilogy: religious ideology, Arabic language, national identity. Their weapons were not military nor political, but a *ulamā* association which transformed itself into a 'true religious party' according to Ali Merad's formula (1967, p. 9), with private schools, cultural circles, youth movements, preaching, newspapers and periodicals in Arabic, an 'effective propaganda machine' to quote Merad again.

How, then, did we shift from the rural armed resistance of the nineteenth century when marabouts and *tariqa*s were omnipresent to the urban cultural opposition of the twentieth century when *'ulamā* had suddenly taken the lead? The answer is not easy to give, but we can suggest various hypotheses to explain why a Muslim country 'almost completely dependent on rural holy men . . . had swung more violently against them' some decades later (Gellner, 1974, p. 285).

A first answer might be given by the continuous decline of the *marabouts*, in proportion to French centralisation of power over the whole of the country. Holy men were losing their appeal bit by bit, as populations could no longer rely on their own resources and ignore the rest of the country. They were also losing their main functions, those of mediators, of 'witnessing oaths', of 'offering personal incarnation of the sacred for tribesmen' (Gellner, 1974, p. 292). There were, after all, few tribesmen left, as more peasants and more rural workers were recruited by settlers who were expanding cultivation, and taking on more hands for growing grapes, citrus and cereals. As Algeria was gaining some kind of a new unity under French rule, *marabouts* who were local and segmented and who could thus answer only local questions became ineffective in dealing with general 'national' problems (Gellner, 1974, p. 293).

A second answer might come from the original strength of the *'ulamā* movement. What it did offer was a new set of rules based on the orthodox tradition but adapted to the necessary modernisation of the world, and which could respond to everyone's needs. By claiming to recruit all Muslims under their banner, the reformists could appear as breaking with segmented politics. They, in fact, provided the different groups with a new image of a larger entity, the nation.

The nation they were talking about could be on a par with the French system of domination, at least for a while. There was a 'national project' which these doctors, bourgeois scholars living in cities for the most part, wrote down through various texts, and especially articles published between 1936 and 1938 by Ben Badis in *El Shihab*.

Ben Badis supported the idea of an Algerian community composed of two major elements: the sociological and the political parts. The first one was said to be permanent, indestructible and purely Algerian. The second (i.e., institutions, legal obligations) could be of foreign origin in the short run, and impose its rule on the Muslim people in Algeria. Later on, the second part would be cut off and Algeria would become an independent political entity, a nation.

So, the future the *'ulamā* were offering was not to be gained through violence and political means, without people having to become overtly nationalistic (i.e., anti-French) but through a cultural and religious conflict with the French. And this could be accepted by the increasing populations of cities. To the bourgeoisie and the petty bourgeoisie, even to the new proletariat in towns, generally attracted by European civilisation, modern standards of living, French culture, the *'ulamā* could offer something to counterbalance all that. Against the French myth of transformation through Western means, they were able to produce another myth, that of an Islamic and Arabic way to attain the same end.

They could even offer the townsmen the pleasure of dismissing the old Islam, that of the tribes, of the brotherhoods in the rural areas, with its mysticism and its purely defensive code, which they said was fit for the past and not for the present. They rejected the *marabouts* who had lost much of their influence anyway; and they presented themselves as the upholders of a new Islam, a purified religion through a return to orthodoxy. They thus legitimated themselves as the true holy men, which meant as the normal leaders of the Moslem community in Algeria.

Between 1920 and 1962, it looked as if the *ulamā*, who had deliberately chosen not to enter political battles and who had left the electoral gambling to other nationalist groups and parties — in which they lost so much energy — had not succeeded in gaining enough support and were politically ruled out. Resistance to the French on religious grounds did not seem to be particularly profitable. But it was quite the opposite. By forcing the other Algerian movements to enter its field (which was cultural) instead of entering their's (which was political), the association of the *'ulamā* led them to share part of its aspirations. The only way out was a Muslim, Arabic-speaking nation. Though they did not share such an option at the beginning, 'rightists' (*Union démocratique du manifeste algérien*, UDMA) or 'leftists' (*Mouvement pour le triomphe des libertés démocratiques*, MTLD) had to take it on the *'ulamā*'s terms, and to fill their own programmes with those of the association. In 1962, the *'ulamā* had lost on the political field, but they had won on the ideological. They had drawn their legitimacy from their reinterpretation of Islam and from the way they had linked religion to nationalism. They had established both Algerian reformism as the official ideology of the independent regime, and themselves as genuine defenders of 'Algerian personality'. In 1962, the elements of secularism put forward by the spokesmen of *Fedération de France* were banned, after the *'ulamā* had rejected the claim. But at the same time they were dispossessed of the moral leadership they had built up bit by bit.

3.5. Why did the *'ulamā* lose the 'capital of legitimacy they had accumulated' (Gellner, 1974) to the benefit of the formal Islam of the 'nation state'? Why was the reformism of the *'ulamā* transformed into a 'state reformism'? For several reasons. First, another form or source of legitimacy had emerged during the war of liberation, when the armed fight against the French had been the only way to put an end to colonisation. The *'ulamā*, of course, could not participate, though some of its representatives had entered the National Liberation Front (FLN). Secondly, the reformists had not been the only ones to ask for independence. Other forces had demanded it more openly and fought for it. Also, they constituted a 'religious party' which could become a political pressure group but which would not transform itself into a political party when politics prevailed. But Reformist Islam was recognised as an established religion. Almost no one questioned it. This had happened because of the conflicts and disputes for political leadership between clans and personalities which led the contenders to appeal to the main source of legitimacy, to the commonly-shared vocabulary: religion as the theoretical instrument of national liberation.

While fighting one another, they had tried to rid themselves of political rivals by demonstrating that the latter were no longer following the national code with its religious implications. By doing so, the claimants ended in 'sacralising' their language with a reformist formula, which tended to become *the* political language of modern independent Algeria.

Afterwards, the message of modernisation and the decision to impose socialism, to promote economic development — implying a marked centralisation of power and a dominant state bureaucracy among other phenomena — had to be passed on to the people through the same well-accepted language. There would be no real independence, it was proclaimed, without socialism and no socialism without Islam. The less legitimacy the men in power had, or thought they had, the more they referred to state reformism and national Islam as justification for their choices and decisions. If Islam was quite compatible with Westernisation according to the Reformist doctrine of the *'ulamā*, it could not fit better with the requirement of an industrial society developing itself while keeping to Arabo-Muslim rules. In other words, modernisation (and modern social organisation as well) could not be obtained without the support of religion. It could be done with reformist Islam, which had stressed both a puritanical observance of the Qur'ān and a transformation of society at the same time.

State reformism, or national Islam in Algeria, means the monopoly of religious affairs by the state, the dominant statist control over Islamic problems, the nationalisation of Qur'ānic schools and institutes, the appointment of *imāms*, *muftīs*, and of a Supreme Islamic Council (*Conseil supérieur islamique*), of *qadis* and of employees of the *mahakmas*, constant propaganda, the enforcement of religious principles for political purposes and, if necessary, a political 'ideology' of religion, as Ali Merad has recently demonstrated. But such a deviation has its counterpart: a criticism which is also based on religious arguments and which tends to use puritanism to justify its claims.

3.6. By noting that puritanism shelters criticism aimed at the political sphere, I would like to evoke the new forms of contestation which have sprung up from time to time since 1962, and which are not well-known.

3.6.1. Although national Islam is manipulated by the 'political class' or 'caste' to legitimise its decisions as well as the new social order and rapid industrialisation, opposition to such processes has not been put to rest. The public debates over the National Charter (*Charte nationale*) in 1976 revealed that the compromise — between those who control the 'industrial-military complex' of Algeria, administrators, state bureaucrats who have technical competence on the one hand and those who have political legitimacy, political leaders and party men on the other — is not completely accepted by the people.

Puritanism is thus a kind of opposition to 'Islamic deviationism'. State reformism could effectively be attacked on the basis that it helps to cover and to protect practices which lead the country, through constant amendments, to abandon its religious principles.

The excessively speedy modernisation of industry for instance, has led to close contacts with Western markets and to effective economic dependence. Such technical or technocratic Westernisation goes along with a Westernisation of morals in the cities and of manners within the ruling elite. The middle class is now imitating what Ernest Gellner calls the 'Mamluks of the Modern World' (1974, p. 203) i.e., those who possess military and administrative skill. Typical aspects of such an imitation can be noticed by those who visit Algeria today.

This widens the gap between official ideology and political speeches of the leaders, highlighting 'islamisation', 'arabisation' on the one hand, and on the other social life and economic habits which tend to imitate the 'European model'.

For the moment, the 'political class' claims a threefold legitimacy:

(1) The religious, which has led to state reformism,
(2) The political, coming from the war of liberation and embodied in the party and the army,
(3) The technical, which is demonstrated through industrialisation.

Its alliances with the bourgeoisie and with the 'Mamluks' have not been questioned since 1965. But there might be some contest arising about religious legitimacy. People begin to realise that pure Islam (puritan Islam) is not compatible with a modern, social organisation that more or less leads to the adoption of Western traditions.

3.6.2. There have been signs of a challenge coming from groups appealing to Ben Badis' spirit to establish their criticism of the official positions. But each time, the regime — which presents itself as the only legitimate heir of the greatest figure of Algerian Reformism — has claimed that every manifestation against its policy on religious grounds would be contrary to the interest of the nation. Reformism was, and is, the only way to enforce development and modernisation.

Whenever censure arose, the political group in command declared that, provided it came from the countryside, those who were expressing their displeasure were in fact trying to return to traditional practices, to superstition, to neo-paganism through the cult of saints and the like.

To take but one example, in 1968 there was a crisis in the eastern area near Mostaganem, along the coast, and where the Alouia (a branch of the Sciadla brotherhood) wanted to give expression to popular dissatisfaction. The official newspaper, *El Moudjahid*, published articles in July 1968 saying that Algeria would be pushed back to obscurantism, mysticism and other dangerous 'isms' (The Minister of *Habous* spoke of 'charlatanism', *Révolution Africaine*, 5 July 1968) if such people were allowed to talk on behalf of the peasants.

Most matters could not be dismissed that way. In that same year, for instance, when it appeared that most of the people seemed to be in favour of birth control, the question of family planning became a controversial issue between the government and traditionalists (*intégristes* in fact). Shaykh Abderrahman El-Jilali condemned birth control openly (*Algérie Actualité*, 28 Jan.–3 Feb.), and the Islamic Superior Council, though it was more cautious, shared the same view (*Al Cha'ab*, 23 Apr.). The state-run *El Moudjahid* could always declare that opponents did not understand the true principles of Islam (17 Apr.), but the Minister of Health and population, and President Boumedienne at the same time, had to retreat. This was a typical subject on which the state was forced to respect the *sharī'a*'s precepts put forward by the conservatives, failing which it might have lost part of its credit.

A new association did its best to play on this somewhat narrow edge, where it was possible to force itself upon the government, while advocating a strong respect of Islamic law. The *Al Qiyam* society, through its periodical *Humanisme musulman* and meetings, made every effort when President Ben Bella was in office to invade the political field and make themselves recognised as the 'new' reformists. They even pushed a bit further after Ben Bella's fall in June 1965. They wanted to appear as the true guardians of pure Islam, as well as of governmental ethics. As a matter of fact, they undermined the legitimacy of people in office. The periodical was banned, and the society was dissolved in 1966. As its members were still active and meeting together, the FLN opened a direct campaign (*Révolution africaine* 14-20 Feb. 1970) which ended in *Al Qiyam* being outlawed (17 March 1970). Less than one year later, the official press reported on the arrest of thirteen 'devout activists' who had created a subversive organisation to force people to respect Islamic principles according to the literal terms of the Qur'ān and the Sunna. *El Moudjahid* (29 Jan. 1971) did not mention whether those extremists were former members of the *Al Qiyam* association but we might guess that some could have participated in its former activities.

3.6.3. Today, the government seems to have mastered the situation, as far as those two kinds of religious criticism are concerned. This does not mean that a part of the petty bourgeoisie — which was not so keen on taking up the traditionalists' cause, but which, on the other hand, feels it is being progressively deprived of the benefits of modernisation — will not develop some kind of opposition based on religion. There are signs of discontent in the cities, and in the countryside which has suffered from the impact of transformation resting mostly on industrialisation as well as from the failure of the 'agrarian revolution'. They can be checked by the state apparatus which seems able to distract or to thwart them. Nothing indicates that the new contenders or critics will turn opponents or become traditionalists and conservatives.

Some groups, however, can very well demand a return to a more puritanical Islam, a more rigid respect of religious norms, which would be compatible with modernisation and even revolution. In this case, there would not be many demands for a return to mysticism, i.e., *maraboutism* or the cult of the saints. What would be most feared by the state is people demanding a transformation through Muslim fundamentalism, and not through Westernisation.

4. Concepts and Interpretations

Is there a general explanation which would take into account the variety of relations between Islam and power in Algeria for almost two centuries? There are several in fact, but I shall limit myself to the main ones, i.e., those based on theories of evolution, through continuity or cycles, and those built upon concepts, such as, crisis and rupture.

4.1. I must confess, in the first place, that the picture I have given can be overly skewed to appear as a progressive evolution; exactly as if a hidden 'mechanism' was making Islam a different force at each stage and as if we were going from popular Islam to state Islam through the religious orders, the *marabouts*, then the *'ulamā*. When I mentioned sufism earlier, I did not mean at all that it suddenly vanished and never came back afterwards. On the contrary, *maraboutism*, reformism, and puritanism may be conceived as natural tendencies which have never been totally eliminated. When one prevailed over the others, those tended to be forgotten but remained in the background, playing their part, although a much smaller one than before.

However, this does not lead to the adoption of the opposite, and to advocacy of some new 'pendulum-swing theory of Islam' (Gellner, 1968), partly because we are not enough at ease with the sociology or anthropology of religions. Nor would I say that the history of Islamic-political relations in Algeria was 'determined' by 'the never ending feud between two cardinal trends': 'The legist interpretation of the faith', with its 'formalistic ritualism' and 'its rival, sufism, Muslim mysticism with its heterogeneous mass of currents' (Khalid, 1978, p. 433).

There is no straight change, no brutal mutation from one state to the other. Neither can we find some kind of evident automatic alternation, one Islam chasing out the other and being replaced by it later on. What do we have then? Perhaps a symbiosis of the two systems.

The nineteenth century first witnessed the domination of the brotherhoods and the part they played in the armed resistance. Later on it witnessed a general return to local *marabouts* and religious leaders in the segmented society who were not deprived of their main functions before the end of the century and perhaps for some areas, not until the First World War. From that moment on, the doctors, the scholars, the theologians and the reformists of the cities became strikingly prominent figures. This has been very well explained by Fanny Colonna (1974), and by Ernest Gellner (1974) who wrote that 'probably no Muslim country was more completely dependent on rural holy men than was 19th century Algeria, and it is doubtful whether any other country has swung more violently against them' (p. 285, see also p. 296).

What followed was the creation of a nation-state, after a war of independence, concomitant with a shift from *'ulamā* reformism to state reformism; the former being displaced in a manner different from its own displacement of the *marabouts* but with a similar result. Technocratic orthodoxy made itself legitimate by claiming that it alone could lead the country both in upholding religion and modernising the country, according to twentieth-century standards. The intercessor betwen God and people is no longer a saint, a prophet, a doctor, a *muftī*, but rather the state apparatus. 'Sufism is the opium of the tribesmen, reformism of the townsmen' noted Gellner (1974, p. 292). We could add that 'statism' is the opium of the citizen.

The consequence is a non-pluralist, 'monopolistic' state, tolerating neither political parties nor social classes seen as disrupting elements that threaten national unanimity, the amalgam of unified 'citizens, workers, brothers' (Gourdon, 1979). We even meet with some 'fundamentalist-revolutionary' Islam in a country not distant from al-Qadhafi's Libya. Ernest Gellner called this recent 'conflation of free floating revolutionary radicalism with such Muslim fundamentalism' a kind of 'reformism-Maoism' (1976, p. 307); a daring label, but one which does illustrate the new situation very well.

4.2. The passage from a dominant Islam to another might also be tackled by means of two concepts: political crisis and social breakdown (or rupture).

To start with the first item (cf. Binder, Coleman *et al.*, 1971), in 1830 there was a crisis, no doubt, which concerned the whole of North Africa, and beyond its frontiers, the Islamic world. European troops which had landed in Algeria on the coast, west of Algiers — for the first time since the Spaniards three centuries before — were forced by Kheireddine to abandon the Peñon, the small fort commanding the port of Algiers. It was a military and political crisis and a moral and religious crisis as well, when the country fell into non-Muslim hands. The responses to such a direct internal menace took the form of rallying to leaders of at least a regional dimension (Ahmed Bey in the east, Abd al-Qādir in the west) and an increase of recruitment among the *tariqas*. This meant a general appeal to men and institutions that were thought to be the most capable of coping with the situation by unfurling the flag of Islam.

Half a century later, a cultural as well as an economic crisis threatened the Algerian part of the population that was shunted aside by the systematic development of the settlers' agro-economy. The danger also came from the extension of French laws and schools, which could have led to a problematic future, to new codes, new values, new rules and a new language. Both the colonial market and the colonial system of education were on the verge of dispossessing the Muslim community of its last valuable assets. The crisis was sustained by the settlers' increasing power over the country. The land and politics were in their hands. They began to develop an ideology of their own ('colonism') and a culture different from the French. They even called themselves 'Algerians'. Among natives who feared cultural extermination, many found in religion, local holy men and *zawiyas*, a last resort.

The identity crisis stemming from French pressure, European influence and the Western economic impact also accounted for the people evoking reformist slogans and propaganda. The strengthening of the *'ulamā*'s position was 'symptomatic of times of crisis and external menaces when the community as a whole is threatened with dissolution and a loss of identity' (Khalid, p. 434). Islam was controlled by the French, or manipulated by *marabouts* and congregations that were unable to provide answers for modern times, for adaptation, incapable of counter-attacking Western dominance. During the period 1930 to 1937 the reformists built a counter-force and discovered an antidote.

Adherence to the FLN in 1954 to 1962 and especially after 1956 was an answer to a new crisis. A community with almost no political rights, with very little access to jobs and careers, had exhausted all legal means. People joined, sometimes reluctantly, a movement which appealed to Islam to undertake a holy war against the French, but which at the same time was suspected of preparing a secularised future.

The constitution of 1963, The *Charte d'Alger* in 1964 and the governments of 1963 and 1965 made clear that Islam would be preserved. Algerians did, however, accept national Islam because, although it was latent, the crisis, of a new type, was none the less there. Reinforcing a young state was the only way to secure independence. Moreover, there was no other structure to answer the needs for development, to help solve the crisis of adaptation to economic development while preserving national unity at the same time. The extraordinary gamble contained in the Charter of Algiers and maintained as the national goal after the coup of 1965, to bring about a social revolution immediately after the political, meant that the people were under permanent pressure whatever they might prefer in their heart of hearts. For some, this might look like an artificial crisis, but most of the people saw it as real and reacted accordingly.

Islam was turned by the state into an ideology of combat (*idéologie de combat*), capable of disarming other ideologies from both global political poles, and especially of resisting Western 'liberal' influence as well as oriental Marxist 'democratic' sway. Islam has become both an instrument of modernisation, for a Third World country, a weapon against 'the popular practices of religious celebrations and customs' and against 'the fatalist quietism of the mystic fraternities' (Khalid, 1978, p. 434) in Algeria itself. State Islam responds to dangers from the inner world as well as from the outer world. *Islamism*, then, reacts to potential crises. It is (a) a counter-ideology opposed to its assumed adversaries (to political crisis from the outside), and (b) a dynamic ideology offering an original way to development (thus solving the crisis of identity).

4.3. To turn now to the notion of 'social rupture', we could say that the term is obviously linked to political, economic and cultural crises. It indicates that such crises have affected society and produced ruptures and clashes between social classes as a consequence.

The way in which Islam and social breaks have mixed at various moments depended on the importance of the rupture, and the resistance the opponents were able to offer. For them, Islam was both a field in which to compete and a matter about which to argue, i.e., a sphere to control and a subject to master.

Most of the time contending parties were not allowed to take centre stage, in the political field. They often fought on issues which could look to observers — and to the French administrators and settlers — as theological debate or petty disputes. But to assert control over the religious sphere meant indirect control over the Muslim community itself. Every important break within society might have led to a recasting of the parts, to groups emerging and others going down.

In short, we shall take but three ten year periods, 1870-80, 1920-30, 1960-70. During the first decade, we note that the military defeat of the Dey's troops had left the *shurfa* and other religious leaders a clear field. We have already pointed out that Abd al-Qādir and the chiefs of the main brotherhoods, who had been kept from politics for a long time, tried to establish themselves as local religious and political leaders and to conquer a territory. The 'religious aristocracy', or what Augustin Berque called 'chapelet aristocracy' (1949), was at its height at that time. So was the 'warrior aristocracy', composed of the main 'commanding families' owning land

and levying troops and taxes.

But when France took over, imposed direct land taxes, small peasants depending on the great families in command had to leave a land because it did not produce enough for them to live, or because they needed no further protection inasmuch as French soldiers could be fought no longer, and *djouad* and *shurfa* had to retreat. They were condemned to accept changes in their socio-economic status. Those who wanted to preserve a portion of their prestige, had to ask the colonial power for a job as caïds, aghas, bachaghas, etc. and later on as departmental delegates (*conseillers généraux*), members of the Economic Algerian Assembly (*Délégation Financières*) generally chosen among aristocratic families. But, as Augustin Berque noted: 'The Algerian nobility was no longer an aristocracy, it hardly was a class' (1949, p. 25).

While the upper class was losing its privileges, the *marabouts* — upon whom France increasingly relied to control the rural areas — did their best to improve the situation and to retrieve some of the prestige attached to religious functions. But (a) they remained segmented and had no general ideal to offer, and they harboured a passive Islam, as we suggested; (b) France did not allow them to do what they liked; (c) what was more important, they did not have an economic base for their desires, or project if any; and (d) the more attractive the cities, the less evident their affluence.

The social group which strove for both position and resources at the time, was the rural petty bourgeoisie. It exploited the land it had kept or bought from ruined peasants. It also seized the opportunity offered by the French to become agents of the colonial system. Among the 700 caïds in the census taken by Augustin Berque, half came from that social stratum. Islam, for them was no longer a daring religion opposed to the coloniser, but an ideology of retreat. This also helped them to concert with the French, play a key role in Franco-Algerian relations and achieve social advancement.

Soon after, a new middle class appeared or, rather, various strata among it were on the verge of formation. A new bourgeoisie, composed mostly of landowners living in cities, of shopkeepers and merchants and of civil servants, began to develop in towns, close to but different from the Moorish tradesmen of the eighteenth century. A part of this entity rapidly became sensitive to social status and French values. The first generation, which had succeeded in raising itself up by taking some of the few ways left open by the colonial system, was ready to send its children to French schools.

French degrees meant jobs and honour. Being associated with the French market meant possible enrichment. Islam, for them, was losing its attraction as well as its uniting force.

During the second decade, which has held our attention, 1920-30, there was another shift, during which a purified Islam was revived as a dynamic and integrative force by a very small number of people, for socio-political reasons. Among upper middle class families, Islam was to become a goal and a weapon at the same time. The members of the then Frenchified group tried to obtain more from the colonial power, in order to impose themselves as the true and only intermediaries between France and the Algerian indigenous community. They praised the Western system of modernisation, while arguing that it should be made possible to remain good Moslems at the same time. The number of their potential followers had been enlarged after Clémenceau's decision, in 1919, to restore local assemblies (*jemaa*) and to 'facilitate the accession of natives to political rights'. But that was not enough to permit the lower middle class to fight its way up through the social hierarchy. Neither was the pro-French group of upper middle class granted the privileges it was asking for. This gave the other stratum of the upper middle class the opportunity to assert itself. Although it enjoyed broadly the same social 'situation', it still did not profit from the same political 'positions', nor did it share the same ideal.

Whatever it feared, social decline or political elimination, it did forge what we referred to as a counter-code or counter-strategy, by putting forward the ideas of a reformed Islam, of a defence of Arabic, of a restoration of the national spirit and will. While making those appeals, it knew it was persuading people to help them to secure and, if possible, to reinforce their own social situation. The reason why the *'ulamā* were at odds with the *évolués* or *élus* was not purely moral, religious or idealistic. It was also a competition between two factions of a class doing their utmost to take control over the largest part of the population. To counter-balance Westernisation, there was no better choice than to borrow from the deep and rich Arabo-Muslim legacy. The religious sphere was apparently but not really 'occupied'. Part had been left to the so-called popular sector, in the country. Part was watched over by the colonial French services and especially by the Director of the *Affaires indigènes* at the *Gouvernement Général* in Algiers, who kept a close watch on what was happening in the countryside, on the *zawiyas*, the mosques, the medresas, the places of pilgrimage and ritual manifestations. The traditional structures and institutions were supervised. But access to a new Islam, to a revival, was not so well guarded.

There are some facts which should be mentioned here, and which have been emphasised by various scholars. We note, first, the somewhat rapid seizure of the 'new Islam's' domain by the religious group of the upper middle class, and its ability to delegitimate traditional Islam, and to develop an ideology of its own, which allowed it to gain enough support among the lower middle class, among those who realised that there was almost no chance to enter the French modernised world. Though their position was none too secure, they succeeded in attracting people, on the pole opposite to that of the *évolués*.

Secondly, the *'ulamā* offered themselves as spokesmen for all the Algerians, by asking the French government to allow them to open private schools and to develop the teaching of Arabic. What they aimed at was to open another way which would lead to jobs entailing a knowledge of Arabic, some degree of Arabo-Muslim culture and of Islamic law. Those who were longing to move upwards and to have their social needs fulfilled, could only become the *'ulamā*'s supporters or clients.

Thirdly, the increasing cultural impact of the *'ulamā* — connected with their battle with the *évolués* for the moral (but in practice political) control over the community — was the hallmark of a change within the social history of Algeria: 'the transition from a segmented society to a class society' (Colonna, 1974, pp. 241-3).

Lastly, we should not forget that some fraction of the lower middle class itself, and the proletariat, did not accept the rival views of the upper middle class. For instance, for most of the workers — relatively few at that time — who had gone to France to find jobs in the industrial sector, neither the programme of the *'ulamā* nor that of the *élus*, appealed to them. All the same, landless peasants, although pious men, were not satisfied by speeches delivered by clerics, sometimes entangled in obscure theological disputes and who, although they had respect for scholars and even for tradesmen, were distant from the cultured who had devoted themselves to letters or rhetoric, from wealthy bourgeois who got their income from land or commerce. For the members of the deprived lower middle class who had launched the uniting of the 'lower classes' through a drastic separatist project — implying an almost direct break with the colonial power — the part was not easy to play. It can, however, help us to understand a twofold consideration. On the one hand, Islam had to be introduced into a programme which was originally a secularising one; leading to a compromise between two discourses: the socialist and the religious. This was supposed to gain twofold support (independent Algeria is still using the two together). On the other hand, it addressed that most deprived stratum that furnished the Algerian movement of liberation with combatants, between 1954 and 1962.

In 1960-70, the picture is different because of other social breaks. During the war of liberation, the part of the upper middle class more or less associated with the French colonial system until 1943 had come to support a programme leading to political independence. In 1947, when the new statute of Algeria was discussed within the French Parliament — with Muslim deputies representing the three departments of Algeria — most of the nationalist political parties and social groups were asked for an autonomous system of government. But they could not come to an agreement with one another on the means of attaining it. The representatives of the upper middle class felt that they could well afford a legal and political dispute with the French about it. The lower middle class representatives were thinking of taking extreme measures. A very small group of them did in fact prepare for war, re-launched the extremist '*organisation secrète*', plunged into underground activities, and finally opened fire on 1 November 1954.

This brutal intervention happened much to everybody's surprise. The French arrested members of political parties who had nothing to do with the shooting and the Algerians remained quite abashed for a while. More than that, the unexpected event threw the socio-political game out of balance. Both the *élus* and the *'ulamā* were suddenly facing a situation they were not expecting. Unknown leaders, arising from the country and various cities, proved ready to set Algeria ablaze. If they were successful, the cultural and political leadership, which the two groups of the upper middle class had established, would have come to an end.

During the first two years of the war of liberation, we still do not know the details of the inner battle which took place among the Algerian movements. But we know that during those months, which culminated in 1956 at the Soumman Congress, the new representatives of the lower middle class did their best to enforce a policy of their own and to take a firm lead. They recruited peasants in the mountains of Aures and Kabylia as well as in the rest of the country and organised them in *wilayas*. They mobilised craftsmen, shopkeepers, trade unionists and enrolled members of the urban sub-proletariat. They also made it clear that those who had fled to join Algerian nationalists in Cairo, Tripoli, Tunis and other places would not govern from afar the country's revolution.

Not only did they disrupt social order and the natural course of politics, but they also took up Islam and reintroduced it as a strategic weapon. A fighting religion, that of the *jihād*, was summoned up, in order to rally Algerians against the French, despite hesitations. People were told not to drink, not to smoke, not to eat during Ramadan. Religious rules were made compulsory for political purposes. A puritan and violent Islam was used against the spineless, the unconvinced and the unfaithful. Algerian and Muslim were made synonymous. Revolutionary chiefs made frequent use of threats and reprisals in the name of Islam. There were moments when a 'religious terror' was put into force. Algerians responded to it though they did not all agree with it.

When it had become obvious that — (a) as more and more members of the upper middle class were joining the *Front de libération nationale* abroad; and (b) as the *wilayas* were losing their efficiency under French military pressure, so that the war could not be won and a diplomatic battle had to ensue — the initiative of the lower middle class was thwarted. The progressive return of the more traditional defenders of an Algerian nation following a calmer process of formation might have irritated some; it might also have pleased those who feared a complete social revolution taking place after the political revolution. The *'ulamā*'s influence was thus reintroduced and its own conception of a more gentle reformist Islam became the main ideal once again. It ended in the political recuperation by those in control of the independent state through a process that has already been mentioned.

Just before independence was proclaimed, a group of the 'new men' who had emerged during the war managed to seize control over some of the revolutionary institutions. They then formed a new coalition, allied with the 'army of the frontier' with Colonel Boumedienne still in command, although he had been dismissed by the provisional government, and fought their way to Algiers — former *gouvernement général*.

The Ben Bella regime had to live up to the people's expectations, to fulfill the claims of its own followers, and to invalidate the fear of its various opponents at the same time. It was led to resist the pressure of those who awaited a 'socialist policy' and a systematic development of *autogestion*. It had to negotiate with others who asked for the implementation of promises made during the war, among others, to members of the former *wilayas*. It was compelled to adopt a policy of compromise about the future and the development of the party. It was faced with a strong army which had assumed and was given important governmental responsibilities, etc.

There were not many ways to meet all those demands. Ben Bella longed for the reduction of political social pressure. He chose to give satisfaction to the most insistent demands such as governmental legislation of land and real estate (houses, flats, shops, business concerns, workshops, etc.) that the Algerians had seized after the Europeans' departure; a vast recruitment of civil servants in the ministries, local administration, the education system, which the lower middle class had dreamt of for decades; employment for former resistance fighters, whose official number was curiously increasing month by month.

In the meanwhile, the new President of the Republic/Secretary General of the FLN developed what would be essential for keeping the Algerian people together: a nationwide appeal to unity, based on the Arabo-Islamic tradition and on a necessary development along socialist lines.

What differentiated President Boumedienne's regime from his predecessor's was not so much his own evolution from dominant Islamism to dominant socialism, but the new changes within the society. Since 1965, there has been a remarkable increase of the lower middle class with better chances to rise within the social hierarchy or, at least, to enjoy better living standards. They have even profited from the post-war period to conclude alliances with the upper middle class, to marry into better-off families. A great number of children entered the schools after the war, obtained degrees, qualified themselves for various jobs and became professionals. For them, there is almost no need to look for 'jobs offered'. The number of public offices, administrative authorities, national firms, the extension of the tertiary sector, of lawyers, of doctors, explains why they profit from the employment situation at that level.

For that dynamic stratum of the lower middle class the official Islam is perfectly suited, because it advocates, both a manifest fondness for the values of a civilisation and allows the Algerians to succeed in modernizing their country according to the requisites of the twentieth century. They did not even think that they were taking advantage of economic development and of the social mobility. They probably imagined that everyone in Algeria could follow the same kind of progress and that the entire Algerian community thought the same. Today they might have a better sense of reality as they look at the other strata of the lower middle class. Furthermore, if they examine the situation of the poor, the unemployed or semi-employed sub-proletariat, the landless peasants, constituting after all the majority of the population, the gap appears evident. It will become wider if what is becoming an independent upper middle class transforms itself into a ruling class, using a more limited system of co-option and reducing its alliances with other social groups.

Until now, we have argued, national ideology has tended to veil the development of other social breaks. Islam more than anything else has served to enforce national unity. But we have also noticed that the deprived stratum of the lower middle class may find within a new puritanism some argument to contest the privileges of the *classe règnante*. Such criticism may also gain some support among the growing number of the 'rejected', those overlooked by a rapidly modernising Algeria.

To those who argue that Islam has been totally secularised in Algeria, we can suggest that if religion had been *the* language of the times when there were no politics, i.e., no independent political structures, religion might also be the language of people who cannot express themselves in political terms.

Note

The present contribution was first drafted for the symposium on 'Islam and Power', held in Rhodes, 2-9 September 1979, under the auspices of the Hellenic Mediterranean Centre for Arabic and Islamic Studies. A revised and enlarged version, written in October–November 1979 was made possible through a French-US Exchange Award (National Science Foundation, Washington, DC — National Center for Scientific Research, Paris) for a period of 12 months at the Near Eastern Studies Department, Princeton University.

Select Bibliography

Abdel Malek, Anouar (1965) *Anthologie de la littérature arabe contemporaine. II Les Essais*, Paris

Abun-Nasr, Jamil (1965) *The Tidjaniya, a Sufi Order of the Modern World*, London

——— (1971) *A History of the Maghrib*, 2nd edn, London

——— (1978) 'Islam und die Algerische National identität', *Die Welt des Islams*, XVIII, 3-4, pp. 178-94

Actes intégraux du 6ème Séminaire pour la connaissance de la pensée islamique, 5 vol. (Alger 24 Juillet–19 Août 1972), Algiers

Actes intégraux du 8ème seminaire pour la connaissance de la pensée islamique, 3 vol. (Bedjaïa, 25 Mars–5 Avril 1974), Algiers (the XIIth seminar was held in Batna 7-14 Septembre 1978)

Ageron, Charles-Robert (1966) *Histoire de l'Algérie contemporaine (1830-1966)* 2nd edn, Paris; 3rd edn, 1969

——— (1968) *Les Algériens musulmans et la France (1871-1919)*, 2 vol., Paris

——— (1972) *Politiques coloniales au Maghreb*, Paris

——— (1977) 'Abd el-Kader et la première résistance Algérienne', *les Africains*, Paris, vol. 1, pp. 17-49

——— (1979) *Histoire de l'Algérie contemporaine. vol. II (1871-1954)*, Paris

André, P.J. (1922) *L'Islam et les races*, 2 vol., Paris

——— (1956) *Contribution à l'étude des confréries musulmanes*, Préface by Jacques Soustelle, Algiers

Arkoun, Mohammed (1973) *Essais sur la Pensée islamique*, Paris

——— (1976a) 'L'Islam et le renouveau des sciences humaines', *Concilium*, pp. 91-101

——— (1976b) *la pensée arabe*, Paris

Aroua, Ahmed (1974) *L'Islam et la science*, Algiers

Basset, René (1901) *Nedromah et les Traras*, Paris

——— (1910) *Recherches sur la religion des Berbères*, Paris

Bel, Alfred (1908) 'La population musulmane de Tlemcen', *Revue des études ethnographiques et sociologiques*, pp. 200-16

——— (1917) 'Coup d'oeil sur l'Islam en Berbérie', *Revue d'histoire des religions*

——— (1938) *La religion musulmane en Berbérie*, I, Paris

Belguedj, M.S. (1973) 'Ben Badis et le Mutazilisme', *Mélanges Le Tourneau, Revue de l'Occident Musulman et de la Méditerranée*, 1-1973, pp. 75-96

Bellah, Robert (1969) *Beyond Belief*, New York

Bennabi, Malek (1954) *Vocation de l'Islam*, Paris

——— (1965) *Mémoires d'un témoin du siècle*, Algiers

Bennoune, Mahfoud (1976) 'Algerian Peasants and National Politics', *Merip Reports*, June 1976, pp. 3-24

Berger, Morroe (1958) 'The Middle Class in the Arab World' in Laqueur, W. (ed.) *The Middle Class in Transition*, New York

Berque, Augustin (1919) 'Essai d'une bibliographie critique des conféries musulmanes algériennces', *Bulletin de la société d'archéologie et de géographie d'Oran*, 3-4/1919, pp. 193-233

——— (1936) 'Un mystique moderniste: le Cheikh Benalioua', *Revue Africaine*, pp. 691-776

——— (1949) 'Esquisse d'une histoire de la seigneurie algérienne', *Revue de la Méditerranée*

——— (1951) 'les capteurs du divin: Marabouts, Oulémas', *Revue des deux mondes*, 43, pp. 286-302

Berque, Jacques (1956) 'Cent vingt-cinq ans de sociologie maghrébine', *Annales E.S.C.*, September

——— (1962a) *Le Maghreb entre deux guerres*, Paris/*French North Africa: The Maghreb between Two World Wars*, London, 1967
——— (1962b) 'Ça et là dans les débuts du réformisme religieux au Maghreb', *Etudes d'orientalisme dédiées à la mémoire de E. Lévi-Provençal*, Paris
——— (1978) 'Introduction méthodologique', *'Islam and Society', Social Compass*, 3/4-1978
Betbeder, Lt. Colonel (1947) *Le réformisme algérien et l'association des oulémas d'Algérie*, Mémoire, Centre des Hautes Etudes d'Administration musulmane, Paris
Binder, L., Coleman, James S., *et al.* (1971) *Crises and Sequences in Political Development*, Princeton, NJ
Bouchene, Abdallah (1975) *Le rôle de l'Islam dans la guerre d'Algérie*, Thesis (3° cycle), Montpellier
Bourdieu, Pierre (1962a) *The Algerians*, Boston (translated from the French edition *Sociologie de l'Algérie*, Paris, 1961)
——— (1962b) 'De la guerre révolutionnaire à la révolution', *L'Algérie de demain*, Paris, pp. 5-13
——— (1963) *et al.*, *Travail et travailleurs en Algérie*, Paris, la Haye
——— (1966) 'Condition de classe et position de classe', *Archives européennes de sociologie*, 2-1966, pp. 201-23
——— (1971) 'Genèse et structure du champ religieux', *Revue française de sociologie*, XII
——— (1973) *Esquisse d'une théorie de la pratique*, Genève
Bousquet, Georges-Henri (1954) *L'Islam maghrébin: Introduction à l'étude générale de l'Islam*, 4th edn, Algiers
Boutemine, Mokhtar (1976) *l'idéologie réformiste en Algérie de 1945 à 1962*, Thesis (3° cycle), Paris III
Boyer, Pierre (1962) *la vie quotidienne à Alger à la veille de l'intervention française*, Paris
——— (1966) 'Contribution à l'étude de la politique religieuse des Turcs de la Régence d'Alger (XVI-XIX siècles)', *Revue de l'occident musulman et de la Méditerranée*, 1.1966, pp. 11-49
Brace, Richard and Brace, Joan (1965) *Algerian Voices*, Princeton, NJ, Toronto, New York, London
Brett, Michael (1977) 'Islam in the Maghrib', *The Maghrib Review*, July–August
——— (1978a) 'Islam in the Maghrib: The Problem of Modernisation', *The Maghrib Review*, Jan.–April
——— (1978b) *Northern Africa, Islam and Modernization*, London
Brosselard, Charles (1859) *Les Khouan. De la constitution des ordres religieux musulmans*, Alger, Paris
Brown, Leon Carl (1964) 'The Islamic Reformist Movement in North Africa', *Journal of Modern African Studies*, 1-1964, pp. 55-65
——— (1966) 'The Role of Islam in North Africa' in Brown, L.C. (ed.) *State and Society in Independent North Africa*, Washington, DC, pp. 97-122
Camau, Michel (1971) *la notion de démocratie dans la pensée des dirigeants maghrébins*, Paris
——— (1978) *Pouvoirs et institutions au Maghreb*, Tunis
Carret, Jacques (1957) 'le problème de l'indépendance du culte musulman en Algérie, *L'Afrique et l'Asie*, 37, pp. 43-58. Also Imprimerie, officielle, Algiers, 1960
——— (1958) 'l'association des oulama réformistes d'Algérie', *L'Afrique et l'Asie*, 43, 1958
——— (1959) *Différents aspects de l'Islam algérien*, Imprimerie officielle, Algiers
Chaliand, Gérard and Minces, Juliette (1972) *l'Algérie indépendante: Billan d'une*

révolution nationale, Paris

Charnay, Jean-Paul (1965) *la vie musulmane en Algérie d'après la jurisprudence de la première moitié du XX Siècle*, Paris

——— (1977) *Sociologie religieuse de l'Islam*, Paris

Charte Nationale (1976) FLN, Alger, Editions Populaires de l'Armée

Chikh, Slimane (1975) *La révolution algérienne. Projet et action (1954-1962)*, thesis, Doctorate in Political Science, Grenoble

Coleman, James S. (1971) 'The Development Syndrome: differentiation–equality–capacity' in Binder, Coleman *et al.*, see above

Collot, Claude and Henry, Jean-Robert (1978) *Le mouvement national algérien. Textes 1912-1954*, Paris

Colonna, Fanny (1974) 'Cultural Resistance and Religious Legitimacy in Colonial Algeria', *Economy and Society*, 3, 3, pp. 232-52

——— (1975) *Instituteurs algériens, 1883-1939*, Paris

——— (1977) 'les débuts de l'Islah dans l'Aurès: 1936-1938', *Revue algérienne des sciences juridiques économiques et politiques*, 2, pp. 277-87

Confluent: Comment les musulmans du Maghreb comprennent, vivent et pratiquent l'Islam? June–July 1964

Cooley, John K. (1967) *Baal, Christ and Mohammed: Religion and Revolution in North Africa*, New York

Coppolani, Xavier (1894) *La confrérie musulmane de Sidi Amar Bou Senna ou l'Ammaria en 1893*, Algiers (see also Depont)

Cote, Marc (1977) *Mutations rurales dans les hautes plaines de l'Est algérien*, thesis, Doctorate in Geography, University of Nice

Cour, Auguste (1921) 'Recherches sur l'état des confréries religieuses musulmanes dans le communes de Oum el Bouaghi, Aïn Beida, Sedrata, Soukh-Aras, Morsott, Tebessa, Meskiana et Khenchela', *Revue Africaine*, pp. 85-139, 291-334

Dabbūz, Muhammad Ali (1965) *Nahdat al-Jazāir al-Hadīta wa ta wratuha al-Mubāraka*, Algiers, 3 vol., 1965-9

Damis, John (1974) 'The Free-school Phenomenon: The Cases of Tunisia and Algeria', *International Journal of Middle East Studies*, 5-1974, pp. 434-49

Danziger, Raphael (1974) *Abd al-Qādir and The Algerians: Resistance to the French and Internal Consolidation (1832-1839)*, Princeton, PhD thesis (published, New York, London, 1977)

Daumas, G.E. (1855) *Moeurs et coutumes de l'Algérie*, Tell, Kabylie, Sahara

——— (1869) *la vie arabe et la société musulmane*, Paris

——— (1971) *The Ways of the Desert*, 9th edn, translated from the French by Sheila M. Ohlendorf, Austin, London

Delpech, A. (1874) 'la zaouia de Sidi Ali Ben Moussa en Ali N'Founas (de la vache)', *Revue africaine*, 18, pp. 81-8

Deppont, A. and Coppolani, X. (1887) *les confréries religieuses musulmanes*, Algiers

Dermenghen, Emile (1954) *Le Culte des saints dans l'Islam maghrébin*, Paris

Desparmet, Joseph (1932) *Le mal magique*, Algiers and Paris

——— (1933a) 'Un reformateur contemporain en Algérie', *Afrique française*, March

——— (1933b) 'Deux manifestes indigènes', *Afrique française*, December

——— (1934) 'les manifestations en Algérie (1933-1934)', *l'Afrique française*, September

——— (1937) 'La politique des Oulémas algériens (1911-1937), *l'Afrique française*, pp. 352-8, 523-7, 557-61

——— (1939) *Coutumes, institutions, croyances des indigènes de l'Algérie* (Translation from Arabic by Peres Henri, Bousquet, G.H.), Algiers, 1st edition in Arabic, 1905; 2nd, 1913; *la vie religieuse (Complément au cours de sociologie de M. Bousquet) Extraits du Tome II*, Centre de formation islamique, Algiers

Doutté, Edmond (1899) 'Notes sur l'Islam maghrébin: les Marabouts', *Revue d'histoire des religions*, 1899, pp. 343-69; and 1900, pp. 22-66, 289-336
——— (1900a) *L'Islam algérien en 1900*, Algiers
——— (1900b) *Les Aissaoua de Tlemcen*, Chalons sur Marne
——— (1908) *La société musulmane du Maghrib. Magie et religion dans l'Afrique du Nord*, Algiers
Duff Gordon, Lady (1845) *The French in Algiers. I. The Soldier of the Foreign Legion (Clemens Lamping); II. The Prisoners of Abd-el-Kader (M. de France)*, New York
Eberhardt, Isabelle and Barrucand, Victor (1906) *Dans l'ombre chaude de l'Islam*, Paris
Eisenstadt, S.N. (1964) 'Social Change, Differentiation and Evolution', *American Political Science Review*
——— (ed.) (1968) *Comparative Perspectives on Social Change*, Boston
——— (1973) *Traditional Patrimonialism and Modern Neo Patrimonialism*, Beverly Hills
Emerit, Marcel (1951) *L'Algérie à l'époque d'Abdel Kader*, Paris
——— (1961) 'L'état d'ésprit des musulmane d'Algérie de 1847 à 1870', *Revue d'histoire moderne*, Apr.–May 1961, pp. 103-20
Encyclopaedia of Islam (1st edn., H.A.R. Gibb *et al.*; 2nd edn, B. Lewis *et al.*, 1965)
Estailleur-Chanteraine, Philippe d' (1947) *Abd el-Kader; l'Europe et l'Islam au XIX siècle*, Paris
——— (1959) *L'Emir magnanime. Abd-el-Kader le croyant*, Paris
Etienne, Bruno (1973) 'le vocabulaire de légitimité en Algérie, *Annuaire de l'Afrique du Nord 1971*
——— (1975) (with Leca, Jean) 'la politique culturelle de l'Algérie', *Annuaire de l'Afrique du Nord*, 1973
——— (1977) *Algérie: cultures et révolution*, Paris
Fanon, Frantz (1965a) *The Wretched of the Earth*, New York (translated from the French *les damnés de la terre*, Paris, 1963)
——— (1965b) *Studies in a Dying Colonialism* (translated from the French *Sociologie d'une révolution l'an V de la révolution algérienne*, Paris)
Faouzi, Adel (1978) 'Islam, réformisme et nationalisme dans la résistance à la colonisation française en Algérie (1830-1930)', *Social Compass*, 3-4
Faure, Adolphe (1969) 'Islam in North West Africa (Maghrib)' in A.J. Aberry (ed.) *Religion in the Middle East*, 2nd vol., London
Flory, Maurice and Mantran, Robert (1968) *Les régimes politiques des pays arabes*, Paris
Fournier, P. (1967) 'l'Etat d'Abdel Kader et sa puissance en 1841, d'après le rapport du sous-intendant militaire Massat', *Revue d'histoire moderne et contemporaine*, Apr.–June 1967, pp. 123-57
Francos, Ania and Séréni, Jean-Pierre (1976) *Un Algérien nommé Boumediene*, Paris
Gallissot, René (1964) 'La guerre d'Abdel Kader ou la ruine de la nationalité algérienne (1839-1847)', *Hespéris-Tamuda*, pp. 119-41
——— (1965) 'Abdel Kader et la nationalité algérienne. Interprétation de la chute de la Régence d'Alger et des premières résistances à la conquête française (1830-1839)', *Revue historique*, 2-1965, pp. 339-68
——— (1976) *Marx, Marxisme et Algérie. Textes de Marx-Engels*, Paris
Gardet, Louis (1946) 'Islam et démocratie', *Revue Thomiste*, 2-1946, pp. 279-321; 3-4, pp. 497-530
——— (1969) *La Cité musulmane, vie politique et sociale*, 3rd edn, Paris
Gaudry, Mathéa (1961) *La société féminine au Djebel Amour et au Ksel; étude de sociologie rurale nord-africaine*, Algiers

Geertz, Clifford (1963) (ed.) *Old Societies and New States*, New York
——— (1967) 'Politics Past, Politics Present', *Archives européennes de sociologie*, 1-1967
——— (1968) *Islam Observed*, Religious Development in Morocco and Indonesia, New Haven
——— (1977) 'The Judging of Nations. Some comments on the assessment of regimes in the new states', *Archives européennes de sociologie*
Gellnèr, Ernest (1963) 'Sanctity, Puritanism, Secularization and nationalism in North Africa: A Case Study', *Archives de Sociologie des Religions*, pp. 71-86
——— (1967) 'Democracy and industrialization', *Archives européennes de sociologie*, 1-1967
——— (1968) 'A pendulum swing theory of Islam', *Annales marocaines de sociologie*, pp. 5-14; also in Robertson (ed.) *Sociology of Religion*, London, 1969
——— (1969) *Saints of the Atlas*, London (formerly a thesis, under the title *The Role and Organization of a Berber zawiya*)
——— (1972) (and Micaud, Charles) (eds.) *Arabs and Berbers: From Tribe to Nation in North Africa*, London, Lexington
——— (1973) 'Post-Traditional Forms of Islam; the Turf and Trade, and Votes and Peanuts', *Deadalus*, Winter
——— (1974) 'The Unknown Apollo of Biskra: The Social Base of Algerian Puritanism', *Government and Opposition*, summer 1974, pp. 277-310
——— (1977) 'Patrons and Clients' in Gellner and Waterbury, John *Patrons and Clients*, London
——— (1979) 'Rulers and tribesmen', *Middle Eastern Studies*, 1-1979, pp. 106-13
Gendzier, Irene L. (1978) 'Algeria and Modernization', *Government and Opposition*, 2-1978, pp. 247-58
Gillespie, Joan (1966) *Algeria, Rebellion 2nd Revolution*, New York
Gordon, David C. (1966) *The Passing of French Algeria*, London, New York
——— (1968) *Women of Algeria: An Essay on Change*, Cambridge, Mass.
Gourdon, Hubert (1979) 'Citoyen, travailleur, frère: la deuxième constitutionnalisation du système politique algérien', *Développements politiques au Maghreb*, Paris, pp. 99-121
Guernier, Eugène (1950) *la Berbérie, l'Islam et la France*, 2 vol., Paris
'Habous et Ministères des Habous en Afrique du Nord depuis les indépendances', *Maghreb*, Etudes et Documents, nov.-dec. 1971, pp. 39-44
Hadj-Sadok, Mohammed (1978) 'De la théorie à la pratique des prescriptions de l'Islam en Algérie contemporaine', *Social Compass*, 3-4/1978
Haim, Sylvia (1962) *Arab nationalism. An Anthology*, Berkeley, Los Angeles
Halpern, Manfred (1963) *The Politics of Social Change in the Middle East and North Africa*, Princeton
Hanoteau, Gal. and Letourneux (1873) *la Kabylie et les coutumes kabyles*, Paris, (3 vol., 2nd edn 1893)
Harbi, Mohamed (1975) *Aux origines du FLN. le populisme révolutionnaire en Algérie*, Paris
Heggoy, Alf Andrew (1972) *Insurgency and Counterinsurgency in Algeria*, Bloomington
Hermassi, El Baki (1972) *Leadership and National Development in North Africa*, Berkeley
——— (1973) 'Political Traditions of the Maghrib', *Daedalus*, 1-1973, pp. 207-24
Hudson, Michael C. (1977) *Arab Politics, the Search for Legitimacy*, New Haven
Huntington, S.P. (1968) *Political Order in Changing Societies*, New Haven
Hutchinson, Martha C. (1978) *Revolutionary Terrorism: The FLN in Algeria, 1954-1962*, Stanford
Ibrahimi, Muhammad Bāsir al- (1963) *'Uyūn al Basā'ir*, Cairo

Joly, Alexandre (1906) 'Etude sur les Chadouliyas', *Revue africaine*, 50, pp. 336-47; 'Saints et légendes de l'Islam', *Revue africaine*, 57, pp. 7-26

Julien, Charles-André (1964) *Histoire de l'Algérie contemporaine. Conquête et colonisation*, Paris

——— (1972) (2nd edn) *l'Afrique du Nord en marche. Nationalismes musulmans et souveraineté française*, Paris

Kaid, Ahmed (1970) *Contradictions de classes et contradictions au sein des masses*, Algiers

Kautsky, John (1972) *The Political Consequences of Modernization*, New York

Kerr, Malcolm H. (1972) 'Socialisme révolutionnaire et tradition islamique', in *Renaissance du monde arabe*, Gembloux and Algiers, pp. 427-34

Khalid, Detlev H. 'The Phenomenon of Re-islamization', *Aussen Politik* (English Edition), 4-1978, pp. 433-53

Knapp, Wilfrid (1977) *North West Africa: A Political and Economic Survey*, 3rd edn, Oxford (on Algeria, pp. 51-173)

Labica, Georges (1966) *Politique et religion chez Ibn Khaldun*, Algiers

Lacheraf, Mostepha (1965) *l'Aglérie, nation et société*, Paris

——— (1965) *la culture algérienne contemporaine: Essai de définition et Perspectives*, Algiers

Lacoste, Yves, Nouschi, André and Prenant, André (1960) *l'Algérie, passé et présent*, Paris

Laroui, Abdallah (1967) *l'idéologie arabe contemporaine*, Pref by M. Rolinson, Paris

Lawless, Richard and Blake, Gerald (1976) *Tlemcen: Continuity and Change in an Algerian and Islamic Town*, Boulder

Layer, Ernest (1916) *Confréries religieuses musulmanes et marabouts. leur état et leur influence en Algérie*, Rouen

Lazreg, Marnia (1976) *The Emergence of Classes in Algeria: Colonialism and Socio-Political Change*, Boulder

Leca, Jean (1974) 'Rencontres d'idéologies en Algérie', *Revue des sciences religieuses*, 48, 4-1974, pp. 323-38

——— (1975a) (with Vatin, Jean-Claude), *l'Algérie politique. Institutions et régime*, Paris (see also Etienne (1975))

——— (1975b) 'Algerian Socialism: Nationalism, Industrialization and State building' in Desfosses, Helen and Levesque, Jacques, *Socialism in the Third World*, New York, pp. 121-60

——— (1979) (with Vatin, J.C.) 'le système politique algérien (1976-1978). Ideologie, institutions et changement social' in *Développements politiques au Maghreb*, Paris

Le Tourneau, Roger (1955a) 'North Africa: Rigorism and Bewilderment' in Von Grunebaum, G. (ed.) *Unity and Variety in Muslim Civilization*, Chicago

——— (1955b) 'Social Change in the Muslim Cities of North Africa', *American Journal of Sociology*, May 1955, pp. 527-35

Lewis, W.H. (1969) 'Politics and Islam in North Africa', *Current History*, March, pp. 136-40, 172-3

Lucas, Philippe (1975) (with Vatin, Jean-Claude) *l'Algérie des anthropologues*, Paris

——— (1979) *Problèmes de la transition au socialisme. le transformisme algérien*, Paris

Mammeri, Moulmoud (1977) 'Culture savante et culture vécue en Algérie', *Libya*, XXIII

Madani, Tawfiq al- (1963) *Kitāb al-Jazʾir*, 2nd edn, Cairo

Marçais, Georges (1946)*La Berbérie musulmane et l'Orient au Moyen Age*, Paris

Marçais, Philippe 'Moslem Civilization' in Dore, Ogrigek (ed.) *North Africa*, New York, pp. 59-84

Marx, Karl and Engels, Friedrich (1944) *On Religion*, Intro. by Reinhold Niebur,

New York
Massignon, Louis (1929) 'Tariqa', *Encyclopaedia of Islam*, 1st edn, IV, pp. 700-5
Mazouni, Abdallah (1969) *culture et enseignement en Algérie et au Maghreb*, Paris
Merad, Ali (1963) 'L'enseignement politique de Muhammad Abduh aux Algériens', *Orient*, 4-1963, pp. 75-123
——— (1967) *Le reformisme musulman en Algérie de 1925 à 1940. Essai d'histoire religieuse et sociale*, Paris
——— (1969) 'Islam et nationalisme arabe en Algérie la veille de la première guerre mondiale', *Oriente-Moderno*, April–May 1969, pp. 213-22
——— (1971) *Ibn Badis, Commentateur du Coran*, Paris
——— (1978) 'Ben Badis (1889-1940) ou la fondation du mouvement réformiste orthodoxe en Algérie', *les Africains*, pp. 89-125
Mercier, Ernest (1869) *les khouans de Sidi Abd el-Kader el Djilali*, Algiers
Mili, Muhammad al (1973) *Ibn Bādīs wa'urūbat al jazā'ir*, Beirut
Miltoun, Francis and McManus, Blanche (1908) *In the Land of Mosques and Minarets*, Boston
Miner, H.M. and Devos, G. (1960) *Oasis and Casbah: Algerian Culture and Personality in Change*, Ann Arbor, Anthropological papers, 15
Moore, Clement-Henry (1970) *Politics in North Africa: Algeria, Morocco and Tunisia*, Boston
——— (1974) 'Old and New Elites in North Africa: The French Colonial Impact in Comparative Perspective' in *Les influences occidentales dans les villes maghrébines à l'époque contemporaine*, Aix-en-Provence, pp. 17-37
Murati, P. (1937) 'Le maraboutisme ou la naissance d'une famille ethnique de la région de Tebessa', *Revue africaine*, pp. 256-315
Nadir, Ahmed (1967) *le mouvement réformiste algérien. Son rôle dans la formation de l'idéologie nationale*, thesis, faculty of letters, Paris
——— (1972) 'les ordres religieux et la conquête française (1830-1851)', *Revue algérienne des sciences juridiques*, 4-1972, pp. 819-72
——— (1976) 'le maraboutisme superstition ou révolte', *l'Algérien en Europe*, 16 July and 1 August
Nellis, J.R. (1977) 'Socialist Management in Algeria' *Journal of Modern African Studies*, 154-1977, pp. 529-54
Neveu, Capitaine de (1845) *Les khouan. Ordes religieux chez les musulmans de l'Algérie*, Paris
Noellat, Col. (1882) *l'Algérie en 1882*, Paris
Nouschi, André (1960) see Lacoste, Y.
——— (1962) *La naissance du nationalisme algérien, 1914-1954*, Paris
Ottaway, David and marina (1970) *Algeria: The Politics of a Socialist Revolution*, Berkeley
Perès, Henri (1957) 'le mouvement réformiste, en Algérie et l'influence de l'orient d'après la presse arabe d'Algérie', *Entretiens sur l'évolution des pays de civilisation arabe*, I, Paris
Pommerol, Mme J. (1902) 'l'Islam saharien. Chez ceux qui guettent', *Journal d'un témoin*, Paris
Quandt, William (1969) *Algeria: Revolution and Political Leadership, 1954-1968*, Cambridge, Mass.
——— (1972) 'The Berbers in the Algerian Political Elite' in Gellner, Ernest and Micaud, Charles (1972), pp. 285-303
Richard, Cdt. (1846) *Étude sur l'insurrection du Dahra (1845-1846)*, Alger
——— (1848a) *Du gouvernement arabe et de l'institution qui doit l'exercer*, Algiers
——— (1848b) *Scènes de moeurs arabes*, Paris
——— (1850) *De la civilisation du peuple arabe*, Paris
Rinn, Louis (1884) *Marabouts et khouan. Etude sur l'Islam en Algérie*, Algiers

——— (1891) *Histoire de l'insurrection de 1871 en Algérie*, Algiers
Roches, Léon (1884) *Dix ans à travers l'Islam, 1834-1844*, Paris
Rodinson, Maxime (1966) *Islam et capitalisme*, Paris (*Islam and Capitalism*, transl. by B. Pearce, New York, 1974)
——— (1972) 'l'Islam et les nouvelles indépendances' in *Marxism et monde musulman*, Paris
Rondot, Pierre (1958) *L'Islam et les musulmans d'aujourd'hui*, Paris
——— (1962) 'L'Algérie de demain et l'Islam', *Documents Nord-Africains*, 6 August
——— (1966) 'Vers une nouvelle inflexion du réformisme musulman en Algérie', *L'Afrique et l'Asie*, 75
Rosenthal, Erwin I.J. (1965) *Islam in the Modern National State*
——— (1967) 'Politics in Islam', *Muslim World*, 1-1967, pp. 3-10
Saadallah, Belkacem (1965) *The Rise of Algerian Nationalism 1900-1930*, thesis. PhD, University of Minnesota
——— (1923) *l'Islam et la psychologie du musulman*, Paris
Schaar, Stuart (1968) 'Reflections on Algeria's Crisis of Participation', *AUFS Reports*, North Africa series, 1-1968, pp. 1-19
Servier, André (1913) *Le péril de l'avenir, le nationalisme musulman en Egypte, en Tunisie,en Algérie*, Constantine
Shinar, Pessah (1961) 'Ibadiyya and Orthodox Reformism in Modern Algeria', *Scripta Hierosolymitana* (Jerusalem) 9, pp. 97-120
——— (1965) 'Abd al-Qadir and Abd al-Krim. Religious Influences of Their Thought and Action', *Asian and African Studies* (Jerusalem), 1, 1965, pp. 139-74
——— (1967) 'Some Observations on Ethical Teachings of Orthodox Reformism in Algeria', *Foreign Affairs Research Series*, no. 5888.
——— (1971) 'The Historical Approach of the Reformist "Ulama" in the Contemporary Maghrib', *Asian and African Studies*, Jerusalem, 7, 1971, pp. 181-210
——— (1977) 'Traditional and Reformist Mawlid Celebrations in the Maghrib', *Studies in Memory of Gaston Wiet*, (ed.) by Rosen-Ayalon, M., Jerusalem, pp. 371-413
Shoemaker, M.M. (1910) *Islam Lands. Nubia, The Sudan, Tunisia, Algeria*, New York, London
Simian, Marcel (1910) *les confréries islamiques en Algérie (Rhamanya-Tidjanya)*, Algiers
Sivers, Peter von (1973) 'The Realm of Justice: Apocalyptic Revolts in Algeria (1849-1870)', *Humanoria Islamica*, 1-1973, pp. 47-60
——— (1979) 'Colonial Elites and Nationalist Politics: The Analysis of Algerian Political and Social Class Structures', *Archives européennes de sociologie*, XX, 1979, pp. 142-8
Smith, Tony (1978) *The French Stake in Algeria, 1945-1962*, Ithaca, NY
Souriau, Christiane (1975) 'L'arabisation en Algérie' in *Introduction à l'Afrique du nord contemporaine*, Centre de Recherches et d'Etudes sur les sociétés Méditerranéennes, Paris, pp. 357-97
Suliman, Hassan Sayed (1976) *Les fondements idéologiques du pouvoir politique au Maghreb*, thesis, doctorate in political science, faculty of law, Aix-en-Provence, 2 vol.
Talibi, Ammar at- (ed.) (1968) *Ibn Bādīs: Hayātuhu wa ataruhu*, Algiers, 4 vol.
Temps Modernes, 375 bis, Octobre 1977, '*Du Maghreb*'
Tillion, Germaine (1957) *l'Algérie en 1957*, Paris (*Algeria. The Realities*, New York, 1958)
Trumelet, C. (1881) *Les saints de l'Islam, légendes hagiologiques et croyances musulmanes algériennes. Les saints du Tell*, Paris

——— (1884) *Etudes sur les régions sahariennes. Histoire de l'insurrection des Ouled Sidi-Ech-Chikh (Sud Algérien) de 1864 à 1880*, Algiers

Turin, Yvonne (1971) *Affrontements culturels dans l'Algérie coloniale. Ecole, médicine, religions, 1830-1880*, Paris

Turner, Bryan (1974) *Weber and Islam: Critical Study*, London

——— (1978) 'Orientalism, Islam and Capitalism', *Islam and Society, Social Compass*, 3-4, 1978

Valin, Raymond (1964) 'Socialisme musulman en Algérie', *l'Afrique et l'Asie*, 2-1964, pp. 21-42, 1-1965, pp. 14-32; (English translation in Zartman, William (ed.) *Man, State and Society in the Contemporary Maghrib*, New York, 1973, pp. 50-64)

Vandevelde, Hélène (1972) *La Participation des femmes algériennes à la vie politique et sociale*, thesis, political science, Algiers

Vatikiotis, P.J. (1966) 'Tradition and Political Leadership: The Example of Algeria', *Middle Eastern Studies*, July 1966; also in Zartman, William (ed.) (1973), pp. 309-29

Vatin, Jean-Claude (1970) 'L'Algérie en 1830. Essai d'interprétation des recherches historiques sous l'angle de la science politique', *Revue algérienne des sciences juridiques*, 4-1970, pp. 977-1058

——— (1972) 'Conditions et formes de la dominiation coloniale en Algérie, 1919-1945', *Revue algérienne*, 4-1972, Paris

——— (1974) *l'Algérie, histoire et société*, Paris

——— (1975) (ed.) *Culture et société au Maghreb*, Paris; see also Leca, J. and Lucas, P.

——— (1977) 'Sur l'approche des mouvements nationaux maghrébins en général et sur l'Algérie des années 1930 en particulier', *Revue algérienne*, 2-1977

Viratelle, Gérard (1970) *Algérie algérienne*, Paris

Waardenburg, Jacques (1978) 'Official and Popular Religion in Islam', *Social Compass*, 3-4/1978, pp. 315-41

Zanattacci, R. (1938) *Les confréries religieuses en Algérie*, Cheam Conference, 20 June 1938, Paris

Zartman, I. William (1963) *Government and Politics in Northern Africa*, New York

——— (1970) 'The Islamic Impact on Socio-Political Change in Algeria', *Foreign Affairs, Research Series*, no. 11794, Washington, DC, Dept. of State, mimeo.

——— (1973) (ed.) *Man State and Society in the Contemporary Maghrib*, New York

——— (1975) 'Algeria: A Post-Revolutionary Elite' in Tachau, Frank (ed.) *Political Elites and Political Development in the Middle East*, New York, pp. 255-92

9 ISLAM AND POWER IN BLACK AFRICA

Donal B. Cruise O'Brien

Introduction: a Mystical Religion?

The ancient tradition of Sufism in Islam is generally associated with ecstatic devotional practices and perhaps with heterodox beliefs, but in black Africa Sufism (in its brotherhood form) may properly be understood as a vehicle for the mass inculcation of a form of Sunni orthodoxy by a literate and learned few. Islamic 'brotherhoods' today still command the devotional allegiances (especially in the rural areas) of the vast majority of black Africa's Muslim population. Each brotherhood (*ṭarīqa*, or 'way') is devotionally distinct in its adoption of a particular additional prayer formula (*wird* or *dhikr*), but such prayers (individual or communal) amount to no more than the repetition of a few simple, conventionally pious phrases. It is therefore on the whole misleading (in most instances) to identify the African *ṭarīqa* as 'mystical'. No African sufi has emulated the theological audacity of the great oriental mystic Al Hallaj — 'Oh God, I have searched for you and I have discovered myself. I am God.'

In the Beginning was the Word

The sacred Arabic script is the initial medium through which the pagan peoples of black Africa came into contact with the world of Islam. Magical properties were ascribed to the written word: the travelling Muslim salesmen of written amulets were familiar figures to pagan peoples centuries before most were ready to adopt Islam as their own religion. The written word could also serve the profane purposes of pagan rulers (court correspondence, records) or of long-distance (notably trans-Saharan) traders. We know that Islam, for these among other reasons, was a familiar presence in much of sub-Saharan West Africa at least as early as the fifteenth century AD. Muslim believers, or devout practitioners, may have been few south of the Senegal river valley, but Islam was widely known, respected (and feared) for hundreds of years before the mass adoption of Muslim belief and practice in the eighteenth and nineteenth centuries.

And the Way Followed the Word

The *ṭarīqa* (especially Qadiriyya and Tijaniyya) was the organisational medium for the diffusion of Muslim belief and practice — diffusion from the learned *zawiya* elite to the mass of newly recruited disciples. The doctrinal links of the *ṭarīqa* with spiritual genealogies stretching to Fez or to Baghdad and with corporate solidarities extending widely through the world of Islam, allowed for the construction of new and broader solidarities in a social world already penetrated by outside forces. The *ṭarīqa* could transcend the local and familial boundaries of pre-existent pagan religion. A gradual process, to be sure (*zawiya* often on pagan sites, 'saint-worship' or popular anthropolatry directed to Muslim holy men), but *ṭarīqa* did permit a limited, circumscribed, popular adherence to the Islamic community. 'Scripturalism' was possible only for a learned, literate few, with rote learning (the recitation of a few Qur'ānic verses) for the illiterate many. The way provided a structure in which the many disciples were taught to seek guidance (on all matters, but firstly sacred ones) from the saintly, learned, few. The disciple might not himself aspire to literacy, but he learned to venerate the authority of those in the *ṭarīqa* who appeared at least to command the skills of Arabic literacy.

Militant Islam

The late eighteenth and nineteenth centuries witnessed the popularisation of new and more rigorous standards of Muslim identity. *Jihad* movements were launched against pagans or against those judged to be no more than nominal Muslims (Futa Jallon, Fulani/Hausaland, etc.). Organisation of the *jihad* had important trans-tribal features, either in a multi-ethnic composition of the sacred army or in the enforced incorporation of new tribes to a newly-puritanical Islam. The organisational medium of religious militancy remained the *ṭarīqa* (especially Tijaniyya in the nineteenth century) and novelty less in sacred doctrine than in insistence that ancient standards be observed (regular prayer, fasting, abstinence from forbidden foods or alcoholic drinks). Attraction of the sacred army lay of course not only in spiritual revival but also in the plunder, subjugation and enslavement of pagans (or semi-pagans). The armed *ṭarīqa* enjoyed the advantages of superior organisation as well as commitment to a transcendent sacred purpose. By the late nineteenth century, that is by the time of European conquest, most of West Africa north of the tropical forest had already joined the world of Islam. And holy war was only, in a desperate last resort, directed against the encroaching European Nazarene.

The Peril of Islam? European Attitudes to Islam at the Time of Colonial Occupation

European mistrust was initially based on some notable instances of armed Muslim resistance in the late nineteenth century, and later concentrated by fears that the Ottoman caliphate might successfully arouse the whole Muslim world against France and Britain in a pan-Islamic revolt. Subsequently, amateur Franco-British alarmism was countered by the reassuring advice of administrators with professional experience of Muslim affairs — Lugard in Nigeria, Arnaud (*et al.*) in French West Africa. European rulers had very quickly learned to live with the *ṭarīqa*, as the *ṭarīqa* had adjusted to alien rule. Many shared interests were involved.

For a World Market, a World Religion? Colonial Rule and the Consolidation of Islam

The modern state in its colonial form established an institutional framework which allowed the *ṭarīqa* new possibilities of expansion. Enforced peace disarmed pagan resistance to Muslim proselytisation. New communications facilities (road and rail) brought the travelling salesmen of Islam together with the trade goods of commercial Europe. And the sacred message met a receptive audience with the spreading market economy and the lessening viability of self-isolated subsistence communities. All this is well enough known (documented) for West Africa, but recent research on colonial Tanganyika further proves the point (from a tiny, coastal trading Muslim minority at the time of German conquest to a 40 per cent Muslim proportion of total population by independence: of the

Muslim total, some 70 per cent affiliated to the Qadiriyya order). At the level of belief, a divinity claiming world power offered some psychic reassurance to people coming under the influence of mysterious alien realities. Locally based pagan belief systems were gradually overwhelmed. A model of such instances can be seen with reference to southern Senegal — the spirit *ufann*, since unseen, retreats into the forest upon the arrival of export agriculture, because he prefers palm wine to the smell of petrol. Allah displaces *ufann* (three-quarters of local population turn to Islam within 15 years of thc arrival of peanut farming), but Allah as mediated by the *ṭarīqa* because that form of Islam was already locally familiar and available. Islam had long been the religion of long-distance trade, providing among other things a moral community for those professionally engaged in trade between remote communities (medieval trans-Saharan trade, colonially redirected to the coast). Islam was capable of adjustment to the colonially sponsored redirection, and to the substantial increase in the scale of trade (prodded by taxes and facilitated by transport). The *ṭarīqa* could also adjust to the new demand for agricultural products, setting the disciples to work partly in the sacred service of their religious guides.

The Nazarene and the Zawiya

European colonial policy did more than establish a framework within which Islam could flourish. Colonial policy (at first somewhat hesitantly, and often inadvertently) positively encouraged the further diffusion of Islam and the institutional consolidation of the Sufi order. Thinly staffed colonial administrations found it useful, sometimes even necessary, to have African intermediaries who could command widespread popular allegiance. And the word (or script) was here again a crucial resource: Muslim intermediaries allowed administrative recourse to a written law (handily translated) as well as a standardised (or standardisable) pattern of authority through the *ṭarīqa*. True, occasional measures were taken to restrict the diffusion of Islam (especially around the time of the First World War) but such measures were half-hearted in application (Governor-General Ponty's policy in 1915 of discontinuing the appointment of Muslim chiefs in pagan areas of French West Africa) and sometimes merely ludicrous in inspiration (in German East Africa in 1913, the proposed importation of pigs in the hope that the African subjects would prefer pork to Islam).

The *ṭarīqa* could offer the colonial government a parallel governing hierarchy. This discovery was first made by France in Algeria (1890s) following Turkish precedent. The *ṭarīqa* could help to keep the colonial peace, collect taxes, provide military volunteers — help at a price, freedom from administrative harassment (and therefore some protection for its disciples). Most Sufi orders came to collaborate willingly, even enthusiastically, with European rulers: the outstanding example, Qadiriyya in northern Nigeria, where emirates originating from *jihād* were fully incorporated into colonial government. Divisions within and between Sufi orders in many cases also facilitated European conquest (Tijaniyya vs. Qadiriyya in Algeria). Few orders attempted a concerted withdrawal from colonial domain (Hajj Umar's branch of Tijaniyya in West Africa), Sanusiyya being particularly (wrongly?) distrusted by France. By making administrative use of the Sufi order, did the Europeans reconstitute (consolidate) the institutional structure of the *ṭarīqa*? 'Brotherhood' evolved as a census category, delimitation of geographical spheres of influence, consolidation of hierarchies and emulation of colonial institutions. From 'order' to 'brotherhood' (but the local lodge cluster within the brotherhood — untranslatable *zawiya* — remains the institutional core). *Zawiya* south of Sahara (unlike, e.g., Algeria) remains at the centre of rural economic change (market agriculture, trade): a flexible, multi-functional institution — monastery, school, inn, market and more.

Promises Sacred and Profane

Within and around the *zawiya* (which is within the Sufi brotherhood, which in turn holds itself to be within the orthodox world of *Sunni* Islam) the disciple is promised much by his sacred, literate, superiors. First he is assured preferential access to paradise, at the price of unquestioning obedience to the *shaykh*. He must (within his means) observe the devotional requirements of Islam, to which each brotherhood adds a few requisite prayer formulas (*wird*, *dhikr*). At a popular level, devotion to the *zawiya*'s sacred few may take heterodox forms ('saint-worship', magical powers imputed to the learned, miracles, spirits, mystical properties of saintly *baraka*). The enthusiasm (and excesses) of popular Sufi Islam can none the less be seen to teach respect for (adulation of) the mysterious gift of literacy.

Literacy has abundant uses for the *zawiya* elite, starting from the mass recognition of authority mediated by the Arabic script. It furnishes the elite with economic tribute (periodic labour services, cash payments, remunerative pilgrimages to saintly tombs) and political deference (quasi-legal arbitration, mediation with state authority).

Authentically aristocratic, the *zawiya* (and brotherhood) elite acts effectively enough to justify popular allegiance in this world — encouraging mass adjustment to changing economic and political realities (including partial protection from the socially disruptive impact of world economy and the modern state). Such social security as is available in the rural world is provided by the *zawiya*. The exploitation and protection in the saint/disciple relation is popularly perceived above all as protection.

Islamic Nationality and the Brotherhoods

The saints' promises include more than paradise in the hereafter, or protection in the present, but also offer the vision of enhanced communal dignity through participation in the total community of the world of Islam. The *umma* may commonly be dimly enough perceived as a global entity, but (a) Islam did provide a popular identity gratifyingly impenetrable to the arrogant European coloniser (vanity or non-existence of Christian missionary efforts in Muslim territory), and (b) Islam in Sufi brotherhood form provided negro black Africa with its own black Muslim leadership, escaping the wounding arrogance of Arab domination.

Brotherhood Islam was thus a balm to the wounded pride of conquered black Africa — long before territorial nationalism, and still today with deeper roots in the popular consciousness. The Muslim brotherhood, via the *zawiya* and the *shaykh*, reduced the perceived extent of the Islamic world, giving a form of priesthood to the faithful. But the brotherhood did also allow some indirect (and even direct, the *hajj* to Mecca for a privileged few) perception of the total world of Islam. Notions of participation in a global religious movement effectively gave added prestige to the brotherhoods (disregard or scorn for brotherhoods in the modern Arab world being largely unperceived). Islam as a universal nation — those who speak Arabic become Arabs — is seen as a difficult but possible aspiration.

A World Divided: Competition and the Muslim Brotherhoods

The brotherhood and the *zawiya* have long thrived on competition, at a local level in the arbitration (at a price) of segmentary conflicts of agricultural/pastoral societies (rights to transhumance or cultivation), at a colonial level in mediating between varied African societies and an alien government. Colonial rule by its (hesitant) introduction of the modern state importantly contributed to the full efflorescence of Muslim brotherhoods in this regard: advantages of having an incontrovertible territorial unit within which to compete and thus have a closely defined social competition to arbitrate. Competition between brotherhoods (notably Qadiriyya/Tijaniyya) was already a salient feature of West Africa in the pre-colonial nineteenth century, and competition between and within brotherhood segments was endemic to local Islam. In addition, some new brotherhoods appeared specifically in response to colonial or post-colonial political situations (Mourides in Senegal, Umariyya in northern Nigeria). West African brotherhoods very seldom (never?) question the existence of the modern state (why should they?) collecting tribute from the subject/disciples at the same time as subsidies and perquisites from the secular rulers. They pretend to be policemen in such a manner as to be popularly regarded as protectors against police authority. Brotherhoods very rarely aspire themselves to constitute a sovereign state (Sanusiyya being an exception), among other reasons because they are unable to constitute a viably united political force. Brotherhoods indeed need the modern state just as the countryside needs the town (albeit with much friction and distrust) in the modern market economy. They thrive on a recognised plural principle, while also lacking the requisite training to assume full control of the modern state.

A World Threatened? The Shadow of Islamic Reform

With the north-west African Maghreb in mind, indeed when viewing reformist currents in the entire contemporary world of Islam, one might expect some reassertion of fundamental Islamic ideals in black Africa. Islam was after all originally diffused south of the Sahara by north African (Arabo-Berber) clerics (from the eleventh century AD), and the militant Tijaniyya revival of the nineteenth century originated in Morocco: black Africa indeed still remains in a certain measure sensitive to the development of Muslim thought and practice to the north (where the reformist movement of the twentieth century has centrally involved a determined, concerted, and on the whole successful assault on the Sufi Muslim brotherhoods). Reform on the Maghreb model originated in the towns, among the Arabic literati (scripturalists), and it may therefore be an ominous portent for black Africa's Sufi brotherhoods to see the general and rapid growth of towns and cities south of the Sahara. Yet, although the fundamentalist current is indeed marginally present in black African Islam (the Wahabiyya, and indeed the Ahmadiyya) one may reasonably be reserved as to its prospects for general extension in the foreseeable future. If the word was in the beginning, so also in the end: the Arabic of the Qur'ān could be 'rediscovered' (systematically taught and diffused) for example by Ben Badis and his associates in colonial Algeria, and used as linguistic medium for their propaganda attack on the previously dominant local Sufi brotherhoods — now accused of having introduced a whole range of heterodox (even heretical) beliefs and practices which had polluted the original purity of Islam (saint worship, sacred tombs, obscurantism in the unwillingness or incapacity of Sufi teachers to teach the language and true content of the Qur'ān, encouragement of popular magic, etc.). But north African reformers (*salafiyya*) could make the return to the Qur'ān a practical possibility: Arabic (albeit in popular dialect form) already was the language used by the majority.

This necessary condition for such Islamic revitalisation is on the whole absent in black Africa. Governing elites speak (and above all write) in the language of the European coloniser — a necessary medium for the political control of colonially demarcated territories. Among the governed masses, there is a very wide range of usually mutually unintelligible indigenous languages, with overall gains for a few vehicular languages (Wolof, Twi, Swahili, etc.) prompted by the amplification of trade and urban growth. Arabic influence is indeed present in most of these vehicular languages (especially religious terms), but such Arabic as is spoken (or written) in black Africa remains on the whole that of a minority within the brotherhood elites.

As long as this linguistic *impasse* obtains, as long as Arabic remains a *zawiya* monopoly, so long it would seem will Sufi brotherhoods remain the privileged organisations of black African Islam. Nor are the brotherhood leaders unaware of their need to demonstrate organisational flexibility in the face of continuing change (economic and political as well as religious) in the surrounding world. Not all may be as adaptable as Senegal's Mourides, partially converting the brotherhood to agrarian trade union, but the brotherhood leaders remain flexible enough to continue to command black Africa's characteristic form of Islam for the foreseeable future. And the basic reason for that, returning for inspiration to Saint John, is that the darkness still comprehendeth not the (Arabic) word.

PART FOUR:

CONCLUSION

10 ISLAMIC RESURGENCE: A CRITICAL VIEW

P.J. Vatikiotis

There is today a prevailing view that the world is witnessing a resurgence of Islam. It is therefore important to determine whether this view is justified, or well founded. In order to do so an understanding of what Islamic resurgence means is needed. Is it a revival of Islamic teachings, or is it a radical religious movement which aims at making Islam the basis of temporal power by the establishment of a theocracy? Or is it both at the same time.

The prevalent view of an Islamic resurgence has been partly forced on observers because of events in Iran, Afghanistan and Pakistan, the public utterances of several rulers and the emergence and activities of several militant religious groups and movements in other Middle Eastern countries. Thus, the Ayatollah Khomeini declares an 'Islamic Republic' in Iran, and General Zia ul-Haq in Pakistan announces the introduction of an Islamic code of law. Afghan rebels, led by their religious teachers, wage a guerilla war against the Soviet invasion of their country and their puppet government in Kabul. The rulers of Saudi Arabia, where Islam has been in power for nearly a century, call for a *jihād* (holy war) to resolve the conflict between the Arabs and Israel. The President of Egypt decrees that the sources and basis of all legislation henceforth shall be the Qur'ān and the *sharī'a* (Sacred Law). Do these developments constitute an Islamic revival? If they do, is it a revival in loyalty to Islamic values? For a broad answer, it is helpful to remember that the invocation of Islam by Muslim societies in times of crisis is not new.

An alternative view of these developments might be that we are witnessing a more vociferous, determined and, in the last decade, better-financed assertion by certain Islamic societies and movements of an Islamic cultural/political identity that wishes to distinguish itself from and challenge another, until recently, internationally-dominant imprint of world 'modernity', based on Western industrial — mainly Christian — civilisation. The financing, needless to say, comes from petroleum. But the use of emotive epithets to describe current events and trends can lead to confusion and misunderstanding. A religious revival, however, which asserts a political role for religion, constitutes a political question of the first order, since it entails essentially a power nexus and a transformation of the perception of authority in society.

There are, of course, historical antecedents and precedents for this proclivity, without necessarily going as far back as the Middle Ages, which help to identify the conditions which tend to give rise to, say, an Islamic resurgence, or, for that matter, any other resurgence. They facilitate a consideration of such questions as whether the Islamic revolution in Iran is an isolated phenomenon, whether it can occur elsewhere, and what it is a reaction to. Recent developments even suggest that those who in the last two hundred, or even thirty, years proclaimed a uniform world culture of progress, development and modernisation, based on the model of Western industrial society, have been hopelessly wrong; that all political questions are ultimately religious and not, as the Marxists assert, economic. On the other hand, they corroborate historical experience which simply underlines the inevitable periodic — and characteristic — response of humankind to major, epochal crises.

The fact remains that ever since the Islamic revolt led by the Ayatollah Khomeini overthrew the late Shah in Iran, there has been a steady preoccupation in the West over the resurgence of Islam and the Islamic revolution. There has been a great deal of writing and broadcasting about them reminiscent in some ways of an earlier Western preoccupation with the 'revival of the East' and 'resurgence of Islam' in the late nineteenth century. The preoccupation in both instances has been due in part to a feeling of potential confrontation. The stakes in both instances, though slightly different, have been high. A century ago they entailed European interests in the East, especially the Suez Canal and British imperial communications, trade and commerce. Today, they relate to the security of vital sources of energy for the West's industry, and strategic advantage in an East-West global contest. Yet the two instances suggest that there have been periodic resurgences of Islam (in Arabia in the eighteenth, in India, Egypt and the Sudan in the nineteenth, and in North Africa in the twentieth centuries), and that the present one, though possibly different in thrust and composition, is not unique or phenomenal. What makes it different is the world circumstances in which it has erupted, and the threat it poses to the stability of a strategically sensitive and important area of the world.

Much of the comment about the Islamic resurgence focuses on the Muslims' rediscovery of their religious-cultural identity, their determination to assert it in the face of an emasculating threat from the industrial civilisation of the West. Implied in this assessment is the proposition that, having tried a period of modernisation through Westernisation, the Muslims have adjudged this avenue as corrupting and therefore now reject it. Their emulation of the West has been disappointing and disastrous, for they believe it has brought upon them social dislocation and national humiliation. In any case, the emulative attempts were confined to small elites which, when in power, expanded the functions and powers of a highly centralised state at the expense of the religion and its institutions, undermined the Islamic ethic of society, and invariably allied themselves with foreign powers to the detriment of their respective societies. With much greater wealth from petroleum, it is now time, they believe, to assert the force of the Islamic ethic and presence at home and abroad. The historic consciousness as well as the perception of that history of the vast majority of the population is Islamic, comprising a glorious past which was lost with the loss of power. It has been impossible to restore that power by the adoption of Western, or European, means. It may be possible to do so by a strict adherence to the ethic and values of Islam. This seems to be the thrust of Khomeini's message in Iran, of the Muslim Brethren's and that of the various militant Islamic groups in Egypt today, or that of the self-styled madhist and radical Wahhabi group which stormed and occupied the Great Mosque in Mecca in 1979. Secular, i.e., state, power, and presumably modernising rulers have failed to cope with the problems and needs of their societies.

If this is a reasonable and plausible characterisation of the causes and motives of Islamic resurgence today, it suggests that the problem it reflects is not so much one which concerns the rest of the world, but Islamic society itself. Nor is it a new problem. Captiously defined, the Islamic revolution today is once again, as in the past, trying to resolve an internal problem: the place of Islam in the modern state, and its role in politics; or in other words, the relation of Islam to political power. To this extent it is essentially a social phenomenon. The difference from the past, however, is significant. Whereas in the past attempts at the regeneration of Islam and its claim for a leading role in the affairs of the state were led by elites of intellectuals and religious teachers, concerned with theological-philosophical disputations and religious reform, today these are carried out by militant leaders who can mobilise and directly involve the armed masses of the population. They are, in other words, populist in character and organisation, translating themselves into 'holy struggles' by 'holy warriors' against evil and corruption and the iniquities of their own rulers, as well as those of hostile outside forces. All evil and corruption, by definition, derives from a deviation from Islam, and conversely all good and progress flow from the assertion of the supremacy of Islam. The dichotomy is simple and exclusive, and therefore revolutionary.

Islam as a Social Force

Although the countries with a predominantly Muslim population are organised into nation-states, Islam has been a potent social force, providing the basis of social cohesion for the majority of their communities, especially the rural ones, and serving as a ready mobilising and unifying agent in the hands of rulers in times of national crisis. At the same time, however, over the last 150 years, Islam, the faith and the law, have been relentlessly relegated to minor roles in the conduct of the affairs of state and of economic and international affairs. This, despite the fact that Islam has been instrumental and played a leading role in nationalist movements of independence from foreign control. This was true in the case of the Arab societies of the Fertile Crescent before and after the Great War, the creation of Pakistan, the Algerian independence movement in the 1950s, and even in post-1952 Egypt. In domestic politics and the politics between states of the Middle Eastern region, Islam has been periodically pushed to the fore, as in Egypt in the 1920s and 1930s over the issues of the Caliphate and the British connection, in Nasser's regional policy, and in the 1960s rivalry between rulers for the leadership of the Arab world. Similarly, in confronting the outside world, there have been periodic arrangements of Islamic conferences and blocs (e.g., meetings of foreign ministers, summits). Islam, in short, remains, with varying degrees of emphasis between these states, a basis of legitimacy, a source of cultural identity and a distinguishing factor from the alien and, in Muslim eyes, often hostile, non-Islamic world.

In the eighteenth and nineteenth centuries, there were reformist Islamic revivals, such as the one in Arabia under the Wahhabis. In the late nineteenth century, there was the wider pan-Islamic movement, seeking to establish a single Islamic state, stretching from Africa to India. In the Sudan there was the revolt of the Mahdi and the Mahdiyya war. In Egypt, there appeared in 1928 the radical religio-political movement known as the Muslim Brethren, seeking to restore an orthodox Muslim state and society. All these have been distinct phenomena, with their own characteristics. What they have had in common is that they all saw the established political order as illegitimate and tyrannical because it was supposed to have deviated from Islamic norms.

In Turkey, nearly thirty years ago, dissatisfaction with 'modern-secular' government was a protest against Atatürk's dictatorial coercion of the Turks to abandon Islam. But recrudescent Islamic sentiment was then dexterously absorbed by new political parties for electoral purposes. Today, under Erbakan, Islamic sentiment in Turkey lies at the one extreme of the political spectrum, with the radical left at the other.

The line between a genuine belief that Islam can really be a political factor in today's world, and its use by rulers or leaders for political purposes, is rather thin. Thus, despite their other differences, the Ottoman Sultan, Abdul Hamid and the Young Turks who deposed him in the first decade of this century both affected a pan-Islamic policy for reasons of state, especially during the Turkish-Italian war over Tripoli and during the Great War. Even Turkey's Arabic-speaking subjects voiced support for their Ottoman masters in their tribulations.

When Atatürk, after the Great War, abolished the caliphate and disestablished official Islam in Turkey, the outcry among Arabic-speaking Muslims was shrill. Their attempts to re-establish the caliphate lasted a decade. (The office of caliph was originally both spiritual and temporal: in its last couple of years it was spiritual only.) The struggle was highlighted by Muslim congresses and marred by murky rivalries for this high office between the rising rulers of the new successor states to the dissolved Ottoman empire in Egypt and Arabia. When Egypt was drafting its new constitution and structuring its independent institutions, between the wars, the country had fierce debates about the right balance between secular and Islamic legislation. In the 1930s there was a crisis over what attitude to take towards Christian missionary activity. This was accompanied by the rapid rise of Muslim-oriented radical movements.

During their war against French rule, in the 1950s and 1960s, the Algerians managed to mobilise most of the population on the basis of their Muslim identity. Even the French reported the casualties among Algerian fighters as the number of 'Muslims' killed. During the invasion of Cyprus in July 1974, mainland Turkey saw an eruption of Islamic sentiment and propaganda in favour of the struggle against the infidel Greek.

In some Arab countries, particularly in the 1950s and 1960s, contests for leadership involved forming Islamic blocs against radical revolutionaries. The latter, in turn, tried to stir up Islamic feeling in support of their own brand of Arab national, or Arab socialist, revolution. The Prophet Muhammad became the first Arab socialist.

In short, historical precedents abound for the use of Islamic sentiment and tradition in political strife. In a world divided into states, and technologically as complex as ours is today, there are still practical uses for Islam. One might explore, for example, the periodic summit meetings of Islamic heads of state or foreign ministers.

Islam and the Modern World

If the ideal Islamic state is supposed to be the one established by the Prophet and his four immediate successors in the seventh century, there has always been sharp controversy ever since over whether, in fact, the Prophet did found a state. Perhaps an Islamic statc simply means limiting temporal power by the Sacred Law, the observance of Islamic tradition and the promotion of Islamic values. The difficulty here is that those who traditionally interpret the Sacred Law became subservient to the power-holders rather early in the course of Islamic history.

There was *never* an 'Islamic republic', properly speaking. The concept is self-contradictory. In strict Islamic terms, only God legislates: he did so once and for all through his Prophet Muhammad in the Qur'ān. Man-made, positive law is, if not excluded, very limited under this premise of divine sovereignty; so is secularism in the sense that nothing is final, but everything may change. No man and no group of men (for example, the people or their elected representatives) can be sovereign, because only God is sovereign. We have the case of Pakistan, which thirty years ago under Jinnah, tried to produce a constitution for an Islamic republic, and failed.

In the meantime, 150 years of relentless secular legislation to regulate the relations between the citizen and the state, public affairs and even certain areas of private conduct, have reduced the scope and jurisdiction of the Sacred Law to matters of personal status. The Sacred Law has little, if anything, to tell us about complex economic matters.

It is therefore ironic that it was relentless modernisation in the last 150 years which has politicised Islam, when secular rulers gradually took over the functions previously performed by traditional religious leaders, and when they used religion for political purposes. It is modernisation which in the last thirty years produced the new urban masses that now express their economic and political grievances in Islamic terms. These simply transported their Islamic idiom and identity from their rural origins to their new urban environment. Many of them moved from participation in traditional *popular* Islam in the countryside (religious brotherhoods) to membership in more militant *populist* religio-political movements in the cities. With their greater involvement in politics, the formulation of political demands and political life itself have become, naturally, more Islamic. Their demands are modern, while their formulation remains traditionally Islamic. They carry with them a cultural idiom which, by sheer weight of numbers, overwhelms the secular one adhered to by tiny elites. The greater the involvement of these new urban masses in politics the more intense the demand for the religious over the secular ambiance.

In the past, Islam did deal successfully with ethnically and religiously diverse societies that came under its political control. But that was under an imperial arrangement. Moreover, Islam then was mainly concerned with confronting other civilisations and cultures, chiefly Christendom, but also the Tatars and Mongols of Asia. Today, Islam is faced with the fragmentation of the Islamic community into national states. They have boundaries, separate administrations and rival interests. Islam is up against the nation-state. It is also exposed to the vagaries of super-power rivalry.

Islamic society today faces internal contradictions, too. Some of these arise from an earlier deliberate choice to move along a more or less secularist path. This essentially elitist choice was exercised against the social reality of the basically Islamic ethic of the populace. This is the reality that has always made it doubtful if 'modernity' can last. This, too, has always forced the elite to justify social and political policies in partly Islamic terms. One way and another, Islam has managed to assert itself as a social force. So it is caught in a great dilemma, one between tradition and modernity, between an Islamic value system and a positivist doctrine of modernity.

Another difficulty lies in a political reality: the religious and ethnic-based separatist movements, even nationalisms, in many Near and Middle Eastern societies. They lie behind events in several of these countries in the last fifty years, especially those in the Fertile Crescent (Iraq, Lebanon, Syria).

The thrust of the Islamic revolution in Iran, for instance, has intensified sectarian and communal conflict. The call for a strict Shīʿi Islamic state has alerted ethnic and sectarian minorities to the possible dangers such a state poses to their survival. Such are the preoccupations of the embattled Kurds, the disaffected Arabs of Khuzistan, the Jews and the Bahais in Iran. Elsewhere in the Middle East too, the general atmosphere created by these events has led to communal clashes and confrontations. Such are the recent episodes of Muslim-Coptic conflict in Egypt, and the sectarian troubles in Syria. There is a proliferation of secret militant Islamic groups of the mahdist variety, which seek to undermine existing regimes, such as *Shabab Muhammad* and *Jamaat al-takfir wa'l hijra*.

Inter-state relations are also exacerbated by calls for the spread of Islamic revolution. Khomeini, for example, has called on Muslims in other states to rise against their rulers and their foreign friends. He has branded the Baath regime in neighbouring Iraq as a usurper and the oppressor of the Shia majority in the country, and called for its overthrow.[1] He has similarly called for the overthrow of the Sadat regime in Egypt for having concluded a peace treaty with the 'enemies of Islam' (Israel) and given asylum to the deposed Shah and his family. Iranian militants have tried to involve themselves in the civil strife in Lebanon. Yet much of this attempt to extend the Iranian brand of Islamic militancy beyond Iran's frontiers is a reflection of existing political differences and conflicting interests between Iran and several other Middle Eastern states. And in any case, militant Islamic movements have existed in countries such as Egypt and the Sudan for several decades now. Their opposition to the regimes there has not been occasioned by the Iranian episode, although it may have been further encouraged by it.

Islamic Reform

To try to revive Islam, without a serious reform of its theological edifice, would be a mere restoration of an anachronistic tradition.

The attempt failed in the past, and there is no evidence that it can succeed now, despite the Ayatollah Khomeini, General Zia and Colonel al-Qadhafi. Most Near Eastern states with an overwhelming Muslim population proclaim Islam as the state religion. They affect deference to Islamic values. But in government and public affairs, they have consistently opted for a largely non-Muslim pattern of behaviour.

This path began with the encroachment of Western modernity on Muslim societies at the end of the eighteenth century. (Napoleon arrived in Egypt in 1798 to gaze at the Pyramids, defeat the Mamluks, and be defeated by Nelson.) Latterly, change has been accelerated by the great wealth from petroleum. In the past, much of this modernity was welcomed, and readily borrowed by rulers in order to increase their power and help them survive. More recently, the accoutrements of material abundance have been adopted by an ever-increasing number of hapless people, caught in the maelstrom of rapid economic and social change. Old ways have been disrupted, bringing dislocation, disorientation and disaffection.

This modernity was of foreign, non-Muslim provenance — Christian, in fact. But it was Muslim autocrats, not colonialists or imperialists, who first superimposed it on traditional Islamic society. It soon caused a crisis of identity, especially in public life. The performance of indigenous rulers, operating within this imported framework of modernity, could be judged by their subjects only according to Islamic standards and perceptions. Disillusionment with the rulers also meant disillusionment with the alien framework.

The encroachment of the West on these societies was not simply one of modernity, of course. It was accompanied by military power, and thus the ability to dominate and control Muslim societies. This did not tally with the Muslims' long-standing perception of the non-Islamic world. It reminded them, with shattering force, of Islam's loss of power. In the last 150 years, the average Muslims' experience of the non-Muslim has been subservience to foreign infidel power. To the traditional conservative Muslim, this has always been as unacceptable as it has been to the secular nationalist, and in recent centuries, indeed, Muslims have had a tradition of being suspicious of their rulers. Most of them have been seen as usurpers, satraps, tyrants, heretical innovators or carriers of infidel ways.

What we are witnessing in Iran and Pakistan now, in the periodic protests in Egypt and Turkey, and in the perorations of Colonel al-Qadhafi in Libya, is the rejection of an alien culture. This includes those native rulers who have tried to borrow, emulate or adopt it in their own countries. Among conservative Muslims, the protest is also a call for the restoration of Islamic power. It is a defiance of the non-Muslims who seem to hold most of the power in the world today.

The Islamic Revolution in Iran

In Iran, the Shia version of Islam is the state religion. There is a tradition that religious teachers give leadership to the faithful. In times of popular resistance to dynastic rulers, in both the nineteenth and twentieth centuries, Shia mullahs have done this. They have greater social and political authority than their counterparts in Sunni (or orthodox) Islam. In the absence of other forms of organised political expression in Iran (except for the bazaar merchants and the Tudeh Communist Party), it was natural for what was perceived as tyrannical rule to be opposed under religious leadership.

But it is one thing for mullahs to lead political rebellions; it is another to assume state power. They never have in the past. The attempt by Ayatollah Khomeini to govern in Iran may yet prove to be his undoing. He supposedly belongs to the Men of the Pen, not the Men of the Sword.

Western interpreters sometimes contrast Shia 'radicalism' with Sunni 'conservatism'. (Saudi Arabia, for example, belongs to the Sunni creed.) But this is a mistake. It is true that one Shia sect, the Ismailis, managed by sedition and revolution to establish a dynasty and an empire in North Africa and Egypt in the tenth century, and set up a rival caliphate to Baghdad. The Ismaili temporal realm, however, was thoroughly authoritarian. Because of the centrality of the Imam, they allowed neither doctrinal nor political differences, let alone opposition. They imposed their own orthodoxy on the community. Iran, however, has had an unbroken tradition of autocracy ever since Herodotus reported on it. The question today is whether autocracy will now be founded on traditional Islamic or non-Islamic premises.

The eruption of a popular Islamic mass protest movement in Iran is neither novel nor phenomenal. Nor is it isolated in kind, only in degree of intensity, if one recalls parallel sporadic episodes in Egypt between 1968 and 1977, the periodic proclamations of Libya's Colonel al-Qadhafi on affairs of state and international affairs, or developments in Pakistan. As stated earlier, Islam has always been a social force in Middle Eastern society. It remains to be seen, however, whether it can also become a potent and workable political factor. What is certain is that its recrudescence or resurgence, including its use by national leaders and rulers for political purposes, is now and will remain for the immediate future, a source of domestic and external conflict and therefore instability. It may even become a new form of power, especially if it is effectively conjoined with economic and military power.

On the other hand, the potent mix in the Middle Eastern mosaic of sectarian divisions and ethnic communal diversity has always been a source of domestic instability and attraction for external interference. It has also exacerbated the conditions of civil peace and strife, inter-state relations and regional contests. The eruption of Islamic sentiment against the alarmingly disrupting and disorienting breakdown of traditional ways as a result of new wealth and the relentless impact of 'modernity' may not be able to deal with internal contradictions. In fact, it may threaten further disintegration in Iran, and perhaps elsewhere in the region.

Observe the situation in Iran. Ayatollah Khomeini has proclaimed his Islamic republic and state, which he seems to govern through an 'invisible' secret government of mullahs and *imāms*, constituted as an Islamic Revolutionary Council. There is an as yet controversial constitution, even though theoretically the *sharī'a* is an Islamic constitution, or the constitution for the Islamic community of the faithful. The new constitution gives Khomeini virtually absolute power, in keeping with his teachings and writings of the last fifteen years about the 'government of the religious jurist'. There is no apparent systematic judiciary other than the Revolutionary Council of the men of religion. In the circumstances, the Ayatollah's word, or his interpretation of the revealed word of God, seems to be the law. It is significant, however, that leading members of the Shia hierarchy in Iran disagree with Khomeini's interpretation of Shia doctrine, and disapprove of the blatantly political use he makes of it. According to Shia doctrine, there is no such formulation or provision as '*wilayat al-faqih*', or the 'guardianship of the jurist' over the state. It is the Imam, a descendent of

Caliph Ali b. Abu Talib's family, who can legitimately govern the state. But the twelfth Imam in line disappeared nearly one thousand years ago. He is 'concealed' and is expected to 'return' in order to establish the just and righteous realm on earth. Some of these Shia religious teachers, therefore, view the role assigned to Khomeini in the new Iranian constitution as a usurpation of the 'expected' Imam's role.

The security situation is utterly confused. When the Army disintegrated and masses of arms fell into the hands of the hapless though angry crowds, and, till then, underground political organisations which surfaced in the heat of the anti-Shah uprising, the inevitable occurred. Neither Khomeini supporters nor the radical groups on the left have been prepared to give up their arms. Praetorian guards abound and proliferate. Inevitably, armed activity by disaffected ethnic groups and religious minorities, such as the Kurds, Azerbaijanis, Baluchistanis or the Arabs in Khuzistan, became common. Given the weakness of the centre in Tehran, this is not surprising. In such a situation, the process of elimination between rivals takes precedence over national policy. It also reintroduces the possibility of military cabals among army officers, as the new order, whatever it will be, proceeds to meet the need for a disciplined military force.

Khomeini's Islamic stance cannot easily admit compromise, nor countenance opposition. His initial tactic of letting a puppet government of his choice grapple with the day-to-day problems of 'modernity' was sound in the context of his religious perception. It has not, however, worked in practice, because of the compromises and concessions it must make to meet the requirements of a state in the late twentieth century. The more intransigent Khomeini becomes, the greater the degree of *stasis* in the country, and the wider the alienation of several groups in Iranian society. His confrontation with the United States can be interpreted, or characterised, in several ways. Beside the declared aim of forcing the United States to return the late Shah to Iran, it served to occupy younger elements among the mass of rebels and distract them from internal problems and anomalies. At the same time, it projects the emotional rejection of the West as represented by its major world power, the United States. In this there are undertones of an older dichotomy and confrontation between the world of Islam and the non-Islamic world. But it also maintains the 'revolutionary momentum' under Khomeini's control, thus postponing for a little while longer the inevitable clash of internal forces over power and the spoils of the revolution.

It is one thing to govern a state with due consideration to the limits set by the Sacred Law; and this usually applies to rulers. It is quite another to insist on the establishment of an 'Islamic republic' in which a strict observance of the letter of the revealed law (especially when *republic* significantly means the rule by the representatives of the people in political association, i.e., constituted as a public) is imposed by force. Pakistan tried it in 1949 and failed.

Even if it were reasonable to accept the interpretation of an Islamic resurgence in Iran — or elsewhere — as a rejection of foreign interference and the excesses of modern industrial society or culture, we cannot from this premise infer that an 'Islamic republic' is possible. According to Shia doctrine itself, a true Islamic state can only be established when the concealed or disappeared, expected Imam will return to earth. Khomeini surely is not that Imam. It is all the same, interesting and important to examine briefly how Khomeini became the symbol of the anti-Shah rebellion by 1977, and the charismatic religio-political leader of post-Pahlavi Iran. This approach suggests that the current Islamic resurgence is a social, not a religious, phenomenon or development.

After 1973, an impatient Shah had his state coffers brimful of money. He quickly proceeded to launch his fifth development plan (ending in March 1978) of instant modernisation. His first mistake perhaps was to utilise capital-intensive instead of labour-intensive means for his economic projects. Soon there were massive capital and commodity imports which not only strained the distributive system, but were also socially disruptive. Short of skilled manpower at home, there was a massive importation of workers form South Korea, Pakistan and India. The presence of this new mass of foreigners generated social tensions. At the same time, the lure of massive capital and commodity imports as well as the launching of development projects, led to an accelerated mass movement of population from the villages to the towns and the capital, Tehran. The lure of industry, commerce and finance was too strong. In twenty years (1956-76) Tehran grew from 1.5 million to 4.5 million, nearly a 200 per cent increase; Isfahan from 250,000 to 670,000. The same increase was registered for Tabriz, Ahwaz, Mashhad and Shiraz. The emigrating masses may have found jobs in the towns and cities, but poor, if any, housing, without services. Slums mushroomed, and the cohesion of rural communities was lost. Significantly though, these were all practising Shia Muslims and, when the time came, they readily responded to their anti-Shah religious teachers. Moreover, the majority of the population is under 20. Their radicalisation in the slums, schools and universities against an ever more repressive police state was not too difficult.

At the same time, more important groups were emerging, some of them the offspring of the Shah's White Revolution and instant modernisation policies. Such was the new class of professionals, mainly Western-educated. The rapid expansion and modernisation of the armed forces, especially the air force, required quick, injudicious, i.e., hasty, promotions. Within twenty years the army increased by 2½ times (125,000 to 285,000); so did the navy, whereas the air force's growth was phenomenal (100,000). No wonder the army collapsed so easily in 1979, with the first signs of sedition in the air force.

The old-style bazaar merchants, resenting new commercial and financial formations, had traditionally allied themselves with the *'ulamā* in resisting or protesting Shah rule. The *'ulamā* themselves resented the government's taking away their accustomed subsidies and other sources of revenue. Khomeini's long-standing opposition to the Shah before and during his long exile gradually rallied dissidents abroad, and capitalised upon the repression of the Shah and his new 'class' until he became pitted in the minds of all Iranian dissidents as the *Imam* against the Shah's own cult of personality. By October 1978 he was able to move to France to co-ordinate the mounting protest movement in Iran. Meanwhile, as early as August 1977, the dismissal of Amir Abbas Hoveida, prime minister for twelve years, signalled the *malaise* within the Shah's establishment and regime. This was followed by a more active campaign by the Shah against Khomeini in January 1978, and martial law later in the year under the new prime minister, General Gholam Riza Azhari. Within a few months, in January 1979, the Shah was out.

Despite the charisma and the religiously derived authority of Khomeini, there are serious uncertainties hanging over his drive to establish an Islamic state. The plebiscite of March 1979 legitimated the proclamation of an 'Islamic republic'. However, it is not clear on what lines. Nor is it clear how the provinces of the multi-ethnic state are to be administered. For the Baluchis, Turkmans, Ahwazis and Kurds the Khomeini-led revolution meant the hope of autonomy, not particularly the return to Islam. The challenge of tribal-ethnic rebellion remains. Furthermore, no national goals have been set beyond the vague proposition that the law of Islam must prevail.

Nor has Islam been the sole component or factor in Iran or its anti-Shah rebellion. Other groups are involved: National Front secularists, Communists, intellectuals, women and autonomy-seeking ethnics. All of these accepted the leadership of the *'ulamā* and mullahs only in order to topple the regime of the Shah. Now one witnesses the struggle for power and the succession to the ousted monarch. It is not fanciful to suggest that whoever succeeds finally in this contest may find himself, after a respectable lapse of time, as a new Shah.

In addition to the internal centrifugal forces which threaten national unity, there is the vexing problem of external relations. Thus the Kurdish problem in Iran may affect relations with Iraq and Turkey — and the Soviet Union. Border disputes with Iraq, in which country the majority of the population is Shia, can become sources of more serious conflict.[2] Unrest among the Baluchis in Iran can lead to difficulties with Pakistan. Irredentist claims over Bahrain and other parts of the Gulf can generate conflict with the Arabs of the Peninsula, especially Saudi Arabia. Any attempt by the Khomeini forces in Iran to promote radical or militant Islamic movements in the Middle East can elicit a sharp response from the Arab regimes, and revive the old Arab–Persian antipathy, antagonism and hostility. In view of Iran's and the Gulf region's strategic importance for oil supplies, most, if not all, of these sources of potential conflict could attract, or invite, foreign power interference.

The radical Islamic political movement of Khomeini in Iran is not simply the reflection of a sense of disillusionment with the West and the main Western ideologies of capitalism and Communism. If the confrontation between Iran and the United States is any indication, it is also a challenge to and defiance of the West, as well as of Western-devised rules and conventions for the conduct of the relations between states; in short, the international order.

For many years, at home and in exile, Khomeini consistently preached the need to establish an Islamic government in Iran, on the basis of his own interpretation of the political duty of Muslims. He called for the guardianship of the state by the religious jurist. In doing so, he also declared Western culture as being irrelevant to Islam and the Muslims, and asserted the ability of Muslims to modernise their society without recourse to Western values. The means he proposed for the achievement of these ends are clear.

These consist of politicising religion and theocratising the state under the leadership — and control — of the religious jurists and teachers. The role of the latter in the pursuit of these ends must be one of sedition against existing tyrannical and oppressive regimes. They must mobilise all Muslims as holy warriors against tyranny for the attainment of the Islamic state. This is not simply the duty of the faithful, but a divine commandment which cannot be ignored or disobeyed. Whereas for centuries the Shia, in particular, dissimulated the 'justice' of their legitimist cause amidst a hostile and mainly Sunni Islamic community, lamented the 'injustices' they have suffered for so long, now they must be released — and unleashed — by their religious leaders actively and militantly to seek to redress the wrongs committed against them, and to establish 'justice and righteousness' on earth. In other words, they must be activated so that they can accelerate and immanentise the 'expected' Imam's realm on earth.

There will be those who will detect echoes of parallel radical religious movements in early fifteenth-century Christian Europe. A subterranean eschatology seems to have erupted in Iran as a highly emotional mass movement of the miserable and the deprived. It may be no more than the acting out of an old man's fantasies. Yet its triumph is accompanied by the vengeance of the apocalyptic tradition of popular religion, which attracts the underprivileged, the oppressed and disoriented. Like the Hussite and Taborite movements in early fifteenth century Europe, the Islamic resurgence in Iran appears as a movement of the common people, caused perhaps by parallel, if not similar, conditions: at the height of prosperity and rapid economic change, ever greater numbers of the population drifted from the rural areas into the towns, and particularly the capital city. The ranks of the urban poor, the dispossessed slum-dwellers swelled up. The political failures of an inefficient and corrupt government contributed to their greater misery — and radicalisation.

After two years of the Islamic revolution, there is as yet no settlement of the political problem in Iran, let alone the establishment of an orderly political regime which can deal authoritatively and decisively with pressing national and international problems. The exercise of terror has not eliminated the threats of sedition and conspiracy against the Khomeini revolution. These acquired renewed significance and poignancy after the abortive American rescue attempt of the hostages in April 1980. But they are also a clear indication of the political chaos in the country, the unrest in the army and the disaffection among wider groups in society.

Islam and Power

In the wider Middle Eastern region, power in the Islamic states rested, for a long time, in the hands of older traditional ruling elites, sectarian and other 'class' minorities, e.g., Sherifs, monarchs and tribal shaykhs, the Sunni minority in Iraq, the Alawite minority in Syria, the Christians in Lebanon, soldiers in many countries, a ruling family in Saudi Arabia. Vast demographic changes in the last decade produced a mass of discarded humanity which now provides radical, populist religious movements with a vast resource of political malcontents for whom Islam is the sole basis of political identity and ethic and a source of solidarity and social cohesiveness. With ready access to money and arms, their transformation into holy warriors or revolutionary forces becomes easier. They can be led not only against their own respective state political establishments, but also against those they presume have obstructed or undermined their cultural autonomy, invariably some foreign power. They are pushed to assert their ability to modernise their societies without recourse to Western, or other alien, values, i.e., without Westernising it. They tend, dangerously, to challenge the internationally recognised boundaries of nation-states as well as the accepted conventions of international relations. In their puritanical and zealous pursuit of the ideal theocracy they threaten the survival of sectarian and ethnic communities in their midst, the territorial disintegration of their own states, and endanger world peace.

The relation between Islam and power has existed ever since the prophet Muhammad established the first Islamic community in Arabia in the early seventh century. There has been controversy between Muslims ever since over the question whether he founded a state, a political order, or merely a community of the faithful. The resolution of the relation between Islam the religion and political power and authority rests on the way the Muslim answers this kind of question. In fact, political conflict and civil strife raged over this very issue soon after the Prophet's death. Arabs distinguished themselves from non-Arabs, orthodox from heterodox Muslims. Yet these divisions were contained and subsumed for a long time under vast Islamic imperial orders. Ever since the division of much of the Islamic world into national states, however, the relation between Islam and power became tenuous; it was, in fact, broken. The question posed by the Iran experience in 1979 is, can it be restored? Shia Muslims — the spiritual descendants of the early legitimists in the inter-Islamic contest for power in the seventh century — have always contended that it can, under the guidance of the expected Imam. But the Imam is not of this world; his ontological essence is eschatological. It is not unfair in the meantime, whether we think of Spain in the fifteenth century, of New England in the seventeenth century, or Iran in the twentieth century, to suggest that when politics becomes religion, one invariably faces the Inquisition, without being able to assert one way or the other whether Islam is a credible vehicle for political change.

On the other hand, given the resurgence of religious sentiment throughout the world, there may be those who feel that we are going through a period akin to that of revolutionary messianism in medieval and reformation Europe. At a time of great social dislocation, economic uncertainty and all kinds of strife men usually seek assurance and certainty and, the unhinged among them, even redemption. There is nothing strange about Muslims in Iran or elsewhere seeking it in their own cultural idiom. This search for assurance by a return to native cultural roots does not, however, necessarily mean the restoration of Islamic states.

In this connection there are other movements in Islam which should not be overlooked or ignored. While a radical, populist and violent variant of Islamic resurgence is holding sway in Iran, there are other approaches regarding the relation between Islam and power which are being argued and developed by Muslims. The most recent and prominent of these is represented by the work of an Egyptian lawyer, Muhammad Said al-Ashmawi, one-time judge and currently counsellor at the Cairo High Court of Appeal, *Uṣul al-Sharīʿa* (*Principles of the Sharia*) (Cairo, 1979).

An Evolutionary Interpretation of Islam

Ashmawi's argument is directed against the static view of the *sharīʿa*, or Sacred Law. He suggests that such a view is the result of the confusion between the religion, the faith, of Islam, its basic teachings and their evolution on the one hand, and religious thought which has developed opinions and theories about it in its historical understanding of the religion and its glosses upon it, on the other. The *Sharī'a*, according to Ashmawi, is not the specific body of rules and regulations governing the conduct of Muslims. Even if it were, these were not revealed once and for all as permanent and immutable. On the contrary, they were revealed in response to specific conditions, circumstances and needs. Thus the Qur'ānic suras revealed to the Prophet in Mecca related exclusively to the faith, the soul of man and its salvation; they did not refer to any problems of the community or society of the faithful. The Qur'ānic verses revealed later in Medina, however, dealt exclusively with matters of personal conduct, communal arrangements and social relations, or relations between the believers. This suggests, argues Ashmawi, the evolutionary nature of the *sharī'a*. The same goes for the Prophetic *hadith*.

The *sharī'a*, therefore, is a guide, a *way*, a programme of action, an ethic for Islam and the Muslims. Subsequent religious rules in the Qur'ān, the Tradition and the exegeses of jurists and religious teachers came to constitute the greater body of the *corpus islamicus*. Moreover, the *sharī'a* as a guide for Islam and Muslims was never divorced, or cut off, from the past. Its link with the past is to be found in the continuity of religious experience centred upon the notions of justice, truth and equity. Furthermore, even its specific rules and regulations ultimately depend on the believer's conscience and faith. The *sharī'a*, that is, is a dynamic ethic.

As for the matter of the Islamic state, Ashmawi asserts that there is no passage in the Qur'ān about such a state and form of government, because the essence of religion, including Islam, is man, without regard to his terrestrial location, racial division or variety. Until the death of the prophet, there was no state in Islam; Medina approximated a city-state. There was only a Muslim community led by the Prophet. The basis of loyalty was religious belief, not any territorial state or nation. The Qur'ān and the *Sharī'a* always addressed themselves to the faithful, not the citizens. In fact, the idea of citizenship was alien and unknown to Islam. There were Muslims in Muslim lands as there were Christians in Christian lands. 'Religion', Ashmawi insists, 'is concerned with man and society, not with states and empires.' The Qur'ān never dealt with the question of the form of government after the Prophet. Nor did the Prophet issue any *hadith* about this subject.

When the first Islamic community was formed in Medina there

was need for legislation to regulate its life and its relations with outsiders (i.e., non-Muslims). Suras were revealed to the Prophet in the form of legal pronouncements. Any government, however, was 'God's government', with God as the sole sovereign ruler. The Prophet was merely the executor of His will. God, not the believers, chose the Prophet as leader of the community. Moreover, such government was based on arbitration, not on rule by force or coercion. Consultation with any members of the community was at the Prophet's discretion; it was not a right of the people. The Prophet's rights and privileges as the executor of God's will were confined and peculiar to his person; they could not be transferred or inherited by another. The basis of his executive rule was revelation and its legitimacy rested on the belief of the community that he was connected to God by revelation. He was not, however, infallible or impeccable.

A 'government of the people' however, is any earthly government, based on social conditions and economic circumstances, and imposed by the realities of power. Unfortunately, after Abu Bakr, the caliphs endowed their own persons and their rule with the attributes of 'the government of God', and adopted or took unto themselves the special rights and privileges of the Prophet.

Ashmawi reminds those who would wish a return to an idealised, pristine Islamic past and a strict adherence to a rigid, static *sharī'a*, that there was only one brief 'religious government' under the Prophet. Even then the *sharī'a* was a guide for the evolutionary development of a body of rules and regulations to meet specific problems. In any case, the idealised past had its human problems too, as is clear from the history of the early caliphate, the Umayyad dynasty and those who succeeded or came after them. Moreover, the *sharī'a* never specified a form of government, whether temporary or permanent. It was the obfuscation of the essence and meaning of the *sharī'a* and its transformation from a guide and ethic, a way to a better life and a means to salvation to a body of permanent, rigid and immutable rules which created the central difficulty in the relation between Islam and power.

Needless to say, Ashmawi's bold evolutionary interpretation of the *sharī'a*, his clear distinction between religion and religious thought, his rejection of any provision for a state by the *sharī'a* and the teachings of the Prophet, i.e., the religion, were bound to elicit the wrath of the Muslim Brethren in Egypt. His work was duly attacked in their journal, *al-Da'wa* (Cairo, October 1979). The fact also that Ashmawi rejects the proposition that Western civilisation is a 'civilisation of sinfulness' irritated the traditional fundamentalists even more. The further fact that he links the development of the *sharī'a* with the historical past, that it was not simply created *ex nihilo*, has revived the whole controversy about the nature of religious belief. Ashmawi's approach also undermines long-held views about war and peace in Islam, legislation, religious belief as a matter of personal conscience versus the observance of a predetermined and rigid set of rules. It also rejects the idea of a specific Islamic state and government.

It remains to be seen, of course, what other currents of Islamic thought will emerge in the next few years. Ashmawi's work represents a rational, historical examination of the evolution of Islam the religion and of religious thought in Islam. It is opposed to and pitted against the tide of a mass popular eruption of Islamic militancy led by those who insist upon the restoration of an idealised Islamic state and order from the past and upon the implementation of the Sacred Law's body of rules and regulations under the control of religious teachers. For Ashmawi, these would be equally usurping the functions of the Prophet, and presenting their order as the 'government of God' when it would be no more than the 'government of man'.

The Prospect of an Islamic Ideology

There is not simply intellectual but also wider disagreement among Muslims over what Islam is. Although Muslims share one faith and a common Islamic sentiment, the social structures in which these prevail differ from one Islamic society or country to another. Historically and in practice, there has been no single or uniform Islamic experience or understanding of Islam. The ethos and tradition of Islam was influenced by different political experiences, in Turkey, Iran, Egypt, the Fertile Crescent, the Arabian Peninsula and Africa, not to mention Africa south of the Sahara, south and south-east Asia. This was as true in its classical and medieval period as it has been in its modern age. It is not surprising then that there is disagreement among Muslims today over what is Islam, since its reality differs from one Muslim community to the other. There has always been a state of tension between the specific psychological, social and historical experiences of Islam on one hand and its ideal universal conception on the other.

Another consideration in assessing the credibility and prospects of the current movements of militant Islam is the effectiveness of Islam as a political ideology. In the recent past (since the nineteenth century) Islam as a political ideology was tried briefly as a defence against the onslaught of the West and quickly abandoned in favour of borrowed secular ideals of nationalism, 'progress' and modernity. The adoption of the latter involved mainly the new Western-educated elites; it has had little effect on the masses of Muslims. To this extent the problem of identity was not resolved. If anything the failure of the borrowed ideology to resolve it compounded it further.

As a historical movement, Islamic revivalism and reformism did play a role in the revitalisation of individual societies a hundred years ago which were undergoing cultural stress deriving from military defeat and foreign political and economic subordination. It was a period of cultural distortion and confusion. It also became a basis for the reformulation of the Muslim's view of the world in religio-cultural terms. The adoption of a substitute cultural model from the modern West was partial at best, confined as it was to very small elites. A wider cultural transformation never occurred. Nevertheless, Islam as a political ideology, or at least as the basis for one, was relegated to the background, whereas Islam as a complex religio-cultural ethos of a particular civilisation, in its several varieties, remained a social reality. As long as the West remained politically powerful, if not wholly ascendant, this uncomfortable coexistence between a borrowed foreign cultural-political and economic model or ideology and a native religio-cultural ethos was sustained.

With the military and political decline of the Western world, however, the precarious relationship could not prevent an Islamic resurgence towards what is considered to be cultural authenticity. At the same time, local social, economic and political factors encouraged this resurgence. The failure of local political leadership to deal with the problems of adaptation and change — of modernity — within the framework of an alien political ideology revived not only the problem of identity but also generated a crisis of legitimacy. Even so, the reappearance of militant Islam in response to these crises is not a single or unified movement; it is not a single 'revolution' with an organisational centre. On the contrary, it is polycentric and diffuse. Its various centres of activity however share certain perceptions and common grievances, such as the failure of the secularised elites, led by such leaders as Atatürk in Turkey, the

Pahlavis in Iran, the old elites of notables in the Fertile Crescent, the old nationalists and their successor military regimes in Egypt, or the Baath in Syria and Iraq, to produce a modern political community, or workable political institutions. They are also perceived as having failed to provide the promised economic development and social justice. What is even worse, their recent military defeat by the enemies of Islam is attributed by militant Muslims to their ineptitude, corruption and heretical deviation from the true faith.

Although not altogether novel, the answer to these shortcomings and failures has been to politicise Islam and activate the Muslim as a Holy Warrior. There are long-standing intellectual roots for this kind of Islamic activism and religious militancy in the puritanism of Muhammad ibn Abdul Wahhab in eighteenth-century Arabia, in the pan-Islamist Afghani and the Mahdi of the Sudan in the late nineteenth century, in Hasan el Banna and the Muslim Brethren in Egypt, in Abu'l Ala' el Mawdudi of Pakistan and Shariat Madari of Iran in this century. The militants of this century in particular have been in a position to take advantage of demographic changes in the Islamic countries as well as economic, political and strategic changes in the world. The last twenty-five years especially saw a process of depoliticisation in many Islamic states, characterised by the increase of state power at the expense of public political participation, leading to the further alienation of the masses from authority. Total governmental control precluded political activity.

Modern conditions of life have corroded further the Islamic ethic. Muslims came to dislike what they saw. The residual heritage of tribalism and factionalism combined with the corrosive effects of the requirements of modernity to frustrate modern notions of loyalty to impersonal political orders, encouraging further fragmentation and contributing to chronic instability. The more traditional social order, based on an intricate web of personal relations, however, remained resilient.

Thus, the answer to the malaise and confusion has been the resurgence of a militant Islam which claims to seek the revitalisation of Islamic society and, by extension, the restoration of its political power. In the face of a declining, devalued radical nationalism since the late 1960s, militant Islam hopes to provide not only the basis of morality and ethic but also to resolve the problem of identity, and furnish the basis for political change along the principles of individual and group dignity, justice and independence.

Militant Islam, however, seeks to do this by recapturing the past in a nostalgic restorative movement. Consequently, it is weak on creativity and innovation. The absence of individual freedom in most Islamic societies cripples any capacity for innovation and predestines the movement to failure. Moreover, militant Islamic movements have to operate in inhospitable environments, that is, in states ruled largely by individuals or groups that are hostile to them. They also arise in an area and a period in which foreign powers have vital interests. Theoretically at least, these powers would be loath to allow Islamic revolutions to jeopardise their interests. Even without these constraints and threats, the restorative — archaic — nature of these movements suggests their inability to cope with the problems of modernity. To this extent, they may be no more than transient phenomena. For the moment, they have acquired an exaggerated significance because of the oil wealth of several Islamic countries, which gives the latter an unreal sense of self-importance. There is no evidence, however, that this wealth is being, or will be in the future, translated into sources of more lasting power.

The dichotomy between authority as perceived by Muslims and the reality of power persists. The sacred Islamic tradition and universal ideal continue to be superseded by force and necessity. Inevitably, these dichotomies and paradoxes nurture conspiracy as a view of history and of political power. They sustain both a traditional alienation of the people from authority and a currently more militant manifestation of this alienation.

It is noticeable that besides prayer, the pilgrimage and holy war, there have been no other institutions providing Muslims with political cohesiveness. The social order became remote and alienated from the political order. The political order may have failed in bringing about the social and political transformation of agrarian peasant and urban communities. But so did the traditional social order and the faith itself fail too. Islam, that is, failed to become the basis of a modern political order, because it could not act as the agent for change. It remained a source of conflict within communities. Nor is there any evidence that leads one to believe that it can become the basis of such an order in the foreseeable future. The modern state remains alien and alienating equally to the devout and the militant Muslim. Islam, in short, may dominate the highly inter-personal basis of a traditional social order, but remains removed from the impersonal political arrangements required by a modern society.

Conclusion

The current Islamic resurgence with its reassertion of an essentially religious political identity in the sense of a declared adherence to the ethic and values of Islam, is the result of the disorientation caused by rapid economic development and the disaffection with social change brought about by the transplantation of certain aspects and appurtenances of modernity. When one also takes into account the existence of armed ethnic-sectarian and national separatist groups from Iran to North Africa, the perception of the Middle Eastern region in comfortable terms of stability is precluded. Moreover, newly-found financial-economic power inevitably affects both the region and the rest of the world. Other conflicts peripheral to the region, such as the one in the Eastern Mediterranean or those in Africa, tend to add to the region's instability.

One observes, nevertheless, that neither in Iran so far nor among any of the militant Islamic movements elsewhere, is there a clear idea of the nature of the Islamic state or government they wish to establish. It might be clear under a prophet, or even in a period of the not-so-distant past when overwhelmingly traditional society was governed by religious precepts. However, in a mass society today, the wedding of Islam to a modern state is not a straightforward proposition. Thus, Saudi Arabia is officially an Islamic state where the *sharī'a* is the supreme law of the land. In most other states of the region Islam is proclaimed in their constitutions as the official state religion. Egypt has recently declared the Qur'ān and the *sharī'a* the fundamental sources and basis for all legislation. Nor, incidentally, is it clear how Muslims will borrow Western technology without any of its underlying ethic, including modes of thought, scale of values and moral presuppositions. It could be argued that precisely because the borrowing was accelerated recently, many of these societies experienced explosive upheavals, suggesting that the internal contradictions of *formally* Islamic states have not been resolved.

On a more superficial level, the Islamic revolution has sharpened the Muslim's consciousness of things Islamic as distinguished from those that are non- or anti-Islamic. Resistance to the relentless uniformity imposed by a world industrial-technological culture on the part of individuals, groups and states has increased. Thus the struggle against neo-colonialism and neo-imperialism is not simply Arab or pan-Arab, or Iranian, but an Islamic one, suggesting the prelude to a civilisational confrontation. A blatant military regime in Pakistan invokes the Sacred Law. Palestine is no longer 'Arab Palestine', but significantly 'Muslim Palestine'. In Afghanistan a tribal struggle against a Communist government and a Soviet invasion is waged under the banner of Islam.

The fact remains that all of these expressions of Islamic rejection, opposition and revolt occur under the aegis of a modern institution, the nation-state, not in the name of a wider or single Islamic dominion or authority. The problem therefore for the new urban masses and their militant Islamic leaders in Iran or elsewhere remains one of coming to terms with modernity, particularly since their traditional world and way of life have been irreparably eroded, dislodged and overwhelmed by the very modernity they seek and which at the same time they anathematise. Their Islamic revolution may be no more than a way of seeking this accommodation. Traditional religiosity, even in their own eyes, is no longer adequate. What they seem to be experimenting with, albeit dangerously, is the use of religion as politics in the hope that it may prove more effective. So far, though, its triumph in Iran has been accompanied by the vengeance of an apocalyptic tradition of popular religion, arbitrary and brutal in its expression, which attracts the underprivileged, the oppressed and the disoriented.

Nevertheless, the Iranian revolution's objective to establish Islam as the formula of political organisation and the sole basis of the political order has yet to be attained. In a way, this is a reflection of the prevailing disagreement among Iranians over the desirability and practicality of this formula. In the meantime, there prevails an essentially archaic, chaotic and blatantly tyrannical rule over the country, characterised by competing loci of power, a capricious application of rough justice, uncertainty and insecurity. This is perhaps the only condition in which a Khomeini, or similar anachronistic phenomenon, can predominate. Equally, the only possible opposition to it can be sedition, which can often be of unknown provenance and, given the Soviet presence in neighbouring Afghanistan, dangerous. Over eighty years old and in poor health, the not unlikely demise of the Ayatollah in the near future, will result in greater strife in Iran. If one accepts that the Islamic revolution in Iran has been a social rather than a religious phenomenon of the revivalist variety, then that revolution has so far failed to deal adequately with the causes of this social upheaval, and is clearly incapable of providing the required remedies for its causes.

Perhaps one of the more ominous consequences of the Islamic

revolution in the last two years is the dilemma in which the regimes of Muslim states find themselves today. While for political reasons they are anxious to support — even promote — the Islamic revival, they are at the same time apprehensive of its mass composition and militant orientation as a potential danger to their own stability and survival, especially when radical Islamic groups challenge their legitimacy. The apprehension is readily translated into plain fear when the destabilising effect of militant Islam attracts a confrontation between the superpowers in the region.

A populist militant Islamic movement could erupt in any of the states where economic change is rapid, as well as in those where there is meagre economic advance. Its chances of overthrowing secular governments, however, are less than in Iran, since Islam, say, in Egypt or Saudi Arabia is both theologically and socially different from Shīʿism in Iran. Nevertheless, Islam will, for some time to come, act as a major revolutionary element both in the struggle to resolve the historical confusion over religion and the state, or religion and politics, in these societies, and in resisting the onslaught of a basically alien modernity. The apparent decline and weakness of the once-worthy-of-emulation Western civilisation will encourage this trend further. On a more practical level, it will heighten ethnic and sectarian tensions in the Middle East, leading to unhappy conflict and strife.

There is, at this time, a worldwide upsurge in religious feeling in both East and West. (Consider the Pope's reception at the conference of Latin-American bishops in Mexico, and his native Poland. Or, alternatively, the proliferation of cults throughout the West, and the vitality of religious orders among Muslim communities.) This reflects a loss of faith in the long-prevailing ideology of progress, both the liberal-Western and Marxist versions. It is also, by extension, a loss of faith in the advantages of an industrial civilisation. In the face of the mounting, and apparently insoluble, economic and social problems caused by rapid change, it is not so extraordinary that people should seek other-worldly formulae of escape, if not deliverance. Cultural perceptions of the 'other' become sharper, and rejection more categorical or at least adamant, in times of crisis. As some of the Muslim states have recently acquired the economic potential for political power, we can expect them to assert their religious and traditional identity. Islam's claim to dominance will become more frequent and vociferous in the immediate future.

The internal contradictions in the Middle East are now being aggravated by the spreading Islamic rejection of an alien order which many Muslims consider unsuitable and inadequate for their societies, even hostile and evil. Their disillusionment with native rulers whose power rests on the use and spread of this imported or transplanted alien political and economic culture is now expressed in a traditional-religious idiom of immense popular force. It reflects the traditional Islamic ethic of the vast populace upon which native rulers and foreign, non-Muslim powers have imposed a secular political, economic and legal order of infidel provenance. How far or well this raw native force can be translated into political power and an effective instrument of policy for the attainment of as yet unclear, undefined objectives is a question that cannot easily be answered at this time. Nor is it certain that Islam can become a credible vehicle for political change, even though it may provide an ideological base for Muslims. The fact remains that it can be ignored by non-Middle Easterners only at their peril. Challenge and defiance in politics or the relations between states, not to speak of cultures or civilisations, are never wholly rational approaches. They unfortunately exceed the limits of political competition and compromise; they tend toward total, salvationist political constructs in the expectation of the ideal polity and universal triumph to come.

Notes

1. The Gulf war between Iraq and Iran broke out exactly a year after this was written.
2. War broke out between Iraq and Iran in September 1980.

NOTES ON CONTRIBUTORS

ALEXANDRE BENNIGSEN is Professor of History at the Universities of Paris and Chicago.

MICHAEL COOK is a Lecturer in History at the School of Oriental and African Studies, University of London.

ALEXANDER CUDSI is Director of Studies at the Hellenic Mediterranean Centre for Arabic and Islamic Studies.

ALI DESSOUKI is Professor of Political Science at Cairo University.

ABBAS KELIDAR is Lecturer in Politics at the School of Oriental and African Studies, University of London.

ANN LAMBTON was Professor of Persian at the University of London before her retirement in 1979.

ALI MERAD is Professor of Sociology at the University of Lyon, France.

THOMAS NAFF is Professor of History and Director of the Center for Near Eastern Studies, University of Pennsylvania.

DONAL CRUISE O'BRIEN is Lecturer in Politics at the School of Oriental and African Studies, University of London.

P.J. VATIKIOTIS is Professor of Politics with reference to the Near and Middle East at the University of London.

JEAN-CLAUDE VATIN teaches at the University of Aix-en-Provence, France. He spent 1979-81 at Princeton University and the Institute of Advanced Study, Princeton.

INDEX

ISLAM AND POWER.   Page 159